Jeff Mackie-Mason
Dept. of Economics

The
Identification
Problem
in Econometrics

The Identification Problem in Econometrics

FRANKLIN M. FISHER

Professor of Economics
Massachusetts Institute of Technology

ROBERT E. KRIEGER PUBLISHING COMPANY
HUNTINGTON, NEW YORK

Original Edition 1966
Reprint 1976, with corrections

Printed and Published by
ROBERT E. KRIEGER PUBLISHING CO., INC.
645 NEW YORK AVENUE
HUNTINGTON, NEW YORK 11743

Library of Congress Cataloging in Publication Data

Fisher, Franklin M.
    The identification problem in econometrics.

    Reprint of the ed. published by McGraw-Hill, New York, issued in the Economics handbook series.
    Bibliography: p.
    Includes index.
    1.   Econometrics.   I.   Title.
[HB139.F57 1975]   330'.01'82   75-23590
ISBN 0-88275-344-4

Printed in U.S.A. by
NOBLE OFFSET PRINTERS, INC.
New York, N.Y. 10003

Preface to the Reissue

IT IS NOW ALMOST ten years since this book was published and I am very glad to see that it is not to be allowed to go out of print. I have found it a useful book to teach from, and I hope that others will continue to do so.

Because the material in the book forms a fairly connected whole, I have not altered the text except to correct such errors as have come to my attention. It seems appropriate, therefore, to spend a little time here discussing work on identification that has appeared since the book was written.

Econometrics is a (usually happy) marriage of the subjects of economics and of mathematical statistics. Different authors, depending on their training or their bent therefore approach the subject in different ways. I have preferred to treat identification, and, indeed, simultaneous equation estimation in general, as primarily a branch of economics. Thus, the present work concentrates largely on identification using restrictions which economists are likely to know about. Other kinds of information, such as detailed information on the distribution of disturbances and the like, are given a much less important place, if, indeed, they are treated at all. Clearly, this is not the only way to discuss identification in econometric models. One can approach the entire subject in terms of mathematical statistics. Two excellent papers which examine the identification problem in a general statistical setting have been written by Thomas J. Rothenberg and Roger Bowden.[1]

There has also been other work, more directly along the lines of the present book than those just cited. In particular, Leon Wegge has examined rather general conditions for the identification of groups

---

[1] Thomas J. Rothenberg, "Identification in Parametric Models," *Econometrica*, vol. 39, no. 3, May, 1971; and Roger Bowden, "The Theory of Parametric Identification," *Econometrica*, vol. 41, no. 6, November, 1973.

of parameters from different equations;[1] in a sense, much other work on identification theory (including a good deal of this book) consists of examining interesting special cases of Wegge's results.

Three such special cases have been examined by Jerry S. Kelly, who has written on identification of parameter ratios; on linear cross equation constraints; and on identification when ratios of disturbance variances are known.[2]

In another area, only lightly touched on in Chapter 6 of this book, E. J. Hannan has written two very important papers on identification in systems with an autoregressive-moving average error structure (ARMA).[3]

Finally, just as all these works appeared too late to be included in the bibliography of this book when first published, so also my daughter, Naomi, appeared too late to be included in its dedication. I trust that I may now be allowed to rectify this lamentable lack of foresight on my part.

FRANKLIN M. FISHER
June, 1975

---

[1] Leon Wegge, "Identifiability Criteria for a System of Equations as a Whole," *Australian Journal of Statistics*, vol. 7, no. 3, November, 1965. Parthasaradhi Mallela, "Dimension Conditions of Identifiability," *International Economic Review*, vol. 2, no. 3, October, 1970, considers identification of sets of equations under linear restrictions.

[2] Jerry S. Kelly, "The Identification of Ratios of Parameters in Unidentified Equations," *Econometrica*, vol. 39, no. 6, November, 1971; "Proportionate Variances and the Identification Problem," *Econometrica*, vol. 40, no. 6, November, 1972; and "Linear Cross-Equation Constraints and the Identification Problem," *Econometrica*, vol. 43, no. 1, January, 1975.

[3] E. J. Hannan, "The Identification of Vector Mixed Autoregressive-Moving Average Systems." *Biometrika*, vol. 56, no. 1, April, 1969; and "The Identification Problem for Multiple Equation Systems with Moving Average Errors." *Econometrica*, vol. 39, no. 5, September, 1971.

To Abraham, Abigail and Naomi

Preface

THIS BOOK PRESENTS a unified treatment of the theory of identification in simultaneous equation estimation. It draws together earlier work of mine and others and contains some new results as well. It is my belief that such an extended treatment of the identification problem can usefully serve in several ways to illuminate the structure of simultaneous equation systems and the theory of the estimation of their parameters as well as be of independent interest. Because the simultaneous equation context is by far the most important one in which the identification problem is encountered, the treatment is restricted to that context.

The book is intended for students of econometrics and is meant to be read in conjunction with the study of simultaneous equation estimation. The first two chapters, in particular, set forth the basic material on identification which all econometrics students should know, and some or all of the remainder of the book may appropriately be assigned to more advanced or interested students. In my own courses at Massachusetts Institute of Technology I have generally used the material of the first three chapters and some of Chaps. 4 and 6 in a first econometrics course and the remainder in a course in advanced topics in econometrics.

It is presumed that the reader has a reasonable familiarity with matrix notation and operations, with concepts of quadratic forms and characteristic values (only occasionally necessary). I have tried, however, to make the book as self-contained as possible by proving explicitly the necessary theorems on matrices with which not every student can be presumed to be familiar.

In the course of my work on the identification problem I have benefited from the comments and criticism of a great number of people, many of whom are thanked in earlier publications. In the course of writing the present volume I have benefited from conversations with Harold Freeman, Edwin Kuh, Paul A. Samuelson, Karl Shell, and Robert M. Solow.

The manuscript was typed by Antoinette Van Beers, and the index was prepared by Beatrice A. Rogers. My wife, Ellen, assisted in improving the clarity of the exposition and in maintaining an environment in which the writing of books such as this is possible.

Finally, I owe a special debt of gratitude to my students in the econometrics courses at M.I.T. who were exposed to experimentation with this material. At least one person in the classroom learned a great deal from that experience.

FRANKLIN M. FISHER

Contents

1

The Nature of the Problem

1.1. Introduction

By far the greater part of empirical work in econometrics consists of structural estimation—the estimation of the parameters of the behavioral and technological relationships whose general nature is indicated by mathematical economic theory. Such work varies from the estimation of the cost curve of an individual firm to large and extremely complex models of an entire economy. It is motivated by the belief that precise quantitative knowledge of the relations of economic theory can provide an indispensable aid to forecasting and an invaluable guide to policy making, whether for a firm or a governmental agency. That knowledge can only be gained from real-world data.

This book is concerned with the situation arising in the very frequent case in which the structural equation to be estimated is part of a system of such equations all of which hold simultaneously. As we shall see, in such a case, the nature of the theoretical model to be estimated itself implies that the parameters of a given equation cannot logically be inferred on the basis of empirical data alone. Structural estimation is impossible without the use of a priori information concerning the equation to be estimated. Such information must be provided from a source outside the real-world data at hand—either from economic theory or from the results of other studies of different types of data.

In a real sense, such a situation does not differ in kind but only in degree from that which arises in the estimation of the parameters of *any* equation. In order to estimate a structural equation, one first has to know what variables appear in it. Indeed, what makes an equation "structural" is the existence of a theory which predicts a relationship among the variables which appear therein. That theory provides necessary a priori information without which the very existence of a structure to be estimated would not be perceived. The simultaneous equation context described above does differ in degree, however, from this general situation. In that context, it does not suffice to know that the equation to be estimated contains precisely a specified list of variables. It is also necessary to know what variables are contained in other simultaneously holding equations or to have other information about the equation in question. Without such additional information, structural estimation is a logical impossibility. One literally cannot hope to know the parameters of the equation in question on the basis of empirical observations alone, *no matter how extensive and complete those observations may be.* Observational information cannot "identify" the equation to be estimated—cannot distinguish it from a host of other possibilities each as capable of generating the observed data as the true one. If structural estimates are to be obtained, additional prior information must be brought to bear. This book is concerned with the requisite properties of such information when that information is of various given types.

1.2. Why Structural Estimation at All?

The question may naturally occur at this point about whether the desirability of structural estimates is really so great as to lead us into an exploration of relatively complicated problems and techniques. (If this question has not yet occurred to the reader, it probably will in the course of this book.) Evidently, the securing of structural estimates in simultaneous equation models relies on a substantial use of theoretical information. That information may not be of uniform reliability. There are clearly situations in which the use of only wholly reliable prior information will not suffice to yield structural estimates. Clearly, it is desirable to confront the relationships of any theory with as much empirical data as possible. If such data do not (and cannot) alone identify the parameters of a given relationship, might it not be better to admit defeat rather than to rely on further theoretical information which will not be empirically tested?

To put the matter differently, observational information is clearly good for something. One can observe historical correlations among variables. Such correlations are the hard facts with which we have to work. Should one not rest content with them? After all, if the objective of science is prediction, one may clearly do rather well by relying on the continuance of historically observed relationships. Is it really desirable to try to do better by introducing further theoretical information? The desirability of structural estimates and indeed the nature of the issues involved may be well indicated by considering an anecdote which points up the fact that "observed relationships" may not be real ones.

There was once a cholera epidemic in Russia. The government, in an effort to stem the disease, sent doctors to the worst-affected areas. The peasants of the province of S____ discussed the situation and observed a very high correlation between the number of doctors in a given area and the incidence of cholera in that area. Relying on this hard fact, they rose and murdered their doctors. (I am indebted to Evsey D. D____ for this tale.)

The point of this story is clear. Historical correlations may indeed be an easy way to forecast correctly so long as nothing happens to disturb the observed associations. It is even likely that in "normal" circumstances such forecasts may do better than alternative predictions based on a knowledge of the causal structure of the processes being studied. When something happens to alter the situation, however, structural information is indispensable. This may occur, as in the story, because it seems desirable to adopt a policy which will affect one or more of the variables of the system or because one enters a period in which historical co-movements are broken up—as when the economy encounters a turning point in the business cycle. Such occasions may (and probably will) be relatively few; they are likely to be just the ones, however, about which accurate prediction is crucial.

1.3. The Marshallian Cross

Having decided, then, that structural estimates are indeed highly desirable, we shall proceed to a somewhat more precise statement of our problem in the context of a particular example. The traditional example in this area is also the most readily understandable one; it is the case of the equilibrium of supply and demand for a given commodity. (This example was used by E. J. Working in his classic paper [38] which first pointed out the nature of the identification problem.)

Suppose that the demand curve for the commodity in question is given by

$$Q = a_0 + a_1 P \qquad (1.3.1)$$

where Q = quantity
P = price
a_0, a_1 = constant parameters

If Eq. (1.3.1) were the only equation relating quantity and price, the observations on Q and P would lie along the straight line whose equation is (1.3.1) and one could infer the values of the structural parameters by connecting any two price-quantity pairs by a straight line. This situation is pictured in Fig. 1a.

Note that no added information could be gained in this nonstochastic example by adding further observations. Because of the existence of

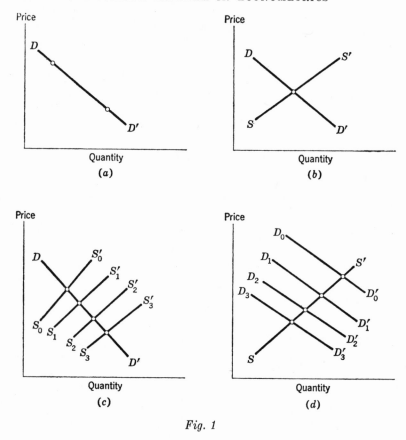

Price

D

D'

Quantity

(a)

Price

D S'

S D'

Quantity

(b)

Price

D S'_0 S'_1 S'_2 S'_3

S_0 S_1 S_2 S_3 D'

Quantity

(c)

Price

D_0 D_1 D_2 D_3 S' D'_0 D'_1 D'_2 D'_3

S

Quantity

(d)

Fig. 1

Eq. (1.3.1) only two observations will be linearly independent. If one thinks of a_0 as the coefficient of a variable which is always equal to unity, one can think of performing two independent experiments by choosing two (identical) values of that variable and two different values of P and letting Q be determined by the equation to be estimated. Clearly, no more than two such independent experiments are possible.

On the other hand, if there is also a supply curve, given by

$$P = b_0 + b_1 Q \qquad b_1 \neq \frac{1}{a_1} \qquad (1.3.2)$$

things are rather different. Now instead of being strung out along the line (1.3.1), observations on P and Q will all be the same; they will all be at the intersection of the two lines given by the simultaneous solution of the two equations. (This is shown in Fig. 1b.) Only *one* independent experiment is available. However, there are *two* parameters to be estimated in Eq. (1.3.1). Clearly, one independent observation will not be enough to determine these parameters. Observational information can tell us only what the intersection of the supply and demand curves is. It can thus rule out possible demand curves which do not pass through the intersection point but cannot by itself distinguish the true demand curve (1.3.1) from any other curve which does pass through the single observed point. Evidently, it is impossible to determine the true parameters of the demand curve (or the supply curve, for that matter) without further information.

It is important to note that the problem is not one of the appropriateness of a particular estimating technique. In the situation described, there clearly exists *no* way using *any* technique whatsoever in which the true demand (or supply) curve can be estimated. Nor, indeed, is the problem here one of statistical inference—of separating out the effects of random disturbance. There is no disturbance in this model, and in the absence of Eq. (1.3.2) it would take only two observations to determine precisely the parameters of Eq. (1.3.1) with complete certainty. It is the logic of the supply-demand equilibrium itself which leads to the difficulty.

The situation is similar when random disturbances are introduced in our two equations. Replace Eq. (1.3.1) by

$$Q = a_0 + a_1 P + u_1 \qquad (1.3.1a)$$

where u_1 is a random disturbance with mean zero. If Eq. (1.3.1a) were the only equation relating quantity and price, the observations on those two variables would be distributed about the straight line (1.3.1) rather than on it. Estimation of the parameters of Eq. (1.3.1a) would then involve some method of eliminating the effects of the disturbance term. The natural procedure would be to regress Q on P, provided that P and u_1 can be assumed to be uncorrelated in the probability limit.

Such a regression procedure can be described as follows. Let X_0 be the variable which is always equal to unity. Taking all sums over all observations and letting T be the number of observations in the sample, the fact that u_1 has mean zero can be written as

$$\mathrm{plim}\left(\frac{1}{T}\right) \sum X_0 u_1 = 0 \qquad (1.3.3)$$

Similarly, because u_1 has zero mean, and denoting the mean of P by $\bar{P}$, we may write the covariance of P and u_1 as

$$
\begin{aligned}
\mathrm{cov}\,(P,u_1) &= \mathrm{plim}\left(\frac{1}{T}\right) \sum (P - \bar{P})(u_1 - 0) \\
&= \mathrm{plim}\left(\frac{1}{T}\right) \sum P u_1 - \mathrm{plim}\,\bar{P}\,\mathrm{plim}\left(\frac{1}{T}\right) \sum u_1 \\
&= \mathrm{plim}\left(\frac{1}{T}\right) \sum P u_1 \qquad (1.3.4)
\end{aligned}
$$

Since P and u_1 are assumed uncorrelated in the probability limit, we have

$$\text{plim} \left(\frac{1}{T}\right) \sum Pu_1 = 0 \tag{1.3.5}$$

We may use Eqs. (1.3.1a), (1.3.3), and (1.3.4) to secure

$$\text{plim} \left(\frac{1}{T}\right) \sum X_0 Q = a_0 \, \text{plim} \left(\frac{1}{T}\right) \sum X_0{}^2 + a_1 \, \text{plim} \left(\frac{1}{T}\right) \sum X_0 P \tag{1.3.6}$$

and

$$\text{plim} \left(\frac{1}{T}\right) \sum PQ = a_0 \, \text{plim} \left(\frac{1}{T}\right) \sum PX_0 + a_1 \, \text{plim} \left(\frac{1}{T}\right) \sum P^2 \tag{1.3.7}$$

Since X_0 is always equal to unity, denoting the mean of Q by $\bar{Q}$, these equations can be simplified and given more familiar form as

$$\text{plim} \, \bar{Q} = a_0 + a_1 \, \text{plim} \, \bar{P} \tag{1.3.8}$$

and

$$\text{plim} \left(\frac{1}{T}\right) \sum PQ = a_0 \, \text{plim} \, \bar{P} + a_1 \, \text{plim} \left(\frac{1}{T}\right) \sum P^2 \tag{1.3.9}$$

The treatment in the text is adopted for the sake of consistency with the later discussion of more general cases.

If one replaces the probability limits in Eqs. (1.3.6) and (1.3.7) with the corresponding sample values, one secures the usual normal equations of least squares, which may be solved to secure consistent estimates of a_0 and a_1.

Those estimates will in fact be unbiased if u_1 is assumed distributed independently of P; this and further properties of least-squares estimates (other than that of consistency) will not concern us here.

Thus, as in the nonstochastic case, one uses precisely two pieces of information to yield consistent estimates of the parameters. In that case one picks two independent sets of values for the two variables X_0 and P. Here one uses the two independent facts, expressed in Eqs. (1.3.3) and (1.3.5), that the average cross product of each of these variables and u_1 is zero in the probability limit.

When a stochastic supply curve, say

$$P = b_0 + b_1 Q + u_2 \tag{1.3.2a}$$

is introduced, the situation is again similar to that in the nonstochastic case. Now the observations will be scattered about the intersection of Eqs. (1.3.1) and (1.3.2) and it will be impossible to tell the true demand curve (1.3.1a) from any other curve whose nonstochastic part passes through that intersection and which has an appropriate additive disturbance.

To put it another way, whereas previously there were two pieces of observational information available, there is now only one—that u_1 has mean zero as expressed in Eq. (1.3.3). One can no longer assume, for example, that P and u_1 are uncorrelated in the probability limit, for it is evident that u_1 affects Q through Eq. (1.3.1a) and that Q in turn affects P through Eq. (1.3.2a). Indeed

$$P = \frac{1}{1 - b_1 a_1} (b_0 + b_1 a_0 + b_1 u_1 + u_2) \tag{1.3.10}$$

so that

$$\text{plim} \left(\frac{1}{T}\right) \sum P u_1 = \text{cov} (u_1, P) = \frac{1}{1 - b_1 a_1} \{b_1 \text{ var } u_1 + \text{cov} (u_1, u_2)\} \tag{1.3.11}$$

which certainly cannot be assumed to be zero without extremely specific further information. It follows that only Eq. (1.3.6) and not Eq. (1.3.7) can be considered as yielding valid information, and this will not suffice.

Another way of putting the problem may be illuminating. Suppose that we add a third parameter to Eq. (1.3.1a) by observing that Q really appears in that equation with a parameter, say c, which has been set equal to unity. By choosing the coefficient of Q equal to unity, we are choosing a normalization rule. Usually (but not always) the choice of a normalization rule can be dispensed with for our purposes. We are usually willing to consider any multiplication of Eq. (1.3.1a) by a nonzero number as an inessential rewriting of that equation and are willing to take consistent estimates of the parameters resulting from such multiplication as just as good as consistent estimates of the original parameters. For definiteness, we have chosen a particular one of the set of trivially equivalent equations resulting from such operations—the one in which $c = 1$.

Now, suppose that we knew how u_1 was distributed. We could try to derive a maximum likelihood estimator of c, a_0, and a_1 {which would be the least-squares estimator if Eq. (1.3.2a) did not exist and if observations on u_1 were normally and independently distributed with common variance}. If Eq. (1.3.2a) did not exist, we could generally do this because the likelihood function in the space of c, a_0, and a_1 would have a ridge along the ray corresponding to the vector of true parameters and its scalar multiples. Indeed, when one considers only the plane given by the normalization rule $c = 1$, the likelihood function would have a unique maximum at the point where that ray intersected that plane.

In the presence of Eq. (1.3.2a), however, this is no longer possible. In the space of the three parameters in question, the likelihood function will attain its maximum everywhere in the two-dimensional subspace spanned by the vectors $(1, a_0, a_1)$ and the vector $(b_1, -b_0, 1)$ derived from Eq.

(1.3.2a). Even imposing the normalization rule that the coefficient of Q is unity will leave the likelihood function with an identical maximum value everywhere on the straight line passing through $(1, a_0, a_1)$ and $(1, -b_0/b_1, 1/b_1)$. Maximum likelihood estimation will therefore not yield a determinate set of estimates for the parameters of the demand curve.

Furthermore, it is evident that the difficulty does not lie with the estimating technique discussed—whether least squares or maximum likelihood—but is embedded in the very structure of the model. Without further assumptions, any estimation technique can at best return to the nonstochastic situation in which the problem still lies. In attempting to secure consistent estimates of the demand (or supply) curve, one is attempting to fit a line to a set of observations which essentially consists of a single point with random disturbances.

What then is to be done? Clearly, in such a situation, nothing can be done without further assumptions. In practice, however, one usually has further information on the equations of the system and can use this information to secure consistent estimates. Such information clearly cannot take the form of knowing which variables are uncorrelated with a given disturbance in the probability limit. As the example makes clear, the logical structure of the model will prevent that sort of information from being sufficient. Rather one needs other types of information.

What sort of information might one then have? Suppose one knew, for example, that for some reason the supply curve shifted a great deal relative to the demand curve. The resulting series of intersections between the demand curve and each of the shifting supply curves would tend to trace out the demand curve as shown in Fig. 1c. If, on the other hand, one knew that the demand curve shifted a great deal relative to the supply curve, the resulting intersections would approximate the supply curve as shown in Fig. 1d. Clearly, if such relative shifts were known to be large enough, one would be able to identify the relatively stable relationship and determine its parameters to any desired degree of approximation.

The knowledge that such shifts occur may be interpreted in two ways. First, we may think of it as a statement about the relative variances of u_1 and u_2—as a statement about the relative amounts of random noise present in the two relationships. Clearly, if one relationship contains an enormous amount of random noise relative to the other, then, in the limit, we are approaching the situation in which only the relatively stable relationship can be said to exist.

Alternatively, if one thinks of disturbances as made up largely or entirely of the effects of variables omitted from the equations, one can interpret a statement about relative shifts as a statement that there is some variable which really appears in one of the equations but not in the other and whose value keeps changing. This amounts to asserting that the shifting curve in fact corresponds to a perfectly stable relationship among Q, P, and an additional variable, but that the presence of that variable shifts the curve in the Q-P plane which is the intersection of that relationship and that plane.

Need such a variable be actually omitted, however? If its presence in the disturbance term leads to identification of one of the equations, then surely, explicit recognition of its influence must also do so. This suggests immediately that if one of the equations contains a variable *not* contained in the other, the equation in which that variable does *not* appear will be identified.

This is in fact the case. Suppose that the demand equation contains income, denoted by Y, in addition to price and quantity. Thus, in place of Eq. (1.3.1a), we substitute

$$Q = a_0 + a_1 P + a_2 Y + u_1 \qquad (1.3.12)$$

Suppose we know that Y is uncorrelated with either u_1 or u_2 in the probability limit. Solve Eqs. (1.3.2a) and (1.3.12) for P and Q in terms of Y, u_1, and u_2 to obtain

$$P = \pi_{10} + \pi_{11} Y + v_1$$
$$Q = \pi_{20} + \pi_{21} Y + v_2 \qquad (1.3.13)$$

where
$$\pi_{10} = \frac{b_0 + b_1 a_0}{1 - a_1 b_1} \qquad \pi_{11} = \frac{b_1 a_2}{1 - a_1 b_1}$$
$$\pi_{20} = \frac{a_0 + a_1 b_0}{1 - a_1 b_1} \qquad \pi_{21} = \frac{a_2}{1 - a_1 b_1} \qquad (1.3.14)$$

and
$$v_1 = \frac{b_1 u_1 + u_2}{1 - a_1 b_1} \qquad v_2 = \frac{u_1 + a_1 u_2}{1 - a_1 b_1} \qquad (1.3.15)$$

Equations (1.3.13) are known as the "reduced form" of the system.

Now, clearly, there is no difficulty in securing consistent estimates of the reduced form parameters π_{10}, π_{11}, π_{20}, and π_{21}. In the nonstochastic case in which u_1 and u_2 (and therefore v_1 and v_2) are zero, this can be done by choosing two different values of Y (two independent observations on X_0 and Y) and observing the effects on P and Q; in the stochastic case, it can be done by least-squares regression of P and Q on Y.

Once consistent estimates of the reduced form parameters are obtained, however, it is clearly possible to obtain consistent estimates of b_0 and b_1, for

$$b_1 = \frac{\pi_{11}}{\pi_{21}} \qquad b_0 = \pi_{10} - b_1 \pi_{20} = \pi_{10} - \frac{\pi_{11}}{\pi_{21}} \pi_{20} \qquad (1.3.16)$$

On the other hand, no way of recovering a_0, a_1, or a_2 exists.

Two features of this example deserve special emphasis. First, it depends on the presence of a variable Y in one of the equations but not the other. If a_2 were zero, we would be back in the earlier case; if Y appeared in the supply curve with a nonzero coefficient, one again could not distinguish the demand and supply curves, and transformations such as Eq. (1.3.16) would not exist. Second, it is the equation in which Y does not appear which is identified. The equation in which it does appear is still not identifiable. While this may seem surprising, it can be expressed in a more intuitively appealing way in the light of our earlier discussion.

Let us suppose that the system really has Y appearing in the supply curve as well as in the demand relationship. Let Y's coefficient in the supply function be denoted by b_2. There are then three parameters which must be estimated in each equation. Empirical, observational information can yield only two pieces of information on the three parameters, by using the facts that

$$\text{plim} \left(\frac{1}{T}\right) \sum X_0 u_i = 0 = \text{plim} \left(\frac{1}{T}\right) \sum Y u_i \qquad (i = 1, 2) \quad (1.3.17)$$

or (in the nonstochastic case) by choosing two independent observations on X_0 and Y and observing the values of P and Q. Prior theoretical information must therefore supply at least one more piece of information if the three parameters of a given curve are to be consistently estimated. This is done for the supply curve by imposing the restriction that $b_2 = 0$— that Y does not appear. The supply curve is then identified, but the demand curve is not, since no parallel information is available for it.

The astute reader may observe at this point that things are not really so simple. Suppose that one knew not only that $b_2 = 0$ but also that $a_2 = 0$. This would not suffice to identify the demand curve. Indeed, it would plunge us back into the original case in which neither relationship was identifiable. The answer is that the prior information which enables us to identify the supply curve really includes information on the demand curve as well—information that Y *does* appear therein. To put it another way, prior information on the supply curve is only of use if it places a restriction on the parameters of that relationship which is not also obeyed by the demand curve. There is no point in knowing that a great many variables do not appear in one if they also do not appear in the other. Information is only of use here if it can be used to *distinguish* the two curves, that is, to identify one in the presence of the other.

We have now seen two ways in which such useful information may be at hand. Both ways happen to imply that one of the curves shifts about substantially relative to the other. While the case of known zero coefficients in one equation for a variable which appears with a nonzero one in another (what we may term "exclusion restrictions") is of particular importance for practical reasons, it and the case of near-zero disturbance variance for one of the equations are by no means the only cases which arise. In general, a priori information takes the form of restrictions on the coefficients of the variables and on the process supposed to generate the random disturbances. Clearly, for example, one might have rather more general restrictions than the exclusion variety on the coefficients of a given equation; or one might be able to specify relations among the coefficients of more than one equation.

Alternatively, one might be willing to specify something about the properties of the disturbances—for example, that u_1 and u_2 in the supply-demand case are uncorrelated. Since this particular type of restriction is of considerable theoretical importance in that, as we shall later see, certain applications of it underlie a great deal of the rationale for simultaneous equation estimation and the treatment of so-called "exogenous variables," its implications for identifiability are worth examining in the present context.

We have already seen that the heart of the problem lies in the fact that observational information alone cannot distinguish the true demand and supply curves from any other curve going through their intersection. Another way of saying this is that the true pair of curves cannot be distinguished from another pair constructed by taking two independent linear combinations of the true equations. That is, if one takes λ times Eq. (1.3.2a) and adds the result to Eq. (1.3.1a), the resulting equation, when solved for Q, will be indistinguishable from Eq. (1.3.1a) so far as observational information is concerned. Similarly, if one takes μ times Eq. (1.3.1a) and adds the result to Eq. (1.3.2a), the resulting equation, when solved for P, will be indistinguishable from Eq. (1.3.2a). The false pair of equations so obtained will be

$$Q = \frac{1}{1 - \lambda b_1} \{a_0 + \lambda b_0 + (a_1 - \lambda)P + u_1 + \lambda u_2\} \qquad (1.3.18)$$

which has the same form as Eq. (1.3.1a), and

$$P = \frac{1}{1 - \mu a_1} \{b_0 + \mu a_0 + (b_1 - \mu)Q + u_2 + \mu u_1\} \qquad (1.3.19)$$

Without further assumptions, so long as $\lambda b_1 \neq 1 \neq \mu a_1$ and the two equations just derived are independent, the true equations cannot be distinguished from any pair of equations in the above form.

On the other hand, if one knows that

$$\text{cov}\,(u_1, u_2)^{\cdot} = \text{plim}\left(\frac{1}{T}\right) \sum u_1 u_2 = 0 \qquad (1.3.20)$$

this is not the case. Denote the terms in Eqs. (1.3.18) and (1.3.19) which involve the disturbances by u_1^* and u_2^*, respectively. If we are to be unable to distinguish the false equations from the true ones, these disturbances must also be uncorrelated with each other in the probability limit. Thus, we must have

$$0 = (1 - \lambda b_1)(1 - \mu a_1) \text{ cov } (u_1^*, u_2^*)$$
$$= (1 + \lambda \mu) \text{ cov } (u_1, u_2) + \lambda \text{ var } u_2 + \mu \text{ var } u_1$$
$$= \lambda \text{ var } u_2 + \mu \text{ var } u_1 \quad (1.3.21)$$

so that

$$\mu = -\lambda \frac{\text{var } u_2}{\text{var } u_1} \quad (1.3.22)$$

In this case, the pairs of equations indistinguishable from the true ones are a one-parameter rather than a two-parameter family. This may not seem much of a gain, but it carries the following implication: If, by reason of *other* information, the demand curve is identified so that only a zero value of λ leads to an equation indistinguishable from the true demand curve (i.e., only the true demand curve has the true demand curve's properties), the restriction on the correlation of the disturbances implies {using Eq. (1.3.22)} that the supply curve is identified also, since then μ must be zero and Eqs. (1.3.19) and (1.3.2a) are identical. The effect of such restrictions is evidently to tie together the identification of different equations. The precise way in which this happens in the general many-equation case will be spelled out in a later chapter.

1.4. A Useful Theorem

Before proceeding to a precise discussion of the identification problem in the general many-equation case, we shall digress to remind the reader of a theorem in matrix algebra which we shall work overtime throughout this book.

Let A be any $n \times c$ matrix. Denote the rank of A by $\rho(A)$. The *null space* (column kernel) of A is the set of vectors mapped into the zero vector by premultiplication by A. We shall usually find it convenient to work with the null space of A', where the prime mark denotes transposition. This space is called the *row kernel*. Formally:

Definition 1.4.1: The *row kernel* of any $n \times s$ matrix A is the set of all n-component row vectors x such that

$$xA = 0 \quad (1.4.1)$$

The row kernel of A will be denoted by $K(A)$ and its dimension by $k(A)$.

The theorem which will prove so useful is:

Theorem 1.4.1: $\qquad \rho(A) + k(A) = n$

Proof: Since A has $\rho(A)$ independent rows, we may, without ·loss of generality, suppose that these are the first $\rho(A)$ rows and partition A as

$$A = \begin{bmatrix} A_1 \\ A_2 \end{bmatrix} \tag{1.4.2}$$

By construction, the set of vectors consisting of the rows of A_1 and any row of A_2 is a dependent set. Thus, there exist $\{n - \rho(A)\}$ vectors in $K(A)$ in the following form:

$$x^i = (x_1{}^i \quad e_i) \qquad \{i = 1, \ldots, n - \rho(A)\} \tag{1.4.3}$$

where e_i has its ith component equal to unity and all other components zero.

We shall prove the theorem by showing that these $\{n - \rho(A)\}$ vectors form a basis for $K(A)$. Since these vectors are obviously independent, it suffices to show that they span $K(A)$. Thus, let y be any vector in $K(A)$ partitioned in the obvious way. We can clearly write

$$y_2 = \sum_{i=1}^{n-\rho(A)} \lambda_i e_i \tag{1.4.4}$$

for some set of scalars $\lambda_1 \cdots \lambda_{n-\rho(A)}$. Form the vector

$$z = y - \sum_{i=1}^{n-\rho(A)} \lambda_i x^i \tag{1.4.5}$$

It is obvious that z lies in $K(A)$ and, partitioning z into z_1 and z_2, that $z_2 = 0$. It follows immediately, however, that $z_1 = 0$ also. To see this, observe that

$$zA = z_1 A_1 + z_2 A_2 = z_1 A_1 = 0 \tag{1.4.6}$$

and the rows of A_1 are independent by construction. Thus $z = 0$ and

$$y = \sum_{i=1}^{n-\rho(A)} \lambda_i x^i \tag{1.4.7}$$

so that the $\{n - \rho(A)\}$ vectors $x^1 \cdots x^{n-\rho(A)}$ form a basis for $K(A)$, and the theorem is proved.

This theorem may be interpreted in a number of ways. Perhaps the most illuminating of these for our purposes is as follows. If the n rows of A were independent, the columns of A would span Euclidean n space. A point in the column space of A would then have n degrees of freedom; it would require n independent conditions to specify it completely, if all that were known of it was that it lay in the column space of A. Every vector in the row kernel of A, however, provides a restriction on the column space of A, for Eq. (1.4.1) shows that some linear combination of the elements of any column must be zero. The dimensionality of the row kernel $k(A)$ is the number of *independent* restrictions obeyed by the columns of A and therefore by every vector in the column space thereof. The number of degrees of freedom of a point in the column space of A must therefore be $\{n - k(A)\}$, since $k(A)$ of the independent conditions required to fix a point in n space have been supplied. The dimension of the column space of A must therefore be $\{n - k(A)\}$, but this is what the theorem asserts, since the dimension of the column space is equal to the rank.

1.5. The General Model to Be Estimated

We are now almost ready to give a formal and precise description of the identification problem. In order to do so, we must first describe the model to be estimated.

We assume that model to consist of M equations in N variables and M random disturbances (which will be identically zero when nonstochastic cases are under discussion). For the most part, and until further notice, those equations will be assumed to be linear in the variables and the disturbances. We thus write

$$A x_t = u_t \tag{1.5.1}$$

where t is a subscript denoting different observations (generally but not necessarily standing for time); A is an $M \times N$ matrix of constant parameters to be estimated; x_t is an N-component column vector, whose typical element x_{it} is the value of the ith variable at the tth observation; and u_t is an M-component vector, whose typical element u_{it} is the (unobservable) value of the ith disturbance at the tth observation.

When a specific matrix is substituted for A and a specific distribution (a specific variance-covariance matrix) assumed for the elements of u, the resulting subcase of the model is called a "structure."

We must now distinguish between two kinds of variables: those which the model determines, given the values of the others, and those which are to be thought of as independently determined. The first type of variable is called "endogenous;" the second type is called "exogenous." Since we may assume that any redundant equations have been eliminated, we may assume:

Assumption 1.5.1: $\rho(A) = M$

Thus there are obviously M endogenous variables, the matrix of whose coefficients is nonsingular.

One is immediately tempted to conclude that there are precisely $N - M$ exogenous variables; this need not be the case, however, and a further distinction is called for. Equation (1.5.1) can be thought of as determining the value at time t of the M endogenous variables, given the value of the other variables and of the disturbances. Not all those other variables need be determined from outside the model, however. Some of them may be previous values of the endogenous variables. We shall call such lagged endogenous variables and the exogenous variables "predetermined"; they have the property that their values can be known before Eq. (1.5.1) is solved at time t for the M values of the M current endogenous variables. Obviously, there are $N - M$ such predetermined variables. We shall be more precise in a later chapter about what constitutes exogeneity and predetermination; for the present, the distinction between endogenous and predetermined variables is that one can logically suppose that one knows the values of the predetermined variables before knowing the values of the endogenous variables. The latter variables are simultaneously determined by the model, given the former variables and the values of the disturbances.

Corresponding to the distinction between endogenous and predetermined variables, we partition x_t, renumbering the variables if necessary, so that the first M components of x_t are the values of the endogenous variables at the tth observation. We denote the M-component vector of those values by y_t, and the $(N - M)$-component vector of the values of the predetermined variables at the tth observation by z_t. We let $\Lambda = N - M$. Similarly, we partition A as

$$A = [B \quad \Gamma] \tag{1.5.2}$$

so that Eq. (1.5.1) may be rewritten as

$$By_t + \Gamma z_t = u_t \tag{1.5.3}$$

Without loss of generality, we may assume that the last predetermined variable is exogenous and has a value equal to unity in every observation. The coefficients of that variable—the last column of Γ—are thus the constant terms of the M equations of the model. If some or all of those equations do not have constant terms, this will be represented by setting the corresponding elements of the last column of Γ equal to zero rather than by deleting the last element of z_t as just defined.

Since B is nonsingular, as remarked following Assumption 1.5.1, we may solve the system (1.5.3) by premultiplication by B^{-1} to obtain an explicit statement of the determination of the values of the endogenous variables in terms of the predetermined variables and the disturbances. Thus

$$y_t = \Pi z_t + v_t \tag{1.5.4}$$

where $\qquad \Pi = -B^{-1}\Gamma \qquad v_t = B^{-1}u_t \tag{1.5.5}$

The system of equations (1.5.4) is called the reduced form of the model

(1.5.1). {In the two-equation example discussed above, the reduced form is given in Eqs. (1.3.13).} Observe that every equation of the reduced form contains precisely one endogenous variable.

We now make two assumptions concerning the predetermined variables. The first of these is:

Assumption 1.5.2: No linear identities connect the predetermined variables. This is an innocuous assumption, since we may always eliminate identities known in advance by direct substitution for one or more of the variables involved. The assumption amounts to agreeing to do this before the system (1.5.1) is written.

Now, let T be the total number of observations in the sample. Denote by Y, Z, U, and V, respectively, the $T \times M$, $T \times \Lambda$, $T \times M$, and $T \times M$ matrices (called "observation matrices") whose tth rows are y_t', z_t', u_t', and v_t', where the prime mark, as before, denotes transposition. We may rewrite Eq. (1.5.3) more compactly as

$$YB' + Z\Gamma' = U \tag{1.5.6}$$

The use of transposes here stems from a desire to maintain the usual notation for least-squares theory while keeping the model in the form which seems most natural for discussion of identifiability.

The second (and crucial) assumption which we shall make concerning the predetermined variables is

Assumption 1.5.3: $\qquad \operatorname{plim}\left(\dfrac{Z'U}{T}\right) = 0$

In other words, the predetermined variables are assumed to be uncorrelated with the disturbances in the probability limit. If we are dealing with the nonstochastic case in which $U = 0$, this presents no problem. In the more general stochastic case, however, it is of such crucial importance as really to be the defining characteristic of predetermined variables. {Note that it arose above in our two-equation example as Eqs. (1.3.3) and (1.3.5), the absence of the latter being a crucial point in our discussion of the example.} When it fails, the problems raised are quite difficult. We shall discuss it in detail in a later chapter, with special regard for the case of lagged endogenous variables (a point which will be slightly amplified in a moment). We shall then need to be concerned in some detail with the defining characteristics of exogeneity and predeterminedness. For the present, we shall simply make Assumption 1.5.3.

Notice that, in view of the definition of the last element of z_t, the last column of Z consists exclusively of unit elements. Assumption 1.5.3 thus includes the assumption that the disturbances have zero mean.

Observe, on the other hand, that a similar assumption cannot be consistently made about the endogenous variables which are clearly influenced by the disturbances. Indeed, using Eqs. (1.5.4) and (1.5.5) and the assumption just made,

$$\text{plim}\left(\frac{Y'U}{T}\right) = \Pi\,\text{plim}\left(\frac{Z'U}{T}\right) + \text{plim}\left(\frac{V'U}{T}\right)$$
$$= B^{-1}\,\text{plim}\left(\frac{U'U}{T}\right) \tag{1.5.7}$$

which, in the stochastic case, cannot generally be assumed even to have particular elements zero without further assumptions on the elements of B and the variance-covariance matrix of the disturbances.

This brings us to the assumptions we shall make concerning that variance-covariance matrix. We shall denote it by Σ and shall assume:

Assumption 1.5.4: Unless we are dealing with the nonstochastic case, or state otherwise, Σ will be assumed to be positive definite. We shall in later chapters deal with more restrictive assumptions on the form of Σ and with the effect of such assumptions on identifiability. (We have already touched on this in our discussion of the two-equation example given above.)

One other property of the disturbances needs to be mentioned before going further. We have not been specific about whether disturbances at one time are allowed to be correlated with disturbances at another time. We shall see in Chap. 6 that the presence or absence of such serial correlation plays an important role in identification when there are lagged endogenous variables present. This is because a lagged endogenous variable is influenced by past disturbances, so that Assumption 1.5.3 is likely to fail with respect to such variables if current and past disturbances are correlated. This means that lagged endogenous variables cannot be treated as predetermined in such circumstances. Without going into further detail, suffice it to observe that Assumption 1.5.3 does imply something about the serial correlation properties of the disturbances if lagged endogenous variables are treated as predetermined. We shall impose that assumption at this time and worry about the implications of serial correlation in a later chapter.

1.6. The Limits of Observational Information

For the sake of definiteness (and without loss of generality), we shall generally be concerned with the estimation of the coefficients of the first equation of Eq. (1.5.1)—the estimation of the first row of A. We denote that row by A_1 and similarly denote the first rows of B and Γ by B_1 and

Γ_1, respectively. In this section we shall examine what observational information can in principle tell us about A_1.

As in the two-equation example discussed above, it may be illuminating first to consider the nonstochastic case in which $U \equiv 0$ and then to go on to the more general case. It will be seen that the two cases have a great deal in common so far as the present problem is concerned. In particular, we shall show that in both cases observational information is in principle capable of putting Λ independent restrictions on the elements of A_1 and no more. It will then follow that at least $M = (N - \Lambda)$ restrictions must generally be secured from outside sources in order to fix A_1.

We begin then with the nonstochastic case. As in the two-equation example, we may think of making ideal experiments to get information on A_1 by choosing values of the predetermined variables and allowing the model to determine the endogenous variables. Thus, suppose that we perform T experiments. Denote by X the $T \times N$ observation matrix

$$X = [Y \quad Z] \tag{1.6.1}$$

whose tth row consists of the values of the variables at the tth experiment (observation). Since Y is determined by the model, given Z, Y and Z must be consistent with the first equation of the model. Thus, in the present nonstochastic case

$$A_1 X' = B_1 Y' + \Gamma_1 Z' = 0 \tag{1.6.2}$$

Thus A_1 lies in the row kernel of X'. Clearly, this is all that such experiments can tell us about A_1.

Unfortunately, however, this is clearly not enough if $M > 1$. Since Y and Z must be consistent with *all* the equations of the model, we must have

$$AX' = BY' + \Gamma Z' = 0 \tag{1.6.3}$$

so that every row of A, and not just the first, lies in the row kernel of X'. Equivalently, since an experiment consists of choosing values for the Λ predetermined variables and letting the model determine the values of the endogenous variables, it is evident that this can in principle be done in only Λ independent ways since no identities connect the predetermined variables. The matrix X' will thus have rank Λ and, since it has N rows, will have a row kernel of dimension $N - \Lambda = M$, by Theorem 1.4.1. Equation (1.6.3) shows that the M independent rows of A form a basis for that row kernel.

If one can perform Λ independent experiments and no more, we may as well discard the redundant information provided by extra experiments and take $T = \Lambda$ (in the nonstochastic case only) and Z nonsingular. Premultiplying Eq. (1.6.3) by B^{-1} and postmultiplying by Z'^{-1}, we obtain after rewriting

$$Y'Z'^{-1} = -B^{-1}\Gamma = \Pi \qquad (1.6.4)$$

by Eq. (1.5.5). It follows that observational information *is* sufficient to yield the parameters of the reduced form.

We now turn to the stochastic case. Here again observational information can, in principle, be used to establish precisely Λ restrictions on the elements of A_1. In this case, these restrictions are secured by the use of Assumption 1.5.3. Thus, writing the model in the transposed form (1.5.6), premultiplying the first equation by Z'/T, denoting the first column of U (the values of u_1) by U^1, and passing to the probability limit, we have

$$\operatorname{plim}\left(\frac{Z'X}{T}\right) A_1' = \operatorname{plim}\left(\frac{Z'Y}{T}\right) B_1' + \operatorname{plim}\left(\frac{Z'Z}{T}\right) \Gamma_1'$$

$$= \operatorname{plim}\left(\frac{Z'U^1}{T}\right) = 0 \qquad (1.6.5)$$

provided all the probability limits exist—which we shall assume without further comment. Since no linear identities connect the predetermined variables, plim $(Z'Z/T)$ is nonsingular and plim $(Z'X/T)$ has rank Λ, so that Eq. (1.6.5) places precisely Λ restrictions on the elements of A_1 and clearly exhausts the observational information available.

As in the nonstochastic case, those restrictions are also obeyed by the other rows of A. Thus

$$\operatorname{plim}\left(\frac{Z'X}{T}\right) A' = \operatorname{plim}\left(\frac{Z'Y}{T}\right) B' + \operatorname{plim}\left(\frac{Z'Z}{T}\right) \Gamma'$$

$$= \operatorname{plim}\left(\frac{Z'U}{T}\right) = 0 \qquad (1.6.6)$$

by Assumption 1.5.3. Every row of A (and not just the first) thus lies in the row kernel of $[\operatorname{plim} (Z'X/T)]'$. Since that matrix has N rows, its row kernel has dimension $N - \Lambda = M$ by Theorem 1.4.1, and the M independent rows of A form a basis for that row kernel.

Again, as in the nonstochastic case, the observational information *does* suffice to determine the parameters of the reduced form. Postmultiply Eq. (1.6.6) by B'^{-1} and premultiply it by $[\operatorname{plim} (Z'Z/T)]^{-1}$ to obtain

$$\operatorname{plim} \{(Z'Z)^{-1}Z'Y\} = \left\{\operatorname{plim}\left(\frac{Z'Z}{T}\right)\right\}^{-1} \operatorname{plim}\left(\frac{Z'Y}{T}\right) = -\Gamma'B'^{-1} = \Pi'$$

$$(1.6.7)$$

This shows, indeed, not only that Π can be consistently estimated, but that ordinary least squares is a consistent estimator when applied to each reduced form equation in turn.

Note that if $M = 1$, the single reduced form equation and the single structural equation are identical, given the convention that the coefficient of the single endogenous variable in the latter equation is -1 when the equation is written with the disturbance on one side and the variables on the other. In this case, least squares is a consistent estimator of the single structural equation.

Since in both the stochastic and the nonstochastic cases the estimates of Π are obtained by a nonsingular transformation of those equations which embody all that observational information can tell us about the parameters of the system, the estimates of Π themselves embody all such information. In particular, we may express the restrictions placed by observation on A_1 in both cases in the following way. Define

$$W = \begin{bmatrix} \Pi \\ I \end{bmatrix} \tag{1.6.8}$$

where I is a $\Lambda \times \Lambda$ identity matrix. Clearly,

$$AW = B\Pi + \Gamma I = B(-B^{-1}\Gamma) + \Gamma = -\Gamma + \Gamma = 0 \tag{1.6.9}$$

and, in particular,

$$A_1 W = 0 \tag{1.6.10}$$

an equation which embodies all the restrictions on A_1 which can be derived from observational information. Such information can lead us only to the statement that A_1 lies in the row kernel of W; however, the dimension of that row kernel is clearly M and every other row of A lies in it as well, the M independent rows of A forming a basis for $K(W)$.

These results may be summarized in a theorem which provides a precise statement of the nature of the identification problem in the present simultaneous linear equations context.

Theorem 1.6.1: An N-component row vector α can be distinguished from the true A_1 on the basis of a posteriori information if and only if α is not a linear combination of the rows of A.

Proof: Suppose first that α is a linear combination of the rows of A, that is, that there exists an M-component row vector h such that

$$\alpha = hA \tag{1.6.11}$$

All a posteriori restrictions on A_1 are given by Eq. (1.6.10); in view of Eq. (1.6.9), however,

$$\alpha W = hAW = 0 \tag{1.6.12}$$

so that α satisfies all those restrictions and thus cannot be distinguished from the true A_1 on the basis of a posteriori information alone.

To prove the converse, suppose that α cannot be so distinguished from the true A_1. Then, certainly

$$\alpha W = 0 \tag{1.6.13}$$

so that α is in $K(W)$. We have already had occasion to remark, however, that the rows of A form a basis for $K(W)$, whence α must be a linear combination of the rows of A, and the theorem is proved.

Thus, observational information can only distinguish the true first equation from candidates which are not linear combinations of the equations of the model. It can do no more. This corresponds to the fact that any linear combination of the equations is clearly in the same form as any single equation in the absence of further information about that form. The fact that equations which are not such linear combinations can be ruled out is a little less obvious but corresponds to the fact that if one has written down all the equations connecting the endogenous variables to the predetermined one, any equation not a linear combination of the true ones must introduce some new variable.

Geometrically, the results may be interpreted as follows. In the non-stochastic case, Eq. (1.6.2) shows that observations satisfying the first equation of the model must lie on an $(N - 1)$-dimensional hyperplane. Unfortunately, that hyperplane is unobservable because Eq. (1.6.3) shows that the observations must lie on the intersection of M such hyperplanes and thus only on a hyperplane of dimension $N - M = \Lambda$. All that can be observed is that intersection, and the hyperplane corresponding to the true first equation cannot be distinguished from any other hyperplane passing through that intersection without the use of further information.

In the stochastic case, the circumstance is much the same, except that the observations are scattered about the intersection just described rather than lying precisely on it. In this case, the situation may be thought of in the following way.

Clearly, the joint distribution of the elements of y, given z, is determined by the joint distribution of the disturbances and the equations of the reduced form (1.5.4), which we write out again as

$$y_t = \Pi z_t + v_t = (-B^{-1}\Gamma)z_t + B^{-1}u_t \tag{1.6.14}$$

Now suppose that we subject the original system to a nonsingular linear transformation with matrix F. That is, we replace each equation of the structure by a linear combination of the structural equations, those linear combinations being independent (to preserve the rank of A when transformed). Thus, we obtain the new structure

$$B^*y_t + \Gamma^*z_t = u_t^* \tag{1.6.15}$$

where
$$B^* = FB \qquad \Gamma^* = F\Gamma \qquad u_t^* = Fu_t \tag{1.6.16}$$

The theorem just proved states that the only equations which can be mistaken for the true first one can be obtained in this way.[1] Suppose that we now write out the reduced form corresponding to the transformed equations. We obtain

$$y_t = \Pi^* z_t + v_t^*$$ (1.6.17)

but $$\Pi^* = -B^{*-1}\Gamma^* = -(FB)^{-1}(F\Gamma) = -B^{-1}\Gamma = \Pi$$ (1.6.18)

and $$v_t^* = B^{*-1}u_t^* = (FB)^{-1}(Fu_t) = B^{-1}u_t = v_t$$ (1.6.19)

Thus both the original and the transformed structure have the same reduced form, and both of them will generate the same observations for the elements of y_t, given the values of the elements of z_t and u_t.

Now suppose that one wanted to tell the original and the transformed structure apart, armed only with the distribution of the elements of u_t. This clearly cannot be done. One is dealing with the same observations in both cases, and the distribution of the elements of y_t, given z_t and a particular distribution for the elements of u_t, is clearly the same (because $\Pi^* = \Pi$, *not* because $v_t^* = v_t$) as that of the elements of y_t, given z_t and the same particular distribution applied to the elements of u_t^*. The likelihood function will have the same value at the point in parameter space corresponding to the transformed structure that it does at the point corresponding to the true one.

Specifically, concentrating again on the first equation, suppose we suppress the parameters of the other equations (as is done in certain estimation methods, of which limited information, maximum likelihood is the leading case) by first maximizing the likelihood function with respect to those parameters and using the resulting first-order maximum conditions to write all terms in the likelihood function involving such parameters as functions of the parameters of the first equation. We now obtain a function in terms only of the parameters of the first equation. This function is called the "concentrated likelihood function," and maximizing it with respect to its arguments clearly finds the maximum of the original likelihood function. The problem in the present situation is that, when we do this, we shall find that the concentrated likelihood function takes on its maximum not just on the hyperplane corresponding to the parameters of the first equation (at a unique point if we agree to fix the scale of the parameters by an appropriate normalization rule) but on every hyperplane passing through the intersection of the M true-equation hyperplanes. That is, it takes on its maximum everywhere in the M-dimensional subspace spanned by the rows of A. Clearly, without

[1] We may always, if necessary, replace the other equations by themselves, taking the last $M - 1$ rows and columns of F to be the unit matrix.

further restrictions, consistent estimators of A_1, or indeed of any row of A, do not exist.

1.7. Admissible Transformations and Structures

Since observational information cannot distinguish any equation of the model from any other linear combination of those equations but can distinguish it from any equation not such a linear combination, it is apparent that structural estimation is possible if and only if there is sufficient a priori information on the parameters of the model to distinguish a given equation from the set of all linear combinations of the equations.

We may put this another way. So far as observational information is concerned, the true set of structural equations cannot be distinguished from a false set in which each structural equation is replaced by a linear combination of the equations. Thus, let F be any $M \times M$ matrix; premultiply Eq. (1.5.1) by F to obtain

$$A^* x_t = u_t^* \qquad (1.7.1)$$

where $\qquad A^* = FA \qquad u_t^* = Fu_t \qquad (1.7.2)$

Observational information cannot distinguish Eq. (1.7.1) from the true model (1.5.1).

There is one exception to this, however. By Assumption 1.5.1, the true A has rank M. Any proposed A^* which does not also have that rank can therefore be eliminated from consideration. It follows that the transformation matrix F must be taken to be nonsingular.

Since, by the theorem of the preceding section, any structure *not* obtained by such a nonsingular transformation of the true structure can be distinguished from the true structure on the basis of observational information, we need consider only the class of "observationally equivalent" structures in discussing the role of a priori information.

Such information can relate either to the elements of the coefficient matrix A or to the process generating the disturbances or both. We shall assume that information on the process generating the disturbances always consists of information about the matrix Σ, that is, the variance-covariance matrix of those disturbances. This means that we must consider the effects of the transformation (1.7.2) on that variance-covariance matrix. We must show how the variance-covariance matrix of the transformed disturbances u_t^* is related to that of the original disturbances.

This is easy to do. Let U^* be the $T \times M$ matrix whose tth row is $u_t^{*'}$. Then $U^* = UF'$. The variance-covariance matrix of the transformed disturbances Σ^* is given by

$$\Sigma^* = \operatorname{plim}\left(\frac{U^{*\prime}U^*}{T}\right) = F\left\{\operatorname{plim}\left(\frac{U'U}{T}\right)\right\} F' = F\Sigma F' \qquad (1.7.3)$$

Clearly, prior information will help by ruling out transformations which result in coefficient matrices A^* or variance-covariance matrices Σ^* which fail to satisfy the restrictions placed by that information on A and Σ, respectively. Formally, we define:

Definition 1.7.1: A linear transformation denoted by an $M \times M$ matrix F is called *admissible* if and only if it has all three of the following properties:
  (a) F is nonsingular.
  (b) $A^* = FA$ satisfies all a priori restrictions on A.
  (c) $\Sigma^* = F\Sigma F'$ satisfies all a priori restrictions on Σ.

Alternatively, it may sometimes be more natural and convenient to work directly with the transformed structure instead of with the transformation producing it and define:

Definition 1.7.2: A structure consisting of an $M \times N$ matrix A^* and an $M \times M$ positive definite matrix Σ^* is called *admissible* if and only if it has all three of the following properties:
  (a) A^* satisfies all a priori restrictions on A.
  (b) Σ^* satisfies all a priori restrictions on Σ.
  (c) There exists a nonsingular $M \times M$ matrix F such that $A^* = FA$ and $\Sigma^* = F\Sigma F'$.

That no ambiguity can arise between the two definitions is shown by the following fairly obvious theorem:

Theorem 1.7.1: There is a one-to-one correspondence between the set of admissible transformations and the set of admissible structures.

Proof: That every admissible transformation corresponds to precisely one admissible structure is obvious. It remains to be proved that every admissible structure can be derived by a unique admissible transformation.

Suppose that this were not the case. Then there exists an admissible structure with coefficient matrix A^* and two admissible transformations with matrices F^1 and F^2, such that $F^1 \neq F^2$ and

$$F^1 A = A^* = F^2 A \qquad (1.7.4)$$

Then
$$(F^1 - F^2)A = 0 \qquad (1.7.5)$$

but this is impossible since at least one row of $(F^1 - F^2)$ must form a nonzero vector in the row kernel of A, violating the assumption that A has rank M. (Note that the theorem does not depend on any properties of Σ. It thus holds in the nonstochastic as well as in the stochastic case.)

In view of the theorem, we may work with either the set of admissible transformations or the set of admissible structures, whichever is more convenient. Note that the identity transformation is always an admissible one, since the true structure is assumed to satisfy all the restrictions on itself.

1.8. Prior Restrictions and Normalization Rules

We are now almost ready to give a precise definition of identification. We shall do this first in terms of a particular equation of the model (1.5.1), this being the context in which the problem generally arises in practice. While we shall later briefly generalize the discussion, most of this book will be concerned with identification of particular equations.

As before, without loss of generality, we may suppose that it is the first equation of the model in which we are interested. Clearly, we shall speak of that equation as identifiable (or identified) if there exists some combination of prior and posterior information which will enable us to distinguish its parameters from those of any other equation in the same form. By the preceding discussion, we know that posterior information will always enable us to rule out candidate equations which are not linear combinations of the equations of the true structure; we need thus only concern ourselves with equations which can form the first equation of admissible structures. It follows that the definition of identification must involve the restriction of admissible structures to those whose first equation is the same as or equivalent to the true first equation of the true structure.

We must be careful here, however, for there are two cases to distinguish. Look back at Eq. (1.6.10), which embodies all posterior information on A_1. Clearly, that equation will be satisfied by any scalar multiple of A_1. In determining what we shall require of prior information in order that the first equation of the model be considered identified, we must decide whether or not we are really interested in distinguishing the true first equation from scalar multiples of itself. (It is for this reason that we referred to equations "the same as or equivalent to" the true one at the end of the preceding paragraph.)

The answer here depends on the nature of our prior information. Multiplication of an equation by a scalar amounts to a choice of a normalization rule—a choice of scale for the parameters. Such rules usually (but not necessarily) take the form of setting the coefficient of a particular endogenous variable equal to unity. The choice of a particular normalization rule may affect the estimates obtained, but, provided that such estimates are consistent, this has nothing to do with identification. If everything we know about an equation is true for all different normalization rules, it is reasonable to say that we are not interested in distinguishing the "true" equation from scalar multiples of itself, since, given any such scalar multiple, we may secure any other one by imposing an appropriate normalization rule.

On the other hand, if we have prior information on the first equation which will not be satisfied by every scalar multiple thereof, the choice of a normalization rule is not arbitrary and we must insist on distinguishing the true first equation from all others including its own scalar multiples.

These two cases can be described formally as follows. Prior information can take the form of either equalities or inequalities. Let the equalities be described by a set of implicit functions of the elements of A and Σ (the latter elements being denoted by σ_{ij} ($i,j = 1, \ldots, M$); thus

$$\Phi^h(A,\Sigma) = 0 \qquad (h = 1, \ldots, H) \qquad (1.8.1)$$

Similarly, let the inequalities be written in vector form as

$$\psi^k(A,\Sigma) > 0 \qquad (k = 1, \ldots, K) \qquad (1.8.2)$$

(We need not concern ourselves here with the distinction between strong and weak inequalities.) Scalar multiplication of the first equation of the model multiplies the first row of A by a scalar and multiplies both the first row and the first column of Σ by the same scalar. Since this will involve the multiplication of σ_{11} (the variance of the first disturbance) by the square of that scalar, it will be convenient to think of the square root of σ_{11} rather than σ_{11} itself as entering the above expressions.

Suppose that every function Φ^h is homogeneous of some degree r_h and every function ψ^k is homogeneous of some degree s_k in the elements of the first row of A, $\sqrt{\sigma_{11}}$, and $\sigma_{12}, \ldots, \sigma_{1M}$. In that case, the restrictions (1.8.1) and (1.8.2) will be satisfied for every scalar multiple of the first equation. We shall call this the homogeneous case and in its presence shall insist only that the first equation be determined up to a normalization rule.

On the other hand, if there is some function Φ^h or ψ^k which is not homogeneous in the listed parameters, the corresponding restriction will generally not be satisfied by every scalar multiple of the first equation.[1] In this case, the choice of a normalization rule is not a matter of indifference; indeed, the prior restrictions themselves may be said to imply a particular normalization rule. We shall call this the inhomogeneous case and, in its presence, shall insist that the first equation of the true model be entirely determined.

In a formal way the two cases may be combined into one in the following manner. Consider the homogeneous case. Choose any normaliza-

[1] This need not be true if it is only an inequality that is involved; however, we shall ignore this overly special case.

tion rule consistent with the prior restrictions[1] and express it as

$$\Phi^{H+1}(A,\Sigma) = G(A_1,\sqrt{\sigma_{11}},\sigma_{12}, \ldots ,\sigma_{1M}) - 1 = 0 \qquad (1.8.3)$$

(As mentioned above, G will generally be a rather simple function.) Equation (1.8.3) can now be considered an inhomogeneous prior restriction, so that its imposition converts the homogeneous case into the inhomogeneous one. This is natural, since the homogeneous restrictions can at best determine the true equation only up to a scalar multiplication; the imposition of the inhomogeneous normalization rule then fixes the scale.

Despite the fact that the two cases can be dealt with jointly by this device, we shall generally consider them separately, since the homogeneous case is of great practical importance.

1.9. Definition of Identifiability for a Particular Equation

We are now in position for the formal definition of the identifiability of an equation of the model (again the first equation, for the sake of definiteness). We begin with the homogeneous case.

Definition 1.9.1: In the homogeneous case, the first equation of the model is said to be *identifiable* under the a priori restrictions if and only if every admissible structure has as its first equation some scalar multiple of the true first equation.

Let e_1 be an N-component row vector whose first element is unity and whose remaining elements are zero. By Theorem 1.7.1, the following is equivalent to the definition just given.

Definition 1.9.1a: In the homogeneous case, the first equation of the model is said to be *identifiable* under the a priori restrictions if and only if the first row of the matrix of every admissible linear transformation is some scalar multiple of e_1.

Similarly, for the inhomogeneous case, we have:

Definition 1.9.2: In the inhomogeneous case, the first equation of the model is said to be *identifiable* under the a priori restrictions if and only if every admissible structure has as its first equation the true first equation.

---

[1] We have not previously mentioned this minor point. In the homogeneous case, multiplication by any scalar is permissible. One generally fixes the scale by imposing a restriction on the parameters of the equation. Obviously, this cannot be done using a restriction which, for example, sets equal to unity a parameter already specified to be zero. This restriction of the choice of normalization rule is not at all the same as that in the inhomogeneous case in which the choice of a rule is severely restricted and even completely determined by the a priori restrictions.

Equivalently:

Definition 1.9.2a: In the inhomogeneous case, the first equation of the model is said to be *identifiable* under the a priori restrictions if and only if the first row of the matrix of every admissible transformation is e_1.

For brevity we shall sometimes omit the words "under the a priori restrictions" where there is no danger of confusion. Moreover, we shall sometimes use "identified" in place of "identifiable" for ease of writing. Since we are concerned with the question of whether there exist ideal experiments which will identify the given equation, identifiable seems the better term.

Definition 1.9.3: An equation which is not identifiable will be called *underidentified.*

We shall in a later chapter wish to distinguish among varying degrees of underidentification. At that time we shall have to worry about the possibility, for example, that the a priori restrictions permit admissible structures to have either the true first equation or one of a *finite* number of other first equations. Such problems need not detain us here, however.

Definition 1.9.4: A set of independent prior restrictions will be said to *just identify* an equation of the model if and only if that equation is identified under all the restrictions in the set but is not identified under any proper subset of the restrictions. If all the available a priori restrictions taken together just identify a particular equation, that equation will be said to be just identified.

In other words, a just identifying set of restrictions is one which identifies but which loses that property if any restriction of the set is removed. The discussion of Sec. 1.6 makes it easy to see the following:

Condition 1.9.1 (Order Condition): Except in rather special circumstances, any just identifying set of restrictions has at least $M - 1$ members in the homogeneous case and at least M members in the inhomogeneous case. It follows that a necessary condition for the identifiability of the first equation of the model will generally turn out to be that there exist at least $M - 1$ independent restrictions in the homogeneous case and M independent restrictions in the inhomogeneous case which involve the parameters of that equation.

To see this, observe that there are N elements of A_1 which must be estimated. By Theorem 1.6.1 and the discussion preceding it, posterior information places $\Lambda = N - M$ restrictions on those coefficients. It is obvious that the remaining restrictions must come from prior information and must generally be at least $N - \Lambda - 1 = M - 1$ or $N - \Lambda = M$ in number in the homogeneous and inhomogeneous cases, respectively. (One fewer restriction is needed in the homogeneous case because A_1 need only be determined up to a scalar multiplication.) That these restrictions must be independent is trivial.

The hedging of the statement of the condition by the phrase "except in rather special circumstances" is done to allow for the fact that equation systems with more unknowns than equations *can* have unique real solutions.[1] This does not usually occur in practice in dealing with identification, however.

We shall meet this condition again in several contexts. It is called the "order condition" because it indicates the order of magnitude of the required information.

As a natural companion of underidentification and just identification, we have:

Definition 1.9.5: An equation will be said to be *overidentified* if and only if there exist two different (but not necessarily disjoint) sets of a priori restrictions each of which just identify the equation in question and the union of the two sets is an independent set of restrictions.

Overidentification is the case in which there is more than enough independent information to distinguish the true equation from all others. Such extra information is not redundant. The restrictions involved cannot be derived from the other restrictions on the parameters of the true equation. Indeed, another way to phrase the definition would be to call an equation overidentified if there exist two distinct (but not necessarily disjoint) sets of a priori restrictions each of which would suffice to just identify the equation in question even if all restrictions in the other set but not in the intersection of the two sets did not hold.

There are a number of ways to describe briefly the relationships among over-, under-, and just identification. One such way is to consider the problem of using the a priori restrictions (and a normalization rule in the homogeneous case) to derive the true first equation from the reduced form. If that equation is just identified, there is a unique way in which this can be done; if it is underidentified, there is no way; if it is overidentified, there are more ways than one.

Another way of looking at the matter reveals the estimation problem which arises in the overidentified case and which is at the heart of all simultaneous equation estimators. If an equation is overidentified, there is available sufficient independent prior and posterior information to place more than N restrictions on its N coefficients. That such restrictions are consistent is guaranteed if the information involved is correct, since the true equation is known to satisfy all of them. On the other hand, while the true equation satisfies all such restrictions, estimates of

[1] For example, the one-equation–two-unknowns system: $x^2 + y^2 = 0$. This matter is discussed more fully in Sec. 5.9 and especially the appendix to Chap. 5.

it derived from using a just identifying set of restrictions need not do so. In general, if one estimates an equation by taking the least-squares estimates of the reduced form and using a particular set of just identifying restrictions to obtain the structural estimates, the resulting estimates will not satisfy the overidentifying restrictions which have not been employed. This will be the case even though the estimates obtained in this way are consistent estimates of an equation which does satisfy all restrictions.

An example may aid here. Returning to the supply and demand example of Sec. 1.3, we rewrite Eq. (1.3.12), which included income in the demand equation, to include also in that equation an additional exogenous variable denoted by Z.

$$Q = a_0 + a_1 P + a_2 Y + a_3 Z + u_1$$
$$P = b_0 + b_1 Q + u_2 \tag{1.9.1}$$

Obtaining the reduced form, we have

$$P = \pi_{10} + \pi_{11} Y + \pi_{12} Z + v_1$$
$$Q = \pi_{20} + \pi_{21} Y + \pi_{22} Z + v_2 \tag{1.9.2}$$

For present purposes, we may concentrate on the coefficients of Y and Z.

$$\pi_{11} = \frac{b_1 a_2}{1 - a_1 b_1} \qquad \pi_{12} = \frac{b_1 a_3}{1 - a_1 b_1}$$

$$\pi_{21} = \frac{a_2}{1 - a_1 b_1} \qquad \pi_{22} = \frac{a_3}{1 - a_1 b_1} \tag{1.9.3}$$

There are two pieces of a priori information on the second equation of Eqs. (1.9.1): the coefficients of both Y and Z are zero. Either piece of information would suffice to identify the equation; the two together over-identify it. This shows up in

$$\frac{\pi_{11}}{\pi_{21}} = b_1 = \frac{\pi_{12}}{\pi_{22}} \tag{1.9.4}$$

so that the true b_1 can be obtained in two independent ways given the true reduced form parameters (which can be consistently· estimated).

While the true structure does have the property that Eq. (1.9.4) is satisfied, it will not be the case in general that estimates of the reduced form derived by simply regressing P and Q on Y and Z will have that property. In particular, it will not generally happen that the ratio of the estimated coefficients of Y in the two regressions will be the same as that of the coefficients of Z. Two *different* estimates of b_1 will thus be available in this overidentified case. Since it is inefficient to throw away some of the restrictions to circumvent this problem, various estimators have been devised which compromise in various ways between such different estimates.

If, then, we look at a least-squares-estimated reduced form, take the estimated parameters thereof as the true ones, and ask how many different versions of a given equation consistent with the a priori restrictions could have formed part of a structure which generated that reduced form (a question of importance, since the reduced form, as we have seen, embodies all our posterior information on the structure), the answer is as follows. If the equation in question is just identified, only one such version exists consistent with the prior restrictions and the estimated reduced form. If it is underidentified, an infinite number are so consistent. If the equation is overidentified, no such equation exists.

The reader should be aware, however, that the distinction between just identification and underidentification is quite different from that between just identification and overidentification despite the apparent symmetry of the terminology and of the ways of looking at the matter just discussed. If an equation is underidentified, there exists *no* way, even in principle, of consistently estimating it. This is the case even when no stochastic elements are present in the system. If an equation is overidentified, there exists more than one way of consistently estimating it, and the difficulty is one of choosing among them. In very large samples that difficulty disappears. It is thus a different kind of problem from that which arises when an equation cannot be known even in principle. The major part of the literature on simultaneous equation estimation is concerned with the resolution of the difficulty in the overidentified case. In this book, we shall be principally concerned with the identification problem itself—with the necessary and sufficient characteristics of a just identifying set of a priori restrictions.

References

For an early account of the identification problem in the two-equation case see Working [38]. A classic and masterful exposition of the subject is Koopmans [21]. For a discussion of the properties of least squares in simultaneous equation systems see Bronfenbrenner [5].

2

Linear Restrictions on the Coefficients of a Single Equation: The Rank and Order Conditions

2.1. Restrictions Discussed in This Chapter

In this chapter we shall begin our discussion of the properties which are necessary and sufficient for the identifiability of a structural equation under a set of prior restrictions of given type. The cases which we shall here discuss are by far the most common in practice. In them, a priori information provides linear restrictions on the coefficients of the variables in the equation to be identified. No information relevant to the disturbances is available other than that involved in the general assumptions of the model; further, nothing is known a priori which links the parameters of the equation to be identified to the parameters of the other equations of the system. Restricting our attention as before to the first equation, all relevant information takes the form of *linear* restrictions known to be obeyed by the elements of A_1.

We shall begin with the case in which those elements are restricted by homogeneous linear equalities. This includes the case of greatest practical importance in which the prior information specifies that certain variables do not appear in the equation in question—that certain elements of A_1 are zero. We shall then go on to discuss the case of inhomogeneous equalities. Finally, the role of linear inequalities in the elements of A_1 will be considered.

2.2. Homogeneous Linear Restrictions

As just stated, the case of greatest practical importance is that in which the prior restrictions involved arise naturally when the model is written

32

down—the case in which all the information on A_1 is the specification that certain of its elements are zero. We have already seen, when discussing the two-equation example of the preceding chapter, that such exclusion of variables from a given equation can identify that equation. Indeed, as we remarked in the course of that discussion, this is one way of interpreting the somewhat heuristic argument that an equation is identified if the other equations of the model shift greatly relative to it. We shall call restrictions in this form "exclusion restrictions."

Important as exclusion restrictions are, however, they are by no means the only case of homogeneous linear restrictions which may arise. Consider for example the case in which the equation to be identified is one which describes the formation of a price as a function of the supplies on the market. If the commodity involved is a homogeneous one, it is reasonable to suppose that supplies from different sources have the same effect on price. In this case, we should have a restriction that the coefficients of two different quantities in the price-formation equation are the same.

To take a different example, consider an accelerator model in which investment depends linearly on change in output as well as on other things. The investment equation would then involve a term in the difference between output at time t and at time $t-1$. Thus, letting I_t be investment at time t and Q_t be output at time t and imposing the obvious normalization rule, the equation would read

$$I_t = a_0 + a_1(Q_t - Q_{t-1}) + \cdots \qquad (2.2.1)$$

where the dots stand for the remaining variables in the equation and for the disturbance term. If either Q_t or Q_{t-1} appear separately in the rest of the model, it may be convenient to rewrite this as

$$I_t = a_0 + a_1 Q_t + a_1' Q_{t-1} + \cdots \qquad (2.2.2)$$

and add the homogeneous linear restriction

$$a_1 + a_1' = 0 \qquad (2.2.3)$$

On the other hand, the latter example suggests that there is really not much difference between general homogeneous linear restrictions and exclusion restrictions. Instead of proceeding as above, we could equally well have added to the model the new (definitional) equation

$$\Delta Q_t \equiv Q_t - Q_{t-1} \qquad (2.2.4)$$

substituted ΔQ_t (which should be treated as endogenous) into Eq. (2.2.1), and imposed the *two* exclusion restrictions that neither Q_t nor Q_{t-1} appear in that equation. The resulting system would have the same identification properties as the original one, since they are trivially equivalent, and would allow us to deal only with exclusion restrictions.

Indeed, this procedure is quite general. Thus, suppose the equation to be studied is

$$a_1x_1 + a_2x_2 + \cdots + a_Nx_N = u_1 \qquad (2.2.5)$$

and we have the homogeneous linear restriction

$$c_1a_1 + c_2a_2 + \cdots + c_Na_N = 0 \qquad (2.2.6)$$

where the c_i are known numbers and at least one of the c_i is nonzero $(i = 1, \ldots, N)$. If only one such c_i is nonzero, the restriction is already an exclusion one; we may therefore suppose (renumbering if necessary) that the first H of the c_i are nonzero and the remainder zero, with $H \geq 2$. Solving for a_H,

$$a_H = k_1a_1 + \cdots + k_{H-1}a_{H-1} \qquad (2.2.7)$$

where $$k_i = \frac{-c_i}{c_H} \qquad (i = 1, \ldots, H - 1) \qquad (2.2.8)$$

Define $H - 1$ new endogenous variables by adding to the model the $H - 1$ equations

$$x_{N+i} = x_i + k_ix_H \qquad (i = 1, \ldots, H - 1) \qquad (2.2.9)$$

and rewrite Eq. (2.2.5) as

$$a_1x_{N+1} + a_2x_{N+2} + \cdots + a_{H-1}x_{N+H-1} + a_{H+1}x_{H+1} + \cdots \\ + a_Nx_N = u_1 \qquad (2.2.10)$$

This is an equation which obviously is identifiable if and only if Eq. (2.2.5) is but in which the single general homogeneous linear restriction (2.2.6) has been replaced by H exclusion restrictions stating that $x_1 \cdots x_H$ do not appear (or appear with zero coefficients).

It is worth noting that we have added $H - 1$ equations and endogenous variables to the model by this procedure. Looking at Condition 1.9.1, the order condition, we observe that whereas in the original form at least $M - 1$ independent restrictions were necessary to identify Eq. (2.2.5), now, with the new equations added, we must have at least $(M + H - 1) - 1$ independent restrictions. On the other hand, we have lost one restriction (2.2.7) but gained H exclusion restrictions. Thus, the number of additional restrictions not involved in this procedure which we must have in order to satisfy the order condition is unchanged. Before the transformation of the system, we needed $(M - 1) - 1 = M - 2$ such additional restrictions. Now we need $(M + H - 2) - H = M - 2$ of them, the same number. This reflects the fact (which can also be proved rigorously from the necessary and sufficient identification conditions given below) that tricks such as the one under discussion cannot possibly alter the identification properties of the prior information. The distance from just identification is unchanged by such procedures.

While it would thus suffice to deal entirely with exclusion restrictions, it is not particularly convenient to do so in the present discussion. (Such convenience is present when considering estimating techniques which are stated in terms of variables present or absent in a given equation.) We shall thus deal directly with the general homogeneous linear case of which exclusion restrictions are the most important subcase. Because of that importance, we shall restate the results in terms of exclusion restrictions whenever it seems illuminating.

We thus suppose that there exists an $N \times K$ matrix ϕ, whose elements are known constants, such that all prior information on the first equation of the model takes the form

$$A_1\phi = 0 \qquad (2.2.11)$$

The coefficients of a particular homogeneous linear restriction—the c_i of (2.2.5)—thus form a column of ϕ. An exclusion restriction which sets the ith element of A_1 equal to zero is expressed by a column of ϕ whose ith element is unity and whose remaining elements are zero.

Thus, for example, a restriction stating that the third element of A_1 is zero is represented by a column of ϕ in the form

$$\begin{bmatrix} 0 \\ 0 \\ 1 \\ 0 \\ \vdots \\ 0 \end{bmatrix}$$

A restriction stating that the first two elements of A_1 are equal is repre-sented by a column of ϕ in the form

$$\begin{bmatrix} 1 \\ -1 \\ 0 \\ \vdots \\ 0 \end{bmatrix}$$

and so forth.

2.3. The Rank and Order Conditions for Identifiability

Equation (2.2.11) exhibits all the restrictions placed on A_1 by prior information in the same form that Eq. (1.6.10) exhibits all the restrictions placed thereon by posterior information. It is natural to proceed by asking what necessary and sufficient conditions will ensure that the two sets of equations will have only one independent solution, since the natural way to attempt to identify the first equation is to try to use Eq. (2.2.11) to recover A_1 from the reduced form {embodied in Eq. (1.6.10)}. (This is the procedure used in the examples of the first chapter.) One would do this by simultaneously solving the two sets of equations for the elements of A_1, if possible.

We shall indeed follow this natural procedure later in this section and show directly that the identifiability condition developed is equivalent to the existence of a unique independent solution. Before doing that, however, we shall prove the same theorem by a far shorter route, making use of the theorems already proved in the preceding chapter. Theorem 1.7.1 enabled us to define identifiability either in terms of the first row of admissible transformations or in terms of the first row of admissible structures, because it assured us that these rows are in one-to-one correspondence. The natural procedure just discussed amounts to working with admissible structures; we shall begin, however, by working with admissible transformations.

Since the prior information takes the form it does, we need concern ourselves only with the first row of the matrix of any admissible transformation, because all our information on the first equation is on it alone and not on its relations to any other equation. Only the first row of a transformation matrix can be restricted by such information.

Suppose that the first equation is not identifiable. Then there exists an admissible transformation with matrix F whose first row, say F_1, is not a scalar multiple of e_1 (the vector with first element unity and remaining elements zero). Since the transformation is admissible, it is nonsingular, so that

$$F_1 \neq 0 \qquad (2.3.1)$$

Further, the transformed structure satisfies all prior restrictions on the true structure, so that {in view of Eq. (2.2.11)}

$$(F_1 A)\phi = F_1(A\phi) = 0 \qquad (2.3.2)$$

On the other hand, suppose that there exists a nonzero N-component row vector, say p, which is not a scalar multiple of e_1 and which satisfies

$$p(A\phi) = 0 \qquad (2.3.3)$$

Then, in view of Eq. (2.2.11), for any scalar λ,

$$(p + \lambda e_1)(A\phi) = p(A\phi) + \lambda e_1(A\phi) = p(A\phi) + \lambda(e_1 A)\phi$$
$$= p(A\phi) + \lambda A_1\phi = 0 \quad (2.3.4)$$

Choose λ such that the vector $(p + \lambda e_1)$ has a nonzero first component. Call that vector F_1 and observe that it is not a scalar multiple of e_1. Consider the matrix

$$F = \begin{bmatrix} F_1 \\ \hline 0 \\ \cdot \\ \cdot & I \\ \cdot \\ 0 \end{bmatrix} \quad (2.3.5)$$

F is nonsingular by construction. The linear transformation corresponding to F is then admissible, however, since: it replaces the equations other than the first by themselves; it replaces the first equation by one which satisfies all prior restrictions thereon; and there is no information relating the other equations to the first. Since F_1 is not a scalar multiple of e_1, the first equation is thus not identifiable.

We have just shown that the first equation is identifiable if and only if the only vectors p satisfying Eq. (2.3.3) are scalar multiples of e_1. Since e_1 is itself such a solution, this is equivalent to the requirement that the row kernel of $A\phi$ have dimension 1. Using Theorem 1.4.1 and the fact that $A\phi$ has M rows, we may restate this result as:

Theorem 2.3.1 (Rank Condition): A necessary and sufficient condition for the identifiability of the first equation of the model under the restrictions (2.2.11) is

$$\rho(A\phi) = M - 1 \quad (2.3.6)$$

We shall discuss this important result below. Now we shall rederive it in the rather more natural way discussed above which shows its direct relevance to the procedure which one would immediately think of using to secure estimates of A_1.

Rewrite the prior restrictions on A_1 (2.2.11) and the posterior restrictions thereon (1.6.10) in one equation as

$$A_1 J = 0 \quad (2.3.7)$$

where
$$J = [\phi \mid W] \quad (2.3.8)$$

Since Eq. (2.3.7) compactly states all that can be known about A_1 and since there are no further restrictions on the first equation, that equation is identifiable if and only if the only vectors satisfying Eq. (2.3.7) are scalar multiples of the true A_1. This is equivalent to requiring that J have a row kernel of dimension 1 or, since J has N rows, that $\rho(J) = N - 1$ (by Theorem 1.4.1). Our alternate proof of the rank condition (Theorem 2.3.1) thus consists of the proof of the following lemma.

Lemma 2.3.1: $\rho(J) = N - 1$ if and only if $\rho(A\phi) = M - 1$

Proof: (a) First suppose that $\rho(J) = N - 1$ but that $\rho(A\phi) \neq M - 1$. Since the first row of $A\phi$ consists of zeros only, this means $\rho(A\phi) < M - 1$ and $k(A\phi) \geq 2$. There thus exist at least two independent row vectors, say b and p, in the row kernel of $A\phi$. Define

$$\tilde{b} = b'A \qquad \tilde{p} = pA \qquad (2.3.9)$$

Now, $\tilde{b}$ and $\tilde{p}$ are independent, for if not, there exist scalars λ_1 and λ_2, not both zero, such that

$$\lambda_1\tilde{b} + \lambda_2\tilde{p} = (\lambda_1 b + \lambda_2 p)A = 0 \qquad (2.3.10)$$

However, since b and p are independent,

$$\lambda_1 b + \lambda_2 p \neq 0 \qquad (2.3.11)$$

so that Eq. (2.3.10) implies the existence of a nonzero vector in the row kernel of A. This is impossible, since A has M rows and $\rho(A) = M$ by Assumption 1.5.1.

Thus $\tilde{b}$ and $\tilde{p}$ are independent vectors and, by construction,

$$\tilde{b}\phi = (bA)\phi = b(A\phi) = 0$$
$$\tilde{p}\phi = (pA)\phi = p(A\phi) = 0 \qquad (2.3.12)$$

Furthermore, by Eq. (1.5.11), $AW = 0$, so that certainly

$$\tilde{b}W = (bA)W = b(AW) = 0$$
$$\tilde{p}W = (pA)W = p(AW) = 0 \qquad (2.3.13)$$

It follows that

$$\tilde{b}J = 0 = \tilde{p}J \qquad (2.3.14)$$

whence $\tilde{b}$ and $\tilde{p}$ are both in the row kernel of J. Since $\tilde{b}$ and $\tilde{p}$ are independent, $k(J) \geq 2$, and since J has N rows, Theorem 1.4.1 implies $\rho(J) < N - 1$, a contradiction.

(b) Now suppose that $\rho(A\phi) = M - 1$ but that $\rho(J) \neq N - 1$. In view of Eq. (2.3.7), this means $\rho(J) < N - 1$ and $k(J) \geq 2$. There thus exist at least two independent vectors, say $\tilde{b}$ and $\tilde{p}$, in the row kernel of J. In view of the definition of J, these two vectors are also in the row kernel of W; as was remarked in obtaining Theorem 1.6.1, however, the rows of

A form a basis for $K(W)$. There thus exist two vectors b and p such that

$$\bar{b} = bA \qquad \bar{p} = pA \qquad (2.3.15)$$

It is obvious that b and p are independent (since otherwise $\bar{b}$ and $\bar{p}$ could not be). By construction, however,

$$b(A\phi) = (bA)\phi = \bar{b}\phi = 0 \qquad (2.3.16)$$
$$p(A\phi) = (pA)\phi = \bar{p}\phi = 0$$

with $\bar{b}$ and $\bar{p}$ both being in $K(\phi)$ since they are in $K(J)$. Thus we have constructed two independent vectors in $K(A\phi)$, whence $k(A\phi) \geq 2$, and since $A\phi$ has M rows, this implies by Theorem 1.4.1 that $\rho(A\phi) < M - 1$. This is a contradiction and the lemma is proved.

This alternate proof shows directly that if and only if the rank condition holds will the attempt to use the prior restrictions to recover A_1 from the reduced form succeed. The use of a just identifying set of restrictions in this way is known as the method of indirect least squares (since the estimates are indirectly obtained from the reduced form which is estimated by least squares). Later in this chapter we shall briefly examine the way in which other commonly used methods of estimation fail in the absence of identifiability.

Before proceeding to a discussion of the rank condition and examples of its use, it is interesting to observe that it immediately implies a version of the very general order condition (Condition 1.9.1) for the present case.

Corollary 2.3.1 (Order Condition): A necessary (but not sufficient) condition for the identifiability of the first equation of the model is that

$$\rho(\phi) \geq M - 1 \qquad (2.3.17)$$

In other words, there must be at least $M - 1$ independent restrictions expressed by Eq. (2.2.11).

Proof: Since the rank of a matrix cannot increase (but can decrease) on premultiplication by another matrix, this follows immediately from the rank condition.

2.4. The Rank and Order Conditions in the Exclusion Restriction Case

The rank and order conditions just derived have somewhat simpler forms when all restrictions are exclusion restrictions. In this case, every column of ϕ has one and only one nonzero element, that element being equal to unity. Any set of such columns will be independent if and only if the unit elements come in different rows. Since the position of a unit element corresponds to a restriction that the corresponding element of A_1 be zero—that the correspondingly numbered variable is excluded from the first equation—the order condition can be restated in this case as:

Corollary 2.4.1 (*Order Condition*): A necessary (but not sufficient) condition for the identifiability of the first equation under exclusion restrictions is that there be at least $M - 1$ variables excluded a priori from that equation.

Similarly, since the matrix $A\phi$ in this case will consist of the columns of A corresponding to the excluded variables, the rank condition becomes:

Corollary 2.4.2 (*Rank Condition*): A necessary and sufficient condition for the identifiability of the first equation under exclusion restrictions is that it be possible to form at least one nonvanishing determinant of order $M - 1$ from the columns of A corresponding to the variables excluded a priori from that equation.

It is instructive to restate the order condition in the exclusion restriction case in alternate form. Suppose that there are $m + 1$ endogenous variables and l exogenous variables *not* excluded a priori from the first equation. The order condition as stated in Corollary 2.4.1 can then be written as

$$(\Lambda - l) + (M - m - 1) \geq M - 1 \qquad (2.4.1)$$

or
$$\Lambda - l \geq m \qquad (2.4.2)$$

In words:

Corollary 2.4.1a (*Order Condition*): A necessary (but not sufficient) condition for the identifiability of the first equation under exclusion restrictions is that the number of exogenous variables excluded a priori from that equation be at least as great as the number of endogenous variables *not* so excluded less one.

The interpretation of this result is as follows. Since exclusion restrictions are all homogeneous, we may select the coefficient of one endogenous variable appearing in the equation and set it equal to unity. This leaves $m + l$ elements of A_1 to be estimated. There would be no identification problem at all if m were zero, for then all remaining variables would be exogenous and ordinary least squares would be a consistent estimator. There is still no problem, in the same sense, as regards the l exogenous variables which do appear in that equation; each of them can be used as in ordinary least squares, by using the l pieces of information that they are uncorrelated with the disturbance term in the probability limit. (Alternatively, in the nonstochastic case, we may think of setting these l variables in l independent ways and observing the corresponding configurations of the remaining $m + 1$ variables.) The m remaining endogenous variables cannot be so used, however; some replacement for such use must be found if the equation is to be identified.   As seen in the preceding chapter, the posterior information obtainable comes from the use of the exogenous variables and the fact that they are uncorrelated with the disturbances in the probability limit.   Having already used the l exogenous variables appearing in the equation, there now remain $\Lambda - l$ pieces of unused posterior information with which to replace the information which could have been gathered if the m remaining endogenous variables had been exogenous.   Clearly, we can succeed in identifying the first equation only if there is at least as much such replacement information as there is information to be replaced.   This is what the present version of the order condition states.

Another equivalent form of the order condition under exclusion restrictions is perhaps the most common in the literature.   Adding l to both sides of Eq. (2.4.2) we obtain

$$\Lambda \geq l + m \qquad (2.4.3)$$

In words:

Corollary 2.4.1b (*Order Condition*)*:* A necessary (but not sufficient) condition for the identifiability of the first equation under exclusion restrictions is that the total number of exogenous variables in the model be at least as great as the number of variables *not* excluded a priori from the equation less one.

The interpretation of this version of the order condition is even more straightforward than that of the preceding one.   Prior information sets some of the coefficients to be estimated equal to zero; a normalization rule sets one more equal to unity.   There remain $l + m$ coefficients to be estimated from observational information.   We saw in Chap. 1, however, that observation can provide only Λ independent pieces of information on the equation in question.   It follows that a necessary condition for the identifiability of that equation is that this be at least as great as the number of unknown coefficients to be estimated from posterior information alone.   This is what is expressed by Corollary 2.4.1b.

2.5. Discussion of the Rank and Order Conditions

An example illustrating the rank and order conditions seems appropriate here.   Consider the following two-equation example in which the y_i are endogenous and the z_j exogenous.   The model to be estimated is

$$a_{11}y_1 + a_{12}y_2 + a_{13}z_1 + a_{14}z_2 = u_1 \qquad (2.5.1)$$
$$a_{21}y_1 + a_{22}y_2 + a_{23}z_1 + a_{24}z_2 = u_2$$

Suppose that it is known that z_1 does not appear in the first equation—that is, that it appears with a zero coefficient. The matrix ϕ then consists of the single column

$$\phi = \begin{bmatrix} 0 \\ 0 \\ 1 \\ 0 \end{bmatrix} \tag{2.5.2}$$

and the restriction is expressed as

$$a_{13} = A_1\phi = 0 \tag{2.5.3}$$

Since ϕ has rank one and $M = 2$ in this case, the necessary order condition is fulfilled. The matrix $A\phi$ of the rank condition is, in this case,

$$A\phi = \begin{bmatrix} a_{13} \\ a_{23} \end{bmatrix} = \begin{bmatrix} 0 \\ a_{23} \end{bmatrix} \tag{2.5.4}$$

using Eq. (2.5.3). This will have rank $M - 1 = 1$ if and only if $a_{23} \neq 0$, so that the latter condition is necessary and sufficient for the identifiability of the first equation of (2.5.1) under the restriction (2.5.3).

This is a result the logic of which is clear and which points up the reason that the rank and not the order condition is sufficient for identification. As we saw in the first chapter, the function of prior restrictions in identification is to distinguish among linear combinations of the equations of the model. In the present case, this is successfully done by the restriction that z_1 fails to appear in the first equation if and only if z_1 does not fail to appear in the second equation also. If a_{23} as well as a_{13} is zero, the restriction fails to add any information which can distinguish between the two equations.

More generally, the order condition gives the minimum number of independent restrictions which must be available in order to distinguish the first equation from the other equations of the model. Even if that number is available, however, the restrictions may not in fact suffice to distinguish that equation. Indeed, they will fail unless there are not only $M - 1$ independent restrictions but also $M - 1$ independent restrictions which are obeyed by the first equation *but not by any other linear combination of the equations of the model*. Prior restrictions on the first equation are important because they are specific to that equation. Restrictions that are not so specific give only limited help.

In particular, restrictions which are obeyed by all the equations of the model give no help whatsoever. Thus, nothing can be gained in attempting to identify the first equation by adding restrictions which specify that variables not in the model are also not in that equation. Such restrictions can easily add to the rank of ϕ and lead to the satisfaction or oversatisfaction of the order condition. They lead only to columns of zeros in the matrix $A\phi$ and add nothing to the rank of that matrix. They thus

do not aid in satisfying the rank condition, which is as it should be, since they obviously are of no use in distinguishing the first equation from the others of the model.

An example which uses a nonexclusion restriction may serve to illustrate the same point. It will be useful also to consider three equations instead of two as some features of the two-equation case are a bit special. Thus, suppose that the model consists of the following three equations

$$a_{11}y_1 + a_{12}y_2 + a_{13}y_3 + a_{14}z_1 + a_{15}z_2 = u_1$$
$$a_{21}y_1 + a_{22}y_2 + a_{23}y_3 + a_{24}z_1 + a_{25}z_2 = u_2 \qquad (2.5.5)$$
$$a_{31}y_1 + a_{32}y_2 + a_{33}y_3 + a_{34}z_1 + a_{35}z_2 = u_3$$

and the prior restrictions on the first equation take the form

$$a_{14} = 0 \qquad a_{12} = a_{13} \qquad (2.5.6)$$

Here the matrix ϕ is

$$\phi = \begin{bmatrix} 0 & 0 \\ 0 & 1 \\ 0 & -1 \\ 1 & 0 \\ 0 & 0 \end{bmatrix} \qquad (2.5.7)$$

so that the restrictions may be written in the canonical form

$$A_1\phi = (a_{14} \quad a_{12} - a_{13}) = 0 \qquad (2.5.8)$$

The rank of ϕ is two, and since $M = 3$ in this example, the order condition is obviously satisfied. The crucial rank condition matrix $A\phi$ is

$$A\phi = \begin{bmatrix} a_{14} & a_{12} - a_{13} \\ a_{24} & a_{22} - a_{23} \\ a_{34} & a_{32} - a_{33} \end{bmatrix} = \begin{bmatrix} 0 & 0 \\ a_{24} & a_{22} - a_{23} \\ a_{34} & a_{32} - a_{33} \end{bmatrix} \qquad (2.5.9)$$

using Eq. (2.5.8).

Clearly, this has the required rank (two) if and only if the last two rows are independent. This may fail in the following ways. First, one of the equations other than the first may obey the same restrictions as the first equation does—then one of the rows in question will be zero. In this case, the prior information available does not distinguish the first equation from the equation in question. Second, the first column of $A\phi$ may be zero, in which case z_1 does not appear in the model and the restriction that it does not appear in the first equation in particular is no aid to identification. Third, the second column of $A\phi$ may be zero. In this case, the coefficients of y_2 and y_3 are the same in all the equations so that nothing is gained by asserting that they are so in the first one. Finally (a general case which includes all the preceding), some linear combination of the last two rows of $A\phi$ may be zero. In this case, the corresponding linear combination of the last two equations of the model forms an equation which obeys all the a priori restrictions on the first equation.

It is interesting to note, on the other hand, that a restriction on the first equation may be of assistance even if it is also obeyed by another equation of the model (so long as it is not obeyed by all of them). If z_1 does not appear in the second equation but does appear in the third, then $a_{24} = 0$, $a_{34} \neq 0$, and $A\phi$ will have the required rank if and only if $a_{22} \neq a_{23}$. Thus, in this case, the first equation will be identified provided that the second restriction is not obeyed by the second equation whether or not it is obeyed by the third. In a sense which will be made precise in a later chapter, the first restriction in this situation identifies the first equation *with respect to the third one;* the remaining restriction must then identify the first equation with respect to the second one if the first equation is to be identified by the two restrictions taken together.

Now, as these examples suggest, there is at least an apparent practical difficulty in the fact that the rank condition and not the order condition is necessary *and* sufficient for identification. Whereas the order condition depends only on the matrix ϕ, a matrix which is completely known a priori, the rank condition depends on the matrix $A\phi$, which is in part a function of the unknown elements of A, the very parameters which are to be estimated. While the question of whether or not the order condition is satisfied can thus be readily settled, the question of whether or not the rank condition is satisfied can apparently not be settled without knowledge of the last $M - 1$ rows of A. Such knowledge can only be attained if the other equations of the model are identifiable, but this is likely to depend on a similar question applied to those equations. It thus cannot be answered without knowledge of A_1. That knowledge can be attained, however, if and only if the rank condition is satisfied for the first equation—the very question to which the answer is being sought.

Fortunately, the problem is more apparent than real. There are two cases to consider.

In the first place, the prior restrictions on the equations of the model other than the first may show that the rank of $A\phi$ is below $M - 1$ for *every* matrix A obeying those restrictions. This is the case, for instance, in the model given in Eqs. (2.5.5) if it is *known* that z_1 does not appear in any equation. In this case, the rank condition may be said to fail identically (as it will if the order condition fails) and this can be known without detailed knowledge of the last $M - 1$ rows of A.

The problem under discussion can thus arise only when the rank condition does not fail identically—that is, when the order condition is satisfied and there exist *some* admissible structures for which the rank condition holds. In this case, there exists at least one determinant of order $M - 1$ which can be formed from the last $M - 1$ rows of $A\phi$ and which is not identically zero for all admissible structures. A determinant is a continuous function of its elements, however, so that the determinant in question is a continuous function of the elements of the last $M - 1$ rows of A and is linear in the elements of any one such row. It follows that such a determinant will be zero and the rank condition will fail only on a set of measure zero in the space of those elements. Loosely speaking, the probability is zero in this situation that the last $M - 1$ rows of A will just happen to be such as to make the rank condition fail. Such failure will occur only by accident. The situation is the same as that encountered when considering the chances that a number picked from the real line happens to be zero. It *can* happen, but one feels rather safe in neglecting such a possibility unless one knows in advance that it *must* happen.

> Strictly speaking, this result will not hold if the prior restrictions on the last $M - 1$ equations of the model are so strong as to lead to only a finite or denumerable number of admissible structures. This never occurs in practice, however.

Thus, if the rank condition does not fail identically it can be assumed to hold in practice. This has frequently led to a neglect of the rank condition in the literature and to a practice of simply checking the order condition. As our discussion shows, however, this is not sufficient. Even if the order condition holds, the rank condition can fail identically and this possibility should always be checked as well.   If the order condition were all that is involved, identification could always be achieved by excluding from the first equation variables which in fact are known not to appear in the model.

2.6. Overidentification and Restrictions on the Reduced Form

In our second proof above of the rank condition, we saw directly that the attempt to recover the parameters of the equation in question by direct solution of the equations giving the prior and posterior information on that equation breaks down if and only if the rank condition fails. That estimation method is called indirect least squares, because it naturally proceeds by least-squares estimation of the reduced form parameters and then uses the prior restrictions to solve for the structural parameters. If the equation to be estimated is just identified, there is only one way to do this; if it is underidentified (that is, not identified) there is no way.   On the other hand, as indicated in the examples of the last chapter, if the equation is overidentified, there is more than one way to go from the reduced form to the structural equation, and the results in a finite sample are not generally independent of the chosen method. In this section, we shall show directly why this is the case.

It should be realized, however, that the difficulty with indirect least squares in the overidentified case is of a very different kind from the problems encountered when the equation to be estimated is not identified. In the latter case, the equations to be solved have an infinite number of solutions; many other equations other than the true structural one satisfy them. This is true no matter how large a sample we consider and no matter how we abstract from problems of sampling error. In the over-identified case, on the other hand, no problem would arise if we could so abstract. We have more than enough restrictions to enable us to fix the parameters of the equation in question. The difficulty arises because in a finite sample there is no assurance that estimates of that equation derived from one just identifying set of restrictions will obey the restrictions not used in the derivation. Since the true equation is known to obey all those restrictions, this is only a finite sample problem. It is thus, in a sense, a practical problem (and one of great importance) rather than a problem of principle.

The simplest way to exhibit the problem involved—other than by examples—is to show that the overidentification of any equation implies the existence of restrictions not only on the structural parameters, which is trivial, but also on the parameters of each of the reduced form equations. Since indirect least squares estimates the reduced form without making use of such restrictions, it follows that the reduced form estimates so obtained will not in general be simultaneously compatible with all the prior restrictions on the structural equation to be estimated. The immediate consequence of this is that when some of those restrictions are used to go from the reduced form parameters to the structural equation in question, the structural parameters so derived will not generally obey the unutilized restrictions.

It is the case, however, that the existence of restrictions on the reduced form is not restricted to the case in which some structural equation is overidentified. Thus, for example, suppose that $M = 3$ and $\Lambda = 2$ and that the only restrictions take the form that neither of the two exogenous variables appears in either of the first two equations. Obviously, none of the three equations is identified; the first two cannot be told apart, and there are no restrictions on the third. Even so, the reduced form matrix is restricted. Once more writing the model in matrix form,

$$By + \Gamma z = u \qquad (2.6.1)$$

and the first two rows of Γ are zero. Since Γ has only three rows, it follows that the two columns of

$$\Pi = -B^{-1}\Gamma \qquad (2.6.2)$$

are linearly dependent.

The general case of the existence of restrictions on the reduced form when the prior restrictions on the structure take the form under discussion is covered by:[1]

Theorem 2.6.1: The a priori restrictions (2.2.11) imply the existence of precisely $\rho(\phi) - \rho(A\phi)$ linear (but not necessarily homogeneous) restrictions on the reduced form matrix Π. These restrictions take the form of linear dependencies among the columns of

$$P = \phi^1 - \Pi\phi^2 \qquad (2.6.3)$$

where ϕ^1 is the submatrix of ϕ consisting of its first M rows and ϕ^2 is the submatrix of ϕ consisting of its remaining Λ rows.

Proof: Without loss of generality, we may obviously assume that the columns of ϕ are independent, so that $\rho(\phi) = K$.

Premultiply $A\phi$ by B^{-1} and rewrite the result to obtain

$$B^{-1}(A\phi) = B^{-1}(B\phi^1 + \Gamma\phi^2) = \phi^1 - \Pi\phi^2 = P \qquad (2.6.4)$$

so that $\rho(P) = \rho(A\phi)$. The prior restrictions (2.2.11) on the first structural equation may be rewritten as

$$B_1 P = 0 \qquad (2.6.5)$$

where B_1 denotes the first row of B. Hence $\rho(P) \leq M - 1$.

Now, from Eq. (2.6.4), every column of P corresponds to a column of ϕ. Choose $\rho(P)$ independent columns of ϕ corresponding to $\rho(P)$ independent columns of P. Call $\tilde{\phi}$ the matrix formed from those columns of ϕ; similarly, denote the corresponding submatrix of P by $\tilde{P}$. Without loss of generality, we may take $\tilde{\phi}$ to consist of the first $\rho(P)$ columns of ϕ.

Now, denote by $P(j)$ the matrix formed by adjoining to $\tilde{P}$ the jth column of P, $j = \rho(P) + 1, \ldots, K$. Every such $P(j)$ has at most M columns, since $\tilde{P}$ has only $\rho(P) < M$ columns. However, every such $P(j)$ has M rows and its columns are obviously dependent. Such dependency is a nontrivial restriction on the columns of P, since it involves no more columns of P than P has rows. Thus such dependency would not exist in the absence of the a priori restrictions (2.2.11) and is thus implied by those restrictions.

It is obvious by construction that the restrictions on the columns of P just described are independent and that there are $\rho(\phi) - \rho(A\phi)$ of them. To see that no more restrictions on the columns of P are possible, observe that each constructed restriction corresponds to a vector in the column

---

[1] See also Malinvaud [25, pp. 561–563]. Malinvaud *defines* overidentification as the presence of restrictions on the reduced form [25, p. 556], a rather awkward usage because under it a structure can be overidentified without containing a single identifiable parameter. Malinvaud realizes this [cf. 25, p. 563].

kernel of P and such vectors are independent. On the other hand, P has $\rho(\phi)$ columns and has rank $\rho(A\phi)$, so that its column kernel has dimension $\rho(\phi) - \rho(A\phi)$ by Theorem 1.4.1.

It remains to show that these restrictions on the columns of P really represent $\rho(\phi) - \rho(A\phi)$ independent restrictions on Π. To this end, let $q = \rho(\phi) - \rho(A\phi)$ and let $\lambda_1, \ldots, \lambda_q$ be independent vectors in the column kernel of P, so that

$$\Pi(\phi^2\lambda_i) = \phi^1\lambda_i \qquad (i = 1, \ldots, q) \qquad (2.6.6)$$

It suffices to show that the vectors

$$\mu_i = \phi^2\lambda_i \qquad (i = 1, \ldots, q) \qquad (2.6.7)$$

are independent.

To see this, suppose that the μ_i were dependent. There would exist scalars $c_1, \ldots, c_q$ not all zero, such that

$$\sum_{i=1}^{q} c_i(\phi^2\lambda_i) = \sum_{i=1}^{q} c_i\mu_i = 0 \qquad (2.6.8)$$

By Eq. (2.6.6), however, this would imply that

$$\sum_{i=1}^{q} c_i(\phi^1\lambda_i) = \Pi \sum_{i=1}^{q} c_i(\phi^2\lambda_i) = 0 \qquad (2.6.9)$$

so that

$$\phi\eta = 0 \qquad (2.6.10)$$

where

$$\eta = \sum_{i=1}^{q} c_i\lambda_i \neq 0 \qquad (2.6.11)$$

by the independence of the λ_i. This would contradict the assumption that the columns of ϕ are independent, and the theorem is proved.[1]

Theorem 2.6.1 immediately implies that the presence of an over-identified structural equation implies the existence of at least one restriction on the reduced form. Thus, from the definition of overidentification, the first equation of the model can be overidentified only if $\rho(\phi) > M - 1$. Since $\rho(A\phi) \leq M - 1$, the desired result on overidentification follows immediately from the following corollary:

Corollary 2.6.1: If $\rho(\phi) > M - 1$, there are at least $\rho(\phi) - (M - 1)$ restrictions on Π.

Now, several points immediately arise in connection with these results.

[1] Exercise: Prove the theorem in another way by proving and making use of the following extension of Lemma 2.3.1:

Lemma 2.6.1: Let ψ be any N-rowed matrix. Define $J(\psi) = [\psi \ W]$. Then $\rho\{J(\psi)\} = \rho(A\psi) + \Lambda$

In the first place, it is clear that the number of restrictions on the reduced form implied by Eq. (2.2.11) is intimately related to the rank and order conditions. If one regards $\rho(\phi) - (M - 1)$ as a measure of the degree of fulfillment (or overfulfillment) of the order condition and similarly takes $\rho(A\phi) - (M - 1)$ as a measure of the degree of fulfillment of the rank condition, the number of restrictions in question is seen to be the difference between the degree of fulfillment of the two conditions.

Moreover, it is natural that $\rho(\phi) - \rho(A\phi)$ should appear in this con-text. If $\rho(\phi) = \rho(A\phi)$ then each prior restriction on A_1 contributes to the degree of identification of the first equation. It tells us something which cannot be obtained *or verified* from observational information. The validity of restrictions on the reduced form, however, can be tested in principle.

Therefore the case $\rho(\phi) = \rho(A\phi)$ cannot lead to restrictions on the reduced form and it is natural in general to obtain $\rho(\phi) - \rho(A\phi)$ as the number of such restrictions because this is the number of prior restrictions on A_1 which can be discarded without affecting the closeness of the first equation to just identification. We shall return to this in Sec. 6.6, where we discuss tests of identifying restrictions.

Secondly, the issue clearly arises of whether some or all of the restric-tions on the reduced form covered in the theorem are really restrictive. This question arises in two ways. On the one hand, the knowledge that the columns of P are dependent may seem not to be restrictive in view of the fact that the vector in the column kernel of P which corresponds to such dependency may very well depend on the coefficients to be estimated.

This is a misleading argument. The fact, shown in the proof of the theorem, that certain submatrices of P with no more columns than rows have dependent columns and that each such column generally involves every row of Π is itself a restriction on Π even though the elements of the vector of coefficients describing that dependency may be unknown. An example may help to clarify the issue here.

Suppose that, after normalization, the model is

$$y_1 = b_{12}y_2 + g_{11}z_1 + g_{12}z_2 + g_{13}z_3 + u_1$$
$$y_2 = b_{21}y_1 + g_{21}z_1 + g_{22}z_2 + g_{23}z_3 + u_2$$

$$(2.6.12)$$

where the notation should by now be familiar. Suppose that the a priori restrictions on the first equation are

$$g_{12} = 0 = g_{13} \qquad (2.6.13)$$

and that the a priori restriction on the second equation is

$$g_{21} = 0 \qquad (2.6.14)$$

The reader should verify that the first equation of Eq. (2.6.12) is thus overidentified provided that $g_{22} \neq 0 \neq g_{23}$ and that the second equation is just identified provided that $g_{11} \neq 0$.

Writing out the reduced form without making use as yet of the restrictions we have

$$y_1 = \pi_{11}z_1 + \pi_{12}z_2 + \pi_{13}z_3 + v_1$$
$$y_2 = \pi_{21}z_1 + \pi_{22}z_2 + \pi_{23}z_3 + v_2 \qquad (2.6.15)$$

where
$$\pi_{1j} = \frac{1}{1 - b_{12}b_{21}}(g_{1j} + b_{12}g_{2j})$$

$$\pi_{2j} = \frac{1}{1 - b_{12}b_{21}}(g_{2j} + b_{21}g_{1j}) \qquad (j = 1, \ldots, 3)$$

and the v_i are linear combinations of the u_i.

Using only the restrictions on the first equation of Eq. (2.6.12), we obtain

$$\begin{bmatrix} \pi_{12} \\ \pi_{22} \end{bmatrix} g_{23} - \begin{bmatrix} \pi_{13} \\ \pi_{23} \end{bmatrix} g_{22} = 0 \qquad (2.6.17)$$

as the (in this case) only restriction on the reduced form parameters. The fact that this restriction involves the parameters g_{23} and g_{33} which could not even be consistently estimated if the restrictions so far used were all that were available would make this restriction pointless if it involved only a particular equation of the reduced form. Since, in fact, it applies to both equations, it clearly implies

$$\frac{\pi_{12}}{\pi_{22}} = \frac{\pi_{13}}{\pi_{23}} \qquad (2.6.18)$$

(the common value of the ratios being b_{12}, as it happens) and this is by no means a vacuous restriction.

As the reader should verify, however, the single restriction on the second structural equation of Eq. (2.6.12) merely provides the necessary equipment with which to secure the parameters of that equation from *any* given set of values for the elements of Π. It implies no restriction on those elements and is thus compatible with any estimate of Π, including those estimates satisfying Eq. (2.6.18).

On the other hand, as already discussed in the preceding section, $\rho(A\phi)$ may not be identically below $\rho(\phi)$ but may fall below it only on a set of measure zero in the parameter space. Where this is the case, the extra restrictions, whose existence due to the reduction in rank of $A\phi$ is implied by the theorem, are obviously not at all restrictive, since at almost every point they fail to hold. Clearly, the theorem should be applied with $\rho(A\phi)$ at the value it achieves almost everywhere in the parameter space.

Where it does happen, however, that $\rho(A\phi) < \rho(\phi)$ identically and the first equation is not almost everywhere identified, so that $\rho(A\phi) < M - 1$, then further restrictions on the reduced form are implied. Clearly, this can only come about as a consequence of prior restrictions on the rows of A other than the first. It is thus a little misleading in this case to speak of the restrictions on the reduced form as implied only by the restrictions on the first row of A (although the theorem is formally correct as stated). The other restrictions on the rows of A enter by lowering the rank of $A\phi$.

This brings us to the question of the total number of independent restrictions on the reduced form implied by the a priori restrictions on all the structural equations. It is clear that summing terms such as $\rho(\phi) - \rho(A\phi)$ over all equations gives an upper bound on that number; it is equally clear, however, that such a total may exceed the true number of *independent* restrictions.

Thus, consider the example given earlier in this section in which $M = 3$, $\Lambda = 2$, and the first two rows of Γ are known a priori to be zero. For the first equation, $\rho(\phi) = 2$, but, in consequence of the fact that both the first two equations obey the same restrictions, $\rho(A\phi) = 1$. The theorem thus implies the existence of one restriction on the reduced form, and we have already observed the proportionality of the two columns of Π in this case. Indeed, denoting the ijth element of Γ by g_{ij}, it is evident that the two columns of Π consist of the third column of B^{-1} multiplied by g_{31} and g_{32}, respectively. On the other hand, $\rho(\phi) - \rho(A\phi) = 1$ for the second equation also; yet there is no additional restriction on Π.

In general, it seems clear that some kind of double counting may be involved when a restriction is used on its own account in applying Theorem 2.6.1 after having been used to reduce the rank of $A\phi$ in dealing with restrictions on the reduced form implied by restrictions on another structural equation. Certainly this is the case when two structural equations obey all the same restrictions. To what extent it is true otherwise and how to deal with this problem in general is as yet an open question.

A final word by way of a digression before closing this section. The example just discussed is one in which restrictions on the first two equations of a three-equation model obviously make it possible to determine the ratio of two parameters of an otherwise unidentifiable equation—the ratio of g_{31} and g_{32}. In that case, a single further restriction which fixed the size of one of those parameters would suffice to enable us to recover both those parameters, although it would not allow us to identify the third equation. (*Why not?*) In the presence of such an additional restriction, it is sensible to regard the two parameters in question as identified by all the restrictions. We mention this only to signal the fact already alluded to that although our discussion runs in terms of the identification of an equation as a whole, there is such a thing as the identification of individual parameters. We shall discuss this briefly in a later chapter; it is a considerably more complicated subject than is identification of an entire equation.

2.7. Identifiability and Two-stage Least Squares

We have already seen the way in which indirect least squares breaks down when the equation to be estimated is not identified. Further, in the previous section, we saw how that estimation method breaks down in quite a different way when the equation in question is overidentified. In this section, we shall examine a class of widely used estimators which do yield consistent estimates in the overidentified case. These estimators do not meet with the difficulties which indirect least squares does. While we shall discuss such estimators in sufficient detail to make the following discussion self-contained, we shall be concerned with the way in which they break down (as they should) in the underidentified case rather than with their properties in the case for which they were designed—the over-identified case. For a summary of the extensive literature on the latter question, the reader may consult any one of a number of standard works (for example, Johnston [20, chaps. 9 and 10]).

For purposes of this discussion, we shall assume that all restrictions on the equation to be estimated are exclusion restrictions. (As seen above, this involves no loss of generality.) It will further be convenient to suppose that the equation in question (which we again take to be the first equation of the model) has already been subjected to a normalization rule so that it has been solved for a particular endogenous variable, which we shall denote by q. We write out that equation, using the exclusion restrictions, and obtain

$$q = \beta y_1 + \gamma z_1 + u_1 \tag{2.7.1}$$

where β and γ are row vectors of parameters to be estimated; y_1 is a column vector of the m endogenous variables other than q appearing in the equation; and z_1 is a column vector of the l exogenous variables appearing in the equation. (We have already used m and l in this way in discussing the order condition in Sec. 2.4.)

Denote the column vector of the $\Lambda - l$ excluded exogenous variables by z_2 and write the equations of the reduced form corresponding to the elements of y_1 only as

$$y_1 = \Pi^{11} z_1 + \Pi^{12} z_2 + v_1 \tag{2.7.2}$$

where v_1 is a column vector of the appropriate reduced form residuals. Similarly, write the reduced form equation corresponding to q as

$$q = \Pi^{q1} z_1 + \Pi^{q2} z_2 + v_q \tag{2.7.3}$$

Define

$$\tilde{\Pi}^1 = \begin{bmatrix} \Pi^{q1} \\ \Pi^{11} \end{bmatrix} \qquad \tilde{\Pi}^2 = \begin{bmatrix} \Pi^{q2} \\ \Pi^{12} \end{bmatrix} \tag{2.7.4}$$

Note that Π^{12} has m rows and $\Lambda - l$ columns. If, therefore, the order condition fails, $\rho(\Pi^{12}) < m$ (see Corollary 2.4.1). This suggests that the rank of Π^{12} may be closely related to the identifiability of Eq. (2.7.1). That this is the case is shown in Theorem 2.7.1 below. First we prove:

Lemma 2.7.1: A necessary and sufficient condition for the identifiability of Eq. (2.7.1) is that $\rho(\tilde{\Pi}^2) = m$.

Proof: If we renumber the variables (if necessary) so that the endogenous variables included in Eq. (2.7.1) come first, the excluded endogenous variables second, the included exogenous variables third, and the excluded exogenous variables last, the matrix ϕ which contains the coefficients of the exclusion restrictions may be written as

$$\phi = \begin{bmatrix} \phi^1 \\ \phi^2 \end{bmatrix} \tag{2.7.5}$$

where $\qquad \phi^1 = \begin{bmatrix} 0 & 0 \\ I^1 & 0 \end{bmatrix} \qquad \phi^2 = \begin{bmatrix} 0 & 0 \\ 0 & I^2 \end{bmatrix} \tag{2.7.6}$

the superscripts being used to denote zero and unit matrices of possibly different orders. Clearly, ϕ^1 has M rows and ϕ^2 has Λ rows.

As in the preceding section {see Eqs. (2.6.4) and (2.6.5)}, by premultiplying $A\phi$ by B^{-1}, the exclusion restrictions can be written in the equivalent form

$$(\tilde{\beta} \quad 0)P = (\tilde{\beta} \quad 0)(\phi^1 - \Pi\phi^2) = 0 \tag{2.7.7}$$

where $\tilde{\beta} = (1 \quad -\beta)$ includes the coefficient of q and we have used the fact that the last $M - (m + 1)$ endogenous variables are known not to appear in the equation to be estimated. In view of the special form taken by ϕ^1 and ϕ^2 in this case, this is equivalent to

$$\tilde{\beta}\tilde{\Pi}^2 = 0 \tag{2.7.8}$$

Now, by the definition of Π,

$$\tilde{\beta}[\tilde{\Pi}^1 \quad \tilde{\Pi}^2] = (\gamma \quad 0) \tag{2.7.9}$$

and the second set of equalities so involved is guaranteed by Eq. (2.7.8). It follows that for any $\tilde{\beta}$ satisfying Eq. (2.7.8) there is a unique corresponding γ obtained from

$$\gamma = \tilde{\beta}\tilde{\Pi}^1 \tag{2.7.10}$$

The $\tilde{\beta}$ and γ so obtained are clearly consistent both with the true reduced form and with the exclusion restrictions. It follows immediately that Eq. (2.7.1) is identified if and only if only scalar multiples of the true $\tilde{\beta}$ satisfy Eq. (2.7.8). Since $\tilde{\Pi}^2$ has $m + 1$ rows, this is equivalent to the desired result. Q.E.D.

Indeed, a result similar to that just obtained holds for $\rho(\Pi^{12})$ which is in fact the same as $\rho(\tilde{\Pi}^2)$. We prove:

Theorem 2.7.1: A necessary and sufficient condition for the identifiability of Eq. (2.7.1) is that $\rho(\Pi^{12}) = m$. (For a direct proof of the equivalence of this to the rank condition, see Koopmans and Hood [22, Appendix A].)

Proof: (a) Sufficiency: Π^{12} is a submatrix of $\tilde{\Pi}^2$. In view of Eq. (2.7.8), the latter matrix has rank at most m; if $\rho(\Pi^{12}) = m$, therefore, $\rho(\tilde{\Pi}^2) = m$ also, and the desired result follows from the preceding lemma.

(b) Necessity: Suppose $\rho(\Pi^{12}) < m$. The m rows of Π^{12} are then dependent and there exists at least one nonzero vector, say λ, in the row kernel of Π^{12}. Premultiply Eq. (2.7.2) by λ, obtaining

$$\lambda y_1 = (\lambda \Pi^{11})z_1 + (\lambda v_1) \tag{2.7.11}$$

This equation is obviously independent of Eq. (2.7.1) but excludes all the variables excluded from the latter equation. Addition of Eqs. (2.7.1) and (2.7.11) thus yields an equation indistinguishable from Eq. (2.7.1) which is thus not identifiable. Q.E.D.

An alternative (and possibly more illuminating) proof of sufficiency may be given as follows:

Suppose that Eq. (2.7.1) is underidentified. Then there exists an equation which is a linear combination of the equations of the model:

$$q = \beta^* y_1 + \gamma^* z_1 + u_1^* \tag{2.7.12}$$

where $(\beta^* \quad \gamma^*)$ is not a scalar multiple of $(\beta \quad \gamma)$. Subtracting Eq. (2.7.1) from Eq. (2.7.12) and rearranging terms we obtain

$$\lambda y_1 = \mu z_1 + e \tag{2.7.13}$$

where $\quad \lambda = \beta - \beta^* \qquad \mu = \gamma^* - \gamma \qquad e = u_1^* - u_1 \quad$ (2.7.14)

Now, Eq. (2.7.13) is a linear combination of the structural equations of the model. Since the reduced form of the model is a nonsingular transformation of the structure, Eq. (2.7.13) is also a linear combination of the reduced form equations. Each endogenous variable, however, appears in one and only one reduced form equation, and it is thus evident that Eq. (2.7.13) can only be a linear combination of the Eqs. (2.7.2) which correspond to y_1. Thus, premultiplication of Eqs. (2.7.2) by λ must give Eq. (2.7.13), whence λ must be in the row kernel of Π^{12}. It follows that the underidentifiability of Eq. (2.7.1) implies $\rho(\Pi^{12}) < m$.

As indicated at the beginning of this section, Theorem 2.7.1 is primarily of interest for the light it casts on the way in which certain estimators break down in the underidentified case. We shall now turn briefly to an examination of the principal one of those estimators, two-stage least squares.

Without going into detail unnecessary for our purposes, the basic idea of two-stage least squares may be stated as follows: The difficulty with applying ordinary least squares to Eq. (2.7.1) is that the elements of y_1 are correlated with u_1 even in the probability limit. However, since y_1 can be expressed as in the reduced form of Eqs. (2.7.2), it is evident that this comes about only because v_1, the reduced form residual, is a function of u_1. Two-stage least squares proceeds by "purging" y_1 by substituting for it in Eq. (2.7.1)

$$\hat{y}_1 = y_1 - v_1 = \Pi^{11}z_1 + \Pi^{12}z_2 \qquad (2.7.15)$$

so that the substitution consists of putting in place of y_1 in Eq. (2.7.15) the expected value of y_1 as calculated from the reduced form equations (estimated by least squares). The result of this substitution is

$$q = \beta\hat{y}_1 + \gamma z_1 + (u_1 + \beta v_1) \qquad (2.7.16)$$

All elements of $\hat{y}_1$ and all elements of z_1 are linear combinations of exogenous variables and are therefore uncorrelated with u_1 in the probability limit. Further, not only are all such elements uncorrelated with v_1 in the probability limit but also their sample values are uncorrelated with the sample time series for v_1 obtained by estimating Eq. (2.7.2) by least squares, since both $\hat{y}_1$ and z_1 are linear combinations of variables on the right-hand side of Eq. (2.7.2). It thus follows from Eq. (2.7.16) that (provided the appropriate probability limits exist) regression of q on the elements of $\hat{y}_1$ and z_1 will yield consistent estimates of β and γ.

This is an intuitively appealing procedure and can be rigorously justified. What has happened to the identification problem, however? So far as the above description is concerned, it appears as though two-stage least squares could be carried out whether or not the equation to be estimated is identifiable.

The catch lies in the second stage—the regression of q on the elements of $\hat{y}_1$ and z_1. This regression will involve the inversion of the variance-covariance matrix of these elements. It turns out that if and only if the equation to be estimated is identified will the matrix be nonsingular in the probability limit. That this is likely to be so can be seen by observing that $\hat{y}_1$ has m elements and z_1 has l elements. On the other hand, every element of each of these vectors is an exact linear function of the Λ elements of z_1 and z_2. If the necessary order condition fails, then $\Lambda < l + m$, and the Λ different variations afforded by the predetermined variables will not provide $l + m$ linearly independent variations in the elements of $\hat{y}_1$ and z_1. These elements will therefore be connected by an exact linear relationship.

Indeed, this result holds even if identifiability fails for reasons other than failure of the order condition. We prove:

Theorem 2.7.2: The elements of $\hat{y}_1$ and z_1 are linearly dependent if and only if Eq. (2.7.1) is not identifiable.

Proof: (a) Suppose that Eq. (2.7.1) is not identifiable. By Theorem 2.7.1, $\rho(\Pi^{12}) < m$, and there exists a nonzero vector λ satisfying Eq. (2.7.11). Subtracting λv_1 from both sides of that equation and rewriting

$$\lambda \hat{y}_1 = \lambda(y_1 - v_1) = (\lambda \Pi^{11}) z_1 \qquad (2.7.17)$$

which gives the linear dependence in question.

(b) Now suppose that such linear dependence exists.[1] Then there exists a nonzero vector, say μ, and another vector, say λ, such that

$$0 = \mu \hat{y}_1 + \lambda z_1 = \mu y_1 + \lambda z_1 - \mu v_1 \qquad (2.7.18)$$

This equation is obviously independent of Eq. (2.7.1), and addition of it to Eq. (2.7.1) yields an equation in the same form as Eq. (2.7.1) which is not simply a scalar multiple thereof. It follows that Eq. (2.7.1) is not identified.

This result has somewhat wider interest than the case of two-stage least squares only. H. Theil [31, pp. 231–232] has shown that there exists a whole class of estimators—the k-class—which contains many of the common simultaneous equation estimators, all having the same asymptotic properties as two-stage least squares. Every one of these estimators involves the inversion of a matrix which approaches the matrix inverted in two-stage least squares in the probability limit. It follows that our result shows that all these estimators break down (as they should) when the equation to be estimated is underidentified.

2.8. Inhomogeneous Linear Restrictions

We have now completed our discussion of the case of homogeneous linear restrictions. As stated at the beginning of this chapter, that case is the one of leading importance in practice. We have therefore spent rather more space on it than will be given to the inhomogeneous case in which the results closely parallel those already obtained.

Indeed, the question may properly be asked: Why discuss the inhomogeneous case at all? The equations to be estimated are all homogeneous in the coefficients; why then be interested in inhomogeneous restrictions?

[1] Note that, by Assumption 1.5.2, no linear identities connect the elements of z_1.

To put it another way, apparently the structural equations would be an equally acceptable explanation of the real world if multiplied by a non-zero scalar; how then can there exist restrictions which prevent such multiplication?

This question is indeed worth raising, and the objection involved is of considerable force. To drive this home, let us consider an example in which what appears at first to be an inhomogeneous restriction really turns out to be a homogeneous one plus a normalization rule. This property is rather general in dealing with inhomogeneous restrictions.

Thus, suppose, for example, that the equation to be estimated is a Cobb-Douglas production function in logarithmic form

$$q = \log \alpha + \lambda \log K + \mu \log L + u \tag{2.8.1}$$

where q = output

K = capital

L = labor

u = a random disturbance

α, λ, μ = parameters to be estimated

If one knows that there are constant returns to scale, one should impose the restriction

$$\lambda + \mu = 1 \tag{2.8.2}$$

which is apparently inhomogeneous.

The difficulty arises in the following way. Rewrite Eq. (2.8.1) *before* normalization with respect to the coefficient of q as

$$\eta q = \log \alpha + \lambda \log K + \mu \log L + u \tag{2.8.3}$$

The inhomogeneous restriction (2.8.2) now becomes the *homogeneous* restriction

$$\lambda + \mu = \eta \tag{2.8.4}$$

and the normalization rule

$$\eta = 1 \tag{2.8.5}$$

When we dealt with homogeneous restrictions in former sections, we generally did so without first imposing a normalization rule. The present example (whose properties are quite general) shows that it is possible to treat inhomogeneous restrictions in precisely the same form—that is, as homogeneous restrictions imposed before a normalization rule. Clearly, dealing with identifiability questions in the presence of Eq. (2.8.4) presents no new problems whatsoever.

The answer is very largely one of convenience. This is particularly so because we shall show below that there always exists a general method of transforming the restrictions which substitutes homogeneous linear restrictions for inhomogeneous linear ones and preserves all identifiability properties. This method must be sharply distinguished, however, from the argument just given and illustrated in the example. The latter argument is not merely that one can always make a transformation which turns inhomogeneous restrictions into homogeneous ones; it asserts that there is a sense in which there is no such thing as a truly inhomogeneous restriction. Inhomogeneous restrictions are made to appear so only because a particular normalization rule has been imposed in one's thinking about them.

There are circumstances, however, in which an inhomogeneous restriction is most conveniently left as is, even if it can be thought of as a homogeneous restriction and a normalization rule. Such circumstances arise when for some reason a "natural" normalization rule is present. For example, we shall deal in the next chapter with restrictions on the variances of the disturbance terms. Such restrictions clearly imply normalization rules; it is generally meaningless to say that the variance of a particular disturbance is known to be less than a certain magnitude unless the scale of the equation in question has been fixed. This is particularly so when the restriction takes the form of a statement on the relative size of the variances of the disturbances in two different equations. The natural procedure is to normalize by making one of the coefficients in each equation equal to unity, so that the units in which the disturbances are measured are fixed. In the presence of such restrictions, inhomogeneous restrictions on the coefficients which might otherwise be treated as in the example above may very well remain inhomogeneous.

In addition, we shall see below that inequalities can be treated as inhomogeneous restrictions with certain parameters. In such cases, it is frequently inconvenient (although still generally possible) to treat the problem as a homogeneous one in the absence of a normalization rule. Indeed, in general, where more than one inhomogeneous restriction is involved, it is often convenient not to think hard about an equivalent homogeneous form but to impose a normalization rule and deal with the inhomogeneous restrictions directly.

Despite such arguments, however, it must be admitted that there is no formal reason for treating inhomogeneous linear restrictions directly as such. This is particularly so because inhomogeneous linear restrictions, as already indicated, can always be turned into homogeneous ones by an appropriate transformation of the system. For this reason, we shall only summarize the extension of our previous results to the inhomogeneous case.

To see that inhomogeneous linear restrictions can be turned into homogeneous ones, write the equation to be estimated in scalar form

$$A_{11}x_1 + A_{12}x_2 + \cdots + A_{1N}x_N = u_1 \qquad (2.8.6)$$

Suppose that an inhomogeneous linear restriction takes the form

$$\sum_{j=1}^{N} c_j A_{1j} = b \qquad (2.8.7)$$

where the c_j and b are known numbers. We may obviously suppose that at least one $c_j \neq 0$, and without loss of generality, we may suppose this to be c_N.

There are two cases to be considered. First, suppose that there has already been a normalization rule imposed, say $A_{11} = 1$. Then we can simply rewrite (2.8.7) as

$$\sum_{j=1}^{N} c_j A_{1j} = b A_{11} \qquad (2.8.8)$$

transforming it into a homogeneous restriction.

It thus suffices to deal with the case in which no previous normalization rule has been imposed. In this case, define

$$k_j = \frac{-c_j}{c_N} \qquad (j = 1, \ldots, N - 1)$$

$$d = \frac{b}{c_N} \qquad (2.8.9)$$

Now, solve (2.8.7) for A_{1N}, obtaining

$$A_{1N} = d + \sum_{j=1}^{N-1} k_j A_{1j} \qquad (2.8.10)$$

Add $N - 1$ endogenous variables, $x_j^*(j = 1, \ldots, N - 1)$, to the system, defined by the additional equations

$$x_j^* = x_j + k_j x_N \qquad (j = 1, \ldots, N - 1) \qquad (2.8.11)$$

Substitute (2.8.10) into the structural equation (2.8.6) and rearrange terms to obtain

$$A_{11} x_1^* + A_{12} x_2^* + \ldots + A_{1N-1} x_{N-1}^* + d x_N = u_1 \qquad (2.8.12)$$

We have now replaced the original inhomogeneous restriction (2.8.7) with $N - 1$ new homogeneous restrictions plus a new inhomogeneous one. The new homogeneous restrictions state that $x_1, \ldots, x_{N-1}$ do not appear in the rewritten structural equation (2.8.12), while the inhomogeneous one states that the coefficient of x_N in that equation is equal to d. Since d is a known number, however, this is a normalization rule. Further inhomogeneous restrictions can now be treated in a manner analogous to that already used in the first case considered above after being rewritten (if necessary), using (2.8.10) to apply them to the coefficients of (2.8.12). They can thus be transformed into homogeneous restrictions. Clearly all identifiability properties are preserved in all this. (Note, in particular, that the number of restrictions and the number of new endogenous variables have both increased by the same amount.)

Having said this, we proceed to a summary of results in the case in which inhomogeneous linear restrictions are not so transformed.

2.9. Summary of Results in the Inhomogeneous Linear Restriction Case

The principal results of interest are of course the extensions of the rank and order conditions to the inhomogeneous case. In place of the restrictions (2.2.11), we write

$$A_1 \psi = \lambda \qquad (2.9.1)$$

where ψ is an $N \times K$ matrix of known numbers and λ is an N-component row vector with at least one nonzero element.

In the present case, we must insist that A_1 be completely determined and not just determined up to a scalar multiplication. Thus, proceeding as in Sec. 2.3, we require that

$$F_1 A \psi = \lambda \qquad (2.9.2)$$

have a *unique* solution in F_1, namely, the vector $(1 \quad 0 \cdots 0)$. This obviously is equivalent to:

Theorem 2.9.1 (Rank Condition): A necessary and sufficient condition for the identifiability of the first equation under the restrictions (2.9.1) is that $\rho(A\psi) = M$.

Again, the obvious corollary is:

Corollary 2.9.1 (Order Condition): A necessary (but not sufficient) condition for the identifiability of the first equation under the restrictions (2.9.1) is that $\rho(\psi) = M$.

As should be expected, the present insistence on restricting A_1 to a point instead of a ray raises the requirement on the restrictions by 1 from $M - 1$ to M.

As almost all our discussion in the homogeneous case carries over to the present case, we shall not trouble to repeat it. Instead, we shall merely observe that the rank and order conditions in the present case are consistent with those already obtained in the homogeneous case. By this we mean that if one adds to the restrictions in the homogeneous case an explicit normalization rule and thus obtains the inhomogeneous case (a normalization rule is an inhomogeneous restriction), the equation to be estimated is identified according to Theorem 2.9.1 if and only if it was identified in the homogeneous sense before the normalization rule was added.

To see this, we add a normalization rule to the restrictions (2.2.11), to which we shall now return. Such a rule must be consistent with the restrictions in that it must not set a zero coefficient equal to unity. Without loss of generality, we may suppose that it is the first element of A_{11} which is set equal to unity. Define

$$\psi = \begin{bmatrix} 1 \\ 0 \\ \cdot \\ \cdot \\ \cdot \\ 0 \end{bmatrix} \phi \qquad \lambda = (1 \quad 0 \cdots 0) \qquad (2.9.3)$$

The full set of homogeneous restrictions plus the normalization rule is then in the form (2.9.1). We need merely show that in this case $\rho(A\psi) = M$ if and only if $\rho(A\phi) = M - 1$.

Write

$$
A\psi = \begin{bmatrix} A_{11} \\ A_{21} \\ \cdot \\ \cdot \\ \cdot \\ A_{M1} \end{bmatrix} A\phi
\tag{2.9.4}
$$

Observe that the first row of $A\phi$ consists of zeros only, in view of Eq. (2.2.11). Take the largest nonvanishing subdeterminant of $A\phi$ (which cannot involve the first row thereof) and border it by the first column and row of $A\psi$. The determinant thus formed is a subdeterminant of $A\psi$ of order one greater than $\rho(A\phi)$. Further, that determinant is clearly nonvanishing, since expansion by the cofactors of the elements of the first row shows that it is equal to A_{11} times the nonvanishing subdeterminant of $A\phi$. A_{11} is not zero, since the normalization rule was assumed consistent. It follows that $\rho(A\psi) = \rho(A\phi) + 1$, whence $\rho(A\psi) = M$ if and only if $\rho(A\phi) = M - 1$, the desired result.

2.10. Linear Inequalities

Perhaps the most frequent type of a priori information available in econometric work, with the possible exception of exclusion restrictions, is information in the form of linear inequalities on the coefficients to be estimated. The most frequently encountered inequalities are those which specify the signs of the coefficients; but there are others. For example, one knows from theory that the marginal propensity to consume is not only positive but also less than unity. Certain commodities may be classified as necessities and thus specified to have an income elasticity of demand less than unity, and so forth.

If the equation to be estimated is identifiable by means of other restrictions, such inequality information can add to the efficiency of estimators if it is incorporated in some manner in the estimation procedure.[1] If, on the other hand, the equation is not identifiable by other restrictions, it is obvious that it is not identifiable with the additional inequality information.

It might seem, therefore, that a discussion of linear inequalities has no place in the present volume. This is not the case. While it is true that linear inequalities cannot identify because they cannot restrict the

---

[1] This may be done by programming techniques or Bayesian analysis. See Theil and Goldberger [33]. The problem of using either of these methods in a simultaneous equation context is very great; however, work is proceeding on Bayesian analysis. See Drèze [6] and the discussion in Sec. 6.5.

set of admissible equations to a sufficient extent, nevertheless, they do provide restrictions which can sometimes yield additional interesting restrictions on the parameters to be estimated when the inequalities are combined with observational information.

An example will be of use before presenting the general theory. Suppose that the equation to be estimated is the first one of the following model

$$y_1 = b_{12}y_2 + g_{11}z_1 + u_1$$
$$y_2 = b_{21}y_1 + g_{21}z_1 + u_2$$
(2.10.1)

Suppose that the only restriction on the first equation is

$$b_{12} > 0$$
(2.10.2)

which for reasons of later notation we choose to write in the form

$$b_{12} = \mu \qquad \mu > 0$$
(2.10.3)

Note that if μ were a known number, the first equation would be identified by the criteria given in the preceding section.

Using the usual notation for the reduced form parameters, observe that the restrictions (1.6.10) placed on the parameters of the first equation by posterior information can be written as

$$-\pi_{11} + b_{12}\pi_{21} + g_{11} = 0$$
(2.10.4)

Combining this with Eq. (2.10.3) yields

$$g_{11} = \pi_{11} - \pi_{21}\mu$$
(2.10.5)

Note that π_{11} and π_{21} can be consistently estimated. Differentiating Eq. (2.10.5) with respect to μ yields

$$\frac{dg_{11}}{d\mu} = -\pi_{21}$$
(2.10.6)

whence $\qquad g_{11} \gtrless \pi_{11} \qquad$ according as $\qquad \pi_{21} \lessgtr 0$ (2.10.7)

Since π_{21} can be consistently estimated, this is a nontrivial result.

Unfortunately, where several inequalities are involved, such an unambiguous result is less likely and will not emerge unless all similar derivatives have the same sign. Nevertheless, it is worth spelling out the general case.

For convenience {because we are going to treat inequalities as inhomogeneous equalities as in Eq. (2.10.3)}, we assume that a normalization rule has been chosen and is one of the prior restrictions. We thus assume that we are in the inhomogeneous case, where any linear equality constraints on A_1 take the form

$$A_1\psi^1 = \lambda^1$$
(2.10.8)

and $\lambda^1 \neq 0$.   The inequality constraints are

$$A_1\psi^2 > \lambda^2 \qquad (2.10.9)$$

and we rewrite these as

$$A_1\psi^2 = \lambda^2 + \mu^2 \qquad \mu^2 > 0 \qquad (2.10.10)$$

where the last inequality is taken to mean that every element of μ^2 is positive.[1]   Define

$$\mu^1 = 0 \qquad \lambda = (\lambda^1 \quad \lambda^2) \qquad \mu = (\mu^1 \quad \mu^2) \qquad \psi = [\psi^1 \mathrel{\vdots} \psi^2] \quad (2.10.11)$$

We may rewrite the restrictions compactly as

$$A_1\psi = \lambda + \mu \qquad (2.10.12)$$

which is in the usual form for inhomogeneous linear restrictions.

There are now three possibilities.   Given μ, the equation to be estimated is either underidentified, just identified, or overidentified by Eq. (2.10.12) according to the criteria developed in the preceding section for identification under inhomogeneous linear restrictions.

If the equation in question is underidentified, its parameters cannot be written as single-valued functions of the elements of μ.   It is still true that those parameters are restricted by Eq. (2.10.12), but it seems unlikely that such restrictions will yield much of interest.

If the equation is just identified, its parameters are completely determined as single-valued linear functions of μ.   Indeed, defining

$$H = [\psi \quad W] \qquad W = \begin{bmatrix} \Pi \\ I \end{bmatrix} \qquad (2.10.13)$$

it is immediate that

$$A_1 = (\lambda + \mu \quad 0)H^{-1} \qquad (2.10.14)$$

(*How do we know that H is nonsingular?   Prove the extension of Lemma 2.3.1 to the inhomogeneous case.*)   From this, we have the value of A_1 when $\mu = 0$ and the (constant) derivatives of each element of A_1 with respect to each element of μ^2. If for some element of A_1 all such derivatives are of the same sign, then we have obtained an inequality on that element.   If all such derivatives are not of the same sign, nothing more can be said without judgment about the possible relative magnitudes of the different elements of μ^2— the relative "strengths" with which the different inequalities in Eq. (2.10.9) hold.   Examination of alternative possibilities may still pay off and, indeed, in the most favorable case, elements of A_1 may actually be bounded by limits which are insensitive to the elements of μ^2.   (For an

[1] For our purposes, there is no particular distinction between strong and weak inequalities; we have written the inequalities as strong ones for convenience.

example of this procedure in practice in a somewhat different context, see Fisher [10, chap. 6].)

Finally, if the equation in question is overidentified under Eq. (2.10.12), two possible procedures are open. The first is to use some consistent estimator such as two-stage least squares and estimate the elements of A_1 as functions of μ. This procedure has the advantage of using all the information at once, but has the disadvantage that, as in the just identified case, all the derivatives of some element of A_1 with respect to the elements of μ^2 may not have the same sign. Efficient estimation of those derivatives may therefore not yield much of interest.

An alternate procedure is to select from Eq. (2.10.12) as many just identifying sets of restrictions as possible and apply the procedure for the just identified case to each of these. This increases the chances of obtaining an unambiguous inequality on elements of A_1. In particular, if there are sufficient equalities in Eq. (2.10.8) to identify the equation in question with the addition of only a single inequality, unambiguous inequalities will result from *every* just identifying set of restrictions which includes only a single inequality and hence only a single element of μ^2. (This is the case in the example given above.) In such a case, it would clearly be foolish to use all inequalities at once as in the first procedure just discussed.

This completes our discussion of the case of linear restrictions on A_1 for the present. We shall resume the discussion in Secs. 3.2 and 3.3 in order to develop concepts needed in that chapter but not required in the present one. Were we to discuss only such linear restrictions, however, those sections would be an integral part of this chapter. In addition, in Chap. 4 we shall consider the combination of such linear restrictions with information on the covariances of the disturbance terms. In Chap. 6 we shall discuss tests of exclusion restrictions and of identifiability under such restrictions.

References

The derivation of the rank and order-conditions is due to Koopmans, Rubin, and Leipnik [23]. The proof by way of Lemma 2.3.1 follows that of Fisher [7].

The discussion of overidentification and the restrictions on the reduced form draws heavily on Fisher [14], while the treatment of inhomogeneous restrictions and inequalities follows Fisher [7].

3

Restrictions on the Variance-Covariance Matrix of the Disturbance Terms, I: The Variances

3.1. Introduction

In the opening chapter we discussed a two-equation supply-demand example and saw that there was a clear intuitive sense in which one equation was identified if the other shifted about relative to it. We observed that there are two ways in which such shifts could come about: first, if the shifting equation contained variables which the equation to be identified did not; and second, if the variance of the disturbance term in the shifting equation is large and the variance of the disturbance term in the equation to be estimated is small. The previous chapter provided a rigorous statement of criteria for identifiability in the multiequation case when variables are excluded from the equation to be identified; in the present chapter we shall be concerned with the alternative case[1] in which prior restrictions on the size of disturbance variances are available. This is the first of two chapters which discuss restrictions on the variance-covariance matrix of the disturbances; the following one will deal with restrictions setting certain covariances equal to zero.

It is interesting to note that there is a sense in which the case of exclusion restrictions includes that in which a particular disturbance variance is known to be zero. A disturbance may be thought of as a sum of the independent effects of unobserved omitted variables, each of whose separate effects is negligible. In this sense, one might suppose that each equation could be thought of as excluding those variables which

[1] The two cases are obviously not mutually exclusive.

go into the disturbance terms of the others.   Unfortunately, this involves the assumption that the same variables are not present in the disturbance terms of more than one equation; this case is precisely that of zero covariance between different disturbances, the case discussed in the next chapter.

On the other hand, not making such an assumption, if we consider each element of u as a separate variable, it is clear that every equation excludes $M - 1$ variables—the other disturbance terms.   It is easy to see that if the disturbances were observable the rank and order conditions for identifiability would be satisfied and each equation identified by such exclusion.   The difficulty with such an argument, however, is precisely that because the disturbance terms are not observable, we cannot distinguish among them without added assumptions.   Thus, without added information, it does us no good to know that the first equation includes u_1 and not u_2; we cannot distinguish u_1 from u_2 or from any linear combination of the two.   In the case, however, in which u_1 is known to be identically zero, we can distinguish the first equation from the others, provided that no linear combination of the other disturbances is identically zero.   In this case, we can think of the first equation as excluding the $M - 1$ "disturbance variables" other than u_1.   This provides the $M - 1$ pieces of prior information satisfying the order condition and the condition that no linear combination of those variables be zero may be thought of as satisfying the rank condition.

Clearly, however, we are not usually concerned with the identification of nonstochastic equations.   We are concerned with the case in which some disturbance variance is known to be small—either absolutely or relative to the other disturbance terms.   In such cases, the sort of argument just made clearly holds approximately, and this chapter is devoted to a precise statement of what is involved and what sort of information is required.

In order to provide that statement, we must first introduce two more definitions of "types" of identification.   This we shall do in the next two sections.   (The next two sections might properly have been placed in Chap. 2, except that we shall need their concepts only in the present and later chapters.)

3.2. Identification with Respect to a Particular Equation

Consider the following three-equation example

$$b_{11}y_1 + b_{12}y_2 + b_{13}y_3 + g_{11}z_1 = u_1$$
$$b_{21}y_1 + b_{22}y_2 + b_{23}y_3 + g_{21}z_1 = u_2 \qquad (3.2.1)$$
$$b_{31}y_1 + b_{32}y_2 + b_{33}y_3 + g_{31}z_1 = u_3$$

Suppose that the only available prior information on the structure is

$$b_{13} = 0 = b_{23} \tag{3.2.2}$$

Obviously, none of the three equations is identified. Yet it is clear that the relationship of the third equation to the first two is rather special. No linear combination of the three equations which gives a nonzero weight to the third one will ever satisfy the restrictions on either the first or the second equation. Any such combination will have a nonzero coefficient for y_3. (This is because B must be nonsingular. In a more general case, a similar statement would be true everywhere except on a set of measure zero.) Thus no such combination could possibly be mistaken for either the first or the second equation. Another way to say this is to observe that the matrix F of any admissible transformation must have the first two elements of its last column zero. It is natural in this situation to speak of each of the first two equations as identified *with respect to the third* and to consider identification of an equation as such to be identification with respect to all other equations in the system.

Returning to the general model, we define:

Definition 3.2.1: The ith equation of the model will be said to be *identified with respect to the jth equation* if and only if the matrix F of any admissible transformation has zero in its ith row and jth column.

In the next chapter we shall develop several ways in which identification with respect to another equation can come about. For the present, we shall generalize the example just discussed by means of a theorem whose relation to the rank condition of the preceding chapter is immediately apparent.

Define $A(j)$ as the matrix formed by striking out the jth row of A. Concentrating once again, for simplicity, on the identifiability of the first equation, suppose that we have the linear and homogeneous restrictions on the elements of A_1:

$$A_1\phi = 0 \tag{3.2.3}$$

We prove:

Theorem 3.2.1: A sufficient condition that the first equation be identified with respect to the jth equation (for any $j = 2, \ldots, M$) is that

$$\rho\{A(j)\phi\} = \rho(A\phi) - 1 \tag{3.2.4}$$

If the only prior restrictions on the first equation are those embodied in Eq. (3.2.3), this is also necessary.

Proof: Let F be the matrix of an admissible transformation, with first row F_1. Then

$$F_1A\phi = 0 \tag{3.2.5}$$

so that F_1 is in the row kernel of $A\phi$. Since $A\phi$ has M rows and rank $\rho(A\phi)$, its row kernel has dimension $M - \rho(A\phi)$ by Theorem 1.4.1.

Now, consider the matrix $A(j)\phi$. It has $M - 1$ rows and has rank $\rho(A\phi) - 1$. Hence its row kernel also has dimension

$$(M - 1) - \{\rho(A\phi) - 1\} = M - \rho(A\phi)$$

Take any vector in the row kernel of $A(j)\phi$ and insert a zero element after the $(j - 1)$st element, so that the resulting new vector has M components and a zero element in the jth place. The vector so constructed lies in the row kernel of $A\phi$. Doing this to $M - \rho(A\phi)$ independent vectors in the row kernel of $A(j)\phi$, we obtain the same number of independent vectors in the row kernel of $A\phi$. These vectors clearly form a basis for the latter row kernel and it is immediate that every admissible F_1 has zero for its jth element.

Now suppose that Eq. (3.2.4) fails to hold. Then, since $A(j)\phi$ is constructed by striking out a row of $A\phi$, it must be the case that $\rho\{A(j)\phi\} = \rho(A\phi)$. The row kernel of $A(j)\phi$ then contains only $M - \rho(A\phi) - 1$ independent vectors, one less than the dimension of the row kernel of $A\phi$. Since no other restrictions on the first equation exist, any nonzero vector in the row kernel of $A\phi$ can be the first row of the matrix of an admissible transformation. Suppose, however, that every such vector had a zero element in the jth place. By striking that element, we would obtain a vector in the row kernel of $A(j)\phi$, so that from $M - \rho(A\phi)$ independent vectors forming a basis for the row kernel of $A\phi$, we would obtain the same number of vectors in the row kernel of $A(j)\phi$. The vectors so constructed would obviously be independent, contradicting the fact that the row kernel of $A(j)\phi$ contains no more than $M - \rho(A\phi) - 1$ independent vectors. Q.E.D.

Some discussion of this result may be in order. Let us begin by examining the example discussed above in terms of the theorem. There ϕ consists of the single column

$$\phi = \begin{bmatrix} 0 \\ 0 \\ 1 \\ 0 \end{bmatrix} \tag{3.2.6}$$

so that
$$A\phi = \begin{bmatrix} 0 \\ 0 \\ b_{33} \end{bmatrix} \tag{3.2.7}$$

making use of the restrictions (3.2.2). This matrix has rank 1, and that rank is maintained if the second row is stricken out but not if the third row is. The theorem then states what we have already observed, namely, that the first equation of Eq. (3.2.1) is identified with respect to the third equation but not with respect to the second one.

Next, the relation of the theorem to the rank condition of the previous chapter is clear. That condition stated that a necessary and sufficient condition for the identification of the first equation under Eq. (3.2.3) is that the rank of $A\phi$ be as high as possible, given Eq. (3.2.3). The present theorem states that the first equation is identified with respect to any other equation which contributes to that rank in an essential way. It is obviously true and not hard to prove directly that if the condition of Theorem 3.2.1 is satisfied with respect to *every* $j = 2, \ldots, M$, then the rank condition holds, and conversely. (*Exercise: Prove it.*)

Indeed, it is also easy to adapt the proof of Theorem 3.2.1 to secure the following more general result which includes both that theorem and the rank condition as special cases:

Theorem 3.2.2: Select a set of r equations other than the first ($r \leq M - 1$). Call that set of equations R. Denote by $A(R)$ the matrix formed by striking out the corresponding r rows of A. A sufficient condition for the first equation to be identified with respect to *each* of the equations in R (and therefore with respect to all of them) is that

$$\rho(A(R)\phi) = \rho(A\phi) - r \tag{3.2.8}$$

If the only prior restrictions on the first equation are those embodied in Eq. (3.2.3), this is also necessary.

The proof is left as an exercise to the reader, as is the simple proof that the rank condition is a corollary of this result.

3.3. Near-identification

Let us return to the example given in the preceding section—to the model (3.2.1). Suppose that a normalization rule is imposed on each of the equations, taking the form of the restrictions[1]

$$b_{ii} = 1 \qquad (i = 1, 2, 3) \tag{3.3.1}$$

Suppose further that in place of the equality restrictions (3.2.2) we have the inequality constraints

$$|b_{13}| < \epsilon > |b_{23}| \tag{3.3.2}$$

where $\epsilon > 0$ is specified to be small. It is clear that in this case there is a sense in which the first equation is "nearly" identified with respect to the third, in that any linear combination of the equations satisfying all

[1] In what follows, the reader should note the convenience of imposing the normalization rules in advance and dealing with the inhomogeneous case.

restrictions on the first equation must give small weight to the third equation relative to the weights given to the first two.

Formally, this may be seen as follows. Let

$$F_1 = (F_{11} \quad F_{12} \quad F_{13})$$

be the first row of the matrix of any admissible transformation. In view of the normalization restriction on the first equation,

$$F_{11} + F_{12}b_{21} + F_{13}b_{31} = 1 \tag{3.3.3}$$

and it should be noted that there is no ambiguity of scale concerning the b_{ij}, since normalization restrictions have been imposed on each equation.

Now, using the fact that b_{33} is restricted to be unity and the restrictions (3.3.2), we have

$$\epsilon > |F_{11}b_{13} + F_{12}b_{23} + F_{13}|$$
$$\geq |F_{13}| - |F_{11}|\,|b_{13}| - |F_{12}|\,|b_{23}| \geq |F_{13}| - (|F_{11}| + |F_{12}|)\epsilon \tag{3.3.4}$$

whence
$$|F_{13}| < \epsilon(1 + |F_{11}| + |F_{12}|) \tag{3.3.5}$$

So far as this is concerned, F_{13} might be absolutely small without being small relative to the absolute magnitudes of F_{11} and F_{12}. Were this to be so, however, the normalization restriction (3.3.3) would be violated, since if all three elements of F_1 were very small, the left-hand side of that equation could not equal unity. To see this, substitute in Eq. (3.3.5) for the unit element on the right-hand side, obtaining

$$|F_{13}| < \epsilon(F_{11} + F_{12}b_{21} + F_{13}b_{31} + |F_{11}| + |F_{12}|)$$
$$\leq \epsilon\{2|F_{11}| + (1 + |b_{21}|)|F_{12}|\} + \epsilon|b_{31}|\,|F_{13}| \tag{3.3.6}$$

For ϵ sufficiently close to zero, $1 - \epsilon|b_{31}| > 0$† and we finally obtain

$$\frac{|F_{13}|}{2|F_{11}| + (1 + |b_{21}|)|F_{12}|} < \frac{\epsilon}{1 - \epsilon|b_{31}|} \tag{3.3.7}$$

Thus, for ϵ sufficiently close to zero, F_{13} must be small *relative* to the other elements of F_1.

Note, however, that there is nothing in this that states that F_{13} must be *absolutely* small. Indeed, indefinitely large absolute values of F_{13} are quite consistent with all the restrictions. What is implied for small ϵ is that if the absolute value of F_{13} is large, the absolute values of either F_{11} or F_{12} or both must be much larger. An admissible linear combination of the three equations will look relatively like a combination of only the first two, in the sense that the distance between the points in

† Note again that there is no ambiguity as to the size of $|b_{31}|$ because of the imposition of the normalization rules.

parameter space represented by the corresponding two combinations of the rows of A will be small relative to the distance from the origin of either one, for small enough ϵ.

One other point should be noted before leaving the example. In the denominator of the left-hand side of the final result (3.3.7) the coefficient of $|F_{12}|$ is $(1 + |b_{21}|)$. Similarly, the coefficient of $|F_{11}|$ can be read as $(1 + |b_{11}|)$, in view of the normalization rules. This is not an accident. In the results obtained below, the elements of A in the same column as the normalized element of A_1 appear similarly.

Turning now to the general case, we shall speak of the first equation as nearly identified with respect to, let us say, the jth equation, if F_{1j} is absolutely small relative to the other elements of F_1. For reasons of the calculus, however, relative sizes of absolute values are an inconvenient measure of this. We shall therefore use squares. For any vector ξ we use $|\xi|$ to mean the length of ξ, that is, the square root of the sum of squares of the elements of ξ; there is absolutely no danger of confusion when ξ is a scalar. In measuring the relative importance of F_{1j} in F_1, we shall thus look at $|F_{1j}|/|F_1|$. It is easy to show, incidentally, that this is the sine of the angle in the space of the elements of F_1 between F_1 and a vector whose elements are all the same as those of F_1 except for the jth element which is zero.

We define:

Definition 3.3.1: Suppose that one or more a priori restrictions are stated in terms of parameters $\epsilon_1, \ldots, \epsilon_S$, where the $\epsilon_i > 0$ are all specified to be small. Let $\epsilon = (\epsilon_1, \ldots, \epsilon_S)$. The ith equation of the model will be said to be *nearly identified with respect to the jth equation* under those restrictions if and only if there exists a function $G(\epsilon)$ such that

    (a) For any admissible transformation with matrix F and sufficiently small ϵ

$$\frac{F_{ij}^2}{F_i'F_i} = \left(\frac{|F_{ij}|}{|F_i|}\right)^2 < G(\epsilon)$$

(b) $\lim_{\epsilon \to 0} G(\epsilon) = 0$

The reason for stating the definition in this way and not simply requiring that $\lim_{\epsilon \to 0} |F_{ij}|/|F_i| = 0$ is that the latter statement is not separately defined. The only sensible way to define it is to require that for any sequence of ϵs approaching zero and any corresponding sequence of admissible Fs, one for each ϵ, the corresponding sequence of $|F_{ij}|/|F_i|$ approaches zero. This is equivalent to (a) and (b) of the definition.

It is natural to add:

Definition 3.3.2: An equation will be said to be *nearly identified* if it is not identified but is either identified or nearly identified with respect to every other equation.

Thus, in the example, the first equation is nearly identified with respect to the third but is not nearly identified. It would be nearly identified if, for example, we knew that

$$b_{12} = 0 = b_{32} \tag{3.3.8}$$

(*Verify this.*)

3.4. Variance Restrictions and Normalization Rules

We shall turn now to the restrictions to be imposed on the disturbance variances. However, it makes no sense to talk of such restrictions without also imposing normalization rules, for such restrictions are inhomogeneous. Thus, the statement that a given disturbance variance is less than some known number has no content if the size of that variance is determined only up to a scalar multiplication. Similarly, a statement that the variance of one disturbance is less than that of another has no content if the units in which each disturbance is measured are not fixed, at least relative to each other. Of course, as in the preceding chapter, we could always alter such inequality constraints to be homogeneous ones, with a normalization rule to be imposed afterwards. This would involve dividing the disturbance variance by the square of the unnormalized coefficient to be set equal to one by the normalization rule. (*Exercise: Write out such a restriction in this form.*) This would lead to a very clumsy (if equivalent) analysis and would be an unnatural way of proceeding. It is clearly better to impose normalization rules at the outset. Accordingly, we assume:

Assumption 3.4.1: Any equation whose disturbance variance is restricted by a priori information of an inhomogeneous type has already been subjected to a normalization rule.

We shall write the normalization rule for the equation (the first) whose identification is studied explicitly below and shall insist that all admissible transformations produce a structure satisfying that rule as well as all other restrictions on that equation. We shall not write the normalization rules on other equations explicitly; we shall use Assumption 3.4.1 on such equations, in the sense that parameters which appear in them will be taken to be unambiguously determined as to scale. (Note that this was explicitly done in the example of the preceding section.)

For reasons of simplicity of discussion we shall now concentrate as before on the identifiability of the first equation. We renumber, if necessary, the equations of the structure other than the first in the following way:

First, if there are any equations with respect to which the first equation is known to be identified by restrictions on the coefficients or for any other reason other than restrictions on the variance of the first disturbance, we place those equations last in the list. If there are $\pi \geq 0$ such equations, therefore, they are renumbered to be equations $M - \pi + 1, \ldots, M$.

Now consider the remaining equations including the first. If necessary, we renumber these so that those equations come first whose disturbances satisfy the same restrictions as does the first disturbance. (The restrictions will be given below.) Note that the first equation is in this set. We assume that there are $\mu \geq 1$ equations in this group which are thus numbered $1, \ldots, \mu$.

Finally, the remaining equations are taken to be λ in number $(\lambda = M - \mu - \pi)$ and given the numbers $\mu + 1, \ldots, \mu + \lambda(= M - \pi)$. These equations are thus those such that (1) the first equation is not already known to be identified with respect to them and (2) the disturbances thereof are not known to obey the restrictions to be placed below on the variance of the first disturbance. While our principal results will hold formally even if there are no equations in this set, it will be apparent below that this case is not of much interest. We shall therefore assume $\lambda > 0$.

It will be convenient to avoid carrying the subscript on F_1 in this chapter and we shall thus denote F_1 by f', where f is a column vector. We partition f and u according to the numbering of equations given above as

$$f = \begin{bmatrix} f^1 \\ f^2 \\ f^3 \end{bmatrix} \qquad u = \begin{bmatrix} u^1 \\ u^2 \\ u^3 \end{bmatrix} \tag{3.4.1}$$

Since, by construction, the first equation is identified with respect to each member of the last set of equations, $f^3 = 0$ for every admissible transformation.

We partition the variance-covariance matrix of the disturbances Σ in a similar way; thus

$$\Sigma = \begin{bmatrix} \Sigma^{11} & \Sigma^{12} & \Sigma^{13} \\ \Sigma^{21} & \Sigma^{22} & \Sigma^{23} \\ \Sigma^{31} & \Sigma^{32} & \Sigma^{33} \end{bmatrix} \tag{3.4.2}$$

Hence, in this notation, Σ^{IJ} denotes the covariance matrix of the elements of u^I (corresponding to the rows) and the elements of u^J {corresponding to the columns $(I, J = 1, 2, 3)$}. We continue to denote individual elements of Σ by σ_{ij} $(i,j = 1, \ldots, M)$.

We are now ready for the restrictions. We impose the following restriction on $\sigma_{11}, \ldots, \sigma_{\mu\mu}$. (Recall that $\mu \geq 1$, with equality allowed.)

Assumption 3.4.2: There exists a scalar $\eta > 0$ such that it is known that

$$\sigma_{ii} < \eta^2 \qquad (i = 1, \ldots, \mu) \tag{3.4.3}$$

Note that by Assumption 3.4.1, this implies the existence of a normalization rule on each of the first μ equations.

Now, in constructing the set of equations $\mu + 1, \ldots, \lambda$, we specified that their disturbances were not known to obey Eq. (3.4.3). As it turns out, we must specify something stronger. Indeed, we must specify first that the disturbances from those equations are known *not* to obey Eq. (3.4.3) and, even stronger, that no suitably normalized linear combination of those disturbances satisfies Eq. (3.4.3). Obviously, it makes no sense to speak of such restrictions without normalization rules on the equations involved; we have already covered this in Assumption 3.4.1. In addition, it is meaningless to impose a lower bound on the variance of any arbitrarily scaled linear combination of those disturbances. Instead, we can impose such a restriction only when the scale of the combination is in turn specified (since otherwise we could take vanishingly small coefficients times each disturbance and violate any such restriction).

Now, let d be a λ-component column vector. Consider $d'u^2$ as any linear combination of the elements of u^2, the disturbances in question. It is easy to see that the variance of $d'u^2$ is given by $d'\Sigma^{22}d$. We shall impose our constraint on the variances of such combinations where d is a vector of unit length. Thus, we assume:

Assumption 3.4.3: There exists a scalar $\rho > \eta > 0$ such that for any λ-component column vector d

$$d'\Sigma^{22}d \geq \rho^2(d'd) \tag{3.4.4}$$

Thus, if d has unit length, $d'\Sigma^{22}d \geq \rho^2$.

As Σ^{22} is positive definite, it is apparent that ρ^2 is its smallest latent root.[1] The size of ρ^2 thus measures the distance of Σ^{22} from singularity.

---

[1] *Proof:* If a matrix A is positive definite, it is orthogonally similar to a diagonal matrix, say D, whose diagonal elements are the latent roots of A. Thus there exists an orthogonal matrix P such that $D = P'AP$. Consider the problem of minimizing $d'Ad$ subject to the constraint that $d'd = 1$. Let $d = Pe$. Then, $d'Ad = e'(P'AP)e = e'De$. Further, $d'd = e'(P'P)e = e'e$, because $P' = P^{-1}$. Thus the problem is equivalent to that of minimizing $e'De$ subject to $e'e = 1$. However, $e'De$ is thus a weighted average of the diagonal elements of D—the latent roots of A—with the weights the squares of the elements of e. The minimum problem is thus solved by putting all the weight on the smallest diagonal element of D; thus the value of the minimized quadratic form is the smallest latent root of A. A similar result holds for maximization.

For a calculus proof of this well-known proposition, cf. Sec. 6.6, Theorem 6.6.1.

To put it another way, if we merely required $\sigma_{jj} \geq \rho^2$ $(j = \mu + 1, \ldots, \lambda)$, it might yet happen that by combining two or more of the equations in the second set we secured a composite equation with disturbance variance less than ρ^2. This would certainly be the case if one of the elements of u^2 were highly correlated with a linear combination of the other elements. Assumption 3.4.3 prevents this from happening.

By Assumption 3.4.1, we have implicitly placed normalization rules on the first $\mu + \lambda$ equations. There is thus no ambiguity about the scale of the elements of the first $\mu + \lambda$ rows of A. We must now explicitly consider the normalization rule imposed on the first equation. We shall take this in the form of setting a particular element of A_1 equal to -1.†
Let h be the column vector formed by the first $\mu + \lambda$ elements of the corresponding column of A. Thus the leading element of h is -1. (Note again that there is no ambiguity about the scale of the elements of h.) Since $f^3 = 0$ for any admissible transformation, the normalization restriction on the first equation may be stated as:

Assumption 3.4.4: For any admissible transformation,

$$(f^{1\prime} \quad f^{2\prime})h = -1 \tag{3.4.5}$$

Finally, define

$$\epsilon = \frac{\eta}{\rho} > 0 \tag{3.4.6}$$

Thus, ϵ^2 is the ratio of the upper bound on the first μ disturbance variances to the lower bound on the variances of normalized linear combinations of the next λ disturbances.

Since we shall be discussing near-identification, we shall let ϵ approach zero. It is therefore not at all restrictive to assume:

Assumption 3.4.5: In what follows, ϵ is small enough that

$$\epsilon^2(h'h) + \epsilon \sqrt{\mu} < 1 \tag{3.4.7}$$

It is important to note that it is ϵ and not η which is to be required to be small. Thus it is the relative size of disturbance variances and not their absolute size which is involved. Nevertheless, Assumption 3.4.2 places an *absolute* upper bound on the variances of the first μ disturbances. Such an upper bound is necessary for what follows. We shall discuss this further after developing the principal theorem of this chapter.

3.5. Lemmas

We shall show in the next section that the assumptions imply that the first equation is nearly identified with respect to equation $\mu + 1, \ldots,$

† We use -1 instead of 1 for reasons of convenience; there is no special reason why 1 cannot be used except for a slight ease of writing below.

$\mu + \lambda$. In this section we shall prove a series of lemmas required for that demonstration. (Henceforth, f will be understood to come from an admissible transformation.)

Lemma 3.5.1: Under Assumption 3.4.4,

$$f'f \geq \frac{1}{h'h} \tag{3.5.1}$$

Proof: We minimize $f'f$ subject to Eq. (3.4.5). Thus, form the Lagrangian function

$$L = f'f + \delta\{(f^{1\prime} \quad f^{2\prime})h + 1\} \tag{3.5.2}$$

where δ is a Lagrange multiplier. Since $f^3 = 0$, this is to be minimized with respect to the elements of f^1 and f^2. Differentiating, the first-order minimum conditions then yield

$$f_j = -\frac{\delta}{2} h_j \qquad (j = 1, \ldots, \mu + \lambda) \tag{3.5.3}$$

which on substitution into Eq. (3.4.5) shows

$$\delta = \frac{2}{h'h} \tag{3.5.4}$$

so that
$$f'f = \frac{h'h}{(h'h)^2} = \frac{1}{h'h} \tag{3.5.5}$$

at the minimum point. Q.E.D.

Since the desired result on near-identification will be trivial if $f^2 = 0$, we shall assume that this is not the case. Further, we prove:

Lemma 3.5.2: $$f^1 \neq 0$$

Proof: Assumption 3.4.2 implies that any admissible transformation must have the property that

$$\eta^2 > f'\Sigma f = f^{1\prime}\Sigma^{11}f^1 + f^{2\prime}\Sigma^{22}f^2 + 2f^{1\prime}\Sigma^{12}f^2 \tag{3.5.6}$$

since $f^3 = 0$ and Σ is symmetric. Suppose that $f^1 = 0$, then Eq. (3.5.6) and Assumption 3.4.3 imply

$$\rho^2(f^{2\prime}f^2) \leq f^{2\prime}\Sigma^{22}f^2 < \eta^2 \tag{3.5.7}$$

so that
$$f^{2\prime}f^2 < \epsilon^2 \tag{3.5.8}$$

In this case, however, we may use Assumption 3.4.5 to obtain

$$(f^{2\prime}f^2)(h'h) < \epsilon^2(h'h) + \epsilon\sqrt{\mu} < 1 \tag{3.5.9}$$

which contradicts Lemma 3.5.1. Q.E.D.

We now define two variables p and q as

$$p = \frac{f^{1\prime}u^1}{|f^1|} \qquad q = \frac{f^{2\prime}u^2}{|f^2|} \tag{3.5.10}$$

Denoting the variance of p by σ_{pp}, the variance of q by σ_{qq}, and their covariance by σ_{pq}, we have

$$\sigma_{pp} = \frac{f^{1\prime}\Sigma^{11}f^1}{f^{1\prime}f^1}$$

$$\sigma_{qq} = \frac{f^{2\prime}\Sigma^{22}f^2}{f^{2\prime}f^2} \tag{3.5.11}$$

$$\sigma_{pq} = \frac{f^{1\prime}\Sigma^{12}f^2}{|f^1|\,|f^2|}$$

Lemma 3.5.3: $\qquad \sigma_{pp} < \mu\eta^2 \qquad$ and $\qquad \sigma_{qq} > \sigma_{pp}$

Proof: Since the largest latent root of a positive semidefinite matrix is no larger than the sum of the diagonal elements, it follows from Eq. (3.5.11), the proof in the footnote on page 74, and Assumption 3.4.2 that

$$\sigma_{pp} \leq \sum_{i=1}^{\mu} \sigma_{ii} < \mu\eta^2 \tag{3.5.12}$$

Furthermore, Assumption 3.4.3 implies

$$\sigma_{qq} \geq \rho^2 \tag{3.5.13}$$

so that $\qquad\qquad\qquad \sigma_{qq} - \sigma_{pp} > \rho^2 - \mu\eta^2 \tag{3.5.14}$

However, since $\epsilon^2(h'h) > 0$, Assumption 3.4.5 implies

$$\frac{\eta\sqrt{\mu}}{\rho} = \epsilon\sqrt{\mu} < 1 \tag{3.5.15}$$

whence $\qquad\qquad\qquad\qquad \sigma_{qq} - \sigma_{pp} > 0 \tag{3.5.16}$

and the lemma is proved.

It is also easy to show:

Lemma 3.5.4: $\qquad -\dfrac{2|f^1|\,|f^2|}{f'f}\dfrac{\sigma_{pq}}{\sigma_{qq}} \leq \dfrac{|\sigma_{pq}|}{\sigma_{qq}} \leq \dfrac{\sqrt{\sigma_{pp}}}{\sqrt{\sigma_{qq}}}$

Proof: Observe that the first inequality is trivial if $\sigma_{pq} \geq 0$. Suppose, therefore, that $\sigma_{pq} < 0$; then $-\sigma_{pq} > 0$, and (recalling that $f^3 = 0$)

$$0 \leq \{(f^{1\prime}f^1)^{\frac{1}{2}} - (f^{2\prime}f^2)^{\frac{1}{2}}\}^2 = f'f - 2|f^1|\,|f^2| \tag{3.5.17}$$

It follows immediately that

$$\frac{2|f^1|\,|f^2|}{f'f} \le 1 \tag{3.5.18}$$

and the first inequality is proved.

To establish the second inequality, let r_{pq} be the correlation between p and q. Then

$$\frac{|\sigma_{pq}|}{\sigma_{qq}} = |r_{pq}| \frac{\sqrt{\sigma_{pp}\sigma_{qq}}}{\sigma_{qq}} \le \frac{\sqrt{\sigma_{pp}}}{\sqrt{\sigma_{qq}}} \tag{3.5.19}$$

Q.E.D.

Now, define the function

$$Z(k) = \frac{\epsilon^2(h'h) - k^2 + k}{1 - k^2} \tag{3.5.20}$$

where k is a scalar. As our final lemma, we prove:

Lemma 3.5.5: $Z'(k) > 0$ for all k such that $0 \le k < 1$

Proof: $Z'(k) = \dfrac{2k\epsilon^2(h'h) + (k^2 - 2k + 1)}{(1 - k^2)^2} > 0$ (3.5.21)

3.6. The Near-identification Theorem for Disturbance Variance Restrictions

We are now ready to use the lemmas just developed to secure our rigorous statement of near-identification under the restrictions on disturbance variances already given. That theorem is:

Theorem 3.6.1: Under Assumptions 3.4.1 to 3.4.5, the first equation of the model is nearly identified with respect to equations $\mu + 1, \ldots, \mu + \lambda$. Specifically, the function $G(\epsilon)$ of Definition 3.3.1 may be taken to be

$$G(\epsilon) = \frac{\epsilon^2\{(h'h) - \mu\} + \epsilon\sqrt{\mu}}{1 - \mu\epsilon^2} < \epsilon^2(h'h) + \epsilon\sqrt{\mu} \tag{3.6.1}$$

Proof: Substitute from Eq. (3.5.11) into Eq. (3.5.6) and divide by $f'f$, to obtain

$$\frac{(f^{1\prime}f^1)}{f'f}\sigma_{pp} + \frac{(f^{2\prime}f^2)}{f'f}\sigma_{qq} + \frac{2|f^1|\,|f^2|}{f'f}\sigma_{pq} < \frac{\eta^2}{f'f} \tag{3.6.2}$$

Since $f^3 = 0$,

$$\frac{f^{1\prime}f^1}{f'f} = 1 - \frac{f^{2\prime}f^2}{f'f} \tag{3.6.3}$$

so that

$$\frac{f^{2\prime}f^2}{f^\prime f}(\sigma_{qq} - \sigma_{pp}) < \frac{\eta^2}{f^\prime f} - \sigma_{pp} - \frac{2|f^1|\ |f^2|}{f^\prime f}\sigma_{pq} \qquad (3.6.4)$$

By Lemma 3.5.3, however, $\sigma_{qq} > \sigma_{pp}$, so that

$$\begin{aligned}\frac{f^{2\prime}f^2}{f^\prime f} &< \frac{\eta^2/f^\prime f - \sigma_{pp} - 2|f^1|\ |f^2|\sigma_{pq}/f^\prime f}{\sigma_{qq} - \sigma_{pp}} \\ &= \frac{(\eta^2/\sigma_{qq})(1/f^\prime f) - \sigma_{pp}/\sigma_{qq} - (2|f^1|\ |f^2|/f^\prime f)(\sigma_{pq}/\sigma_{qq})}{1 - \sigma_{pp}/\sigma_{qq}} \qquad (3.6.5)\end{aligned}$$

As already observed, however, $\sigma_{qq} \geq \rho^2$, and this, together with Lemmas 3.5.1 and 3.5.4, yields

$$\frac{f^{2\prime}f^2}{f^\prime f} < \frac{\epsilon^2(h^\prime h) - \sigma_{pp}/\sigma_{qq} + \sqrt{\sigma_{pp}}/\sqrt{\sigma_{qq}}}{1 - \sigma_{pp}/\sigma_{qq}} \qquad (3.6.6)$$

By Lemma 3.5.3 and Assumption 3.4.5

$$0 \leq \frac{\sigma_{pp}}{\sigma_{qq}} < \frac{\mu\eta^2}{\rho^2} = \mu\epsilon^2 < 1 \qquad (3.6.7)$$

and the theorem now follows from Lemma 3.5.5 with $k = \sqrt{\sigma_{pp}/\sigma_{qq}}$, the inequality in Eq. (3.6.1) being an easy consequence of Assumption 3.4.5.

3.7. Discussion of the Theorem

Theorem 3.6.1 presents the rigorous statement of the intuitive result on disturbance variances with which we began. Several features of it require discussion.

In the first place, it is important to note the way in which absolute and relative restrictions on the variance of the first disturbance enter. The original restrictions (Assumptions 3.4.2 and 3.4.3) are in terms of the absolute size of the disturbance variances. Despite this, the crucial parameter in the result (ϵ) is clearly a relative one. It may thus seem that a restriction on relative variances is all that is required and that the absolute restrictions are overly strong.

To see that this is not the case, it suffices to consider an example with only two equations. If all that is specified is that the second disturbance has a large variance relative to that of the first, the only restriction on admissible transformations is that the transformed version of the second equation must continue to have a disturbance variance which is large relative to that of the transformed version of the first equation. Unless the second equation is itself identified by other restrictions, there is no reason why this cannot be accomplished by giving the transformed version of the second disturbance a very large variance and choosing f_2 (the second element of f) very large relative to f_1 (the first element) but still small enough not to violate the restriction. This cannot be done if an upper bound is available on either variance in question; but then we have an absolute restriction. It is thus not true that the large shifting of one equation relative to another helps identify the one which shifts relatively less, if such shifts come only from the disturbance term. One must also know something about the absolute size of the variances involved.

How, then, can such knowledge be available? The above discussion indicates two appropriate ways in which this can happen. First, one may be willing to impose both an upper bound on the variance of a disturbance other than the first *and* a restriction on the relative size of the first disturbance variance. If such restrictions are tight enough, this is equivalent to the restrictions given in Assumptions 3.4.2 and 3.4.3. Second, the first disturbance variance may be known to be small relative to the variance of a disturbance from an equation identified by other restrictions. In such a case, the size of the latter variance can be consistently estimated, so that an absolute restriction on the first disturbance variance can be derived. In either case, note that the absolute restriction required need *not* require that the first disturbance be absolutely small, only that it be bounded from above by a number which is small relative to a known lower bound on certain other disturbance variances. We shall return in the next section to the question of whether our assumptions are necessary as well as sufficient for the result of the theorem.

Next, it is important to realize that near-identification with respect to certain of the equations is not equivalent to near-identification. Unless $\mu = 1$, so that there are no disturbances other than the first whose variances satisfy Assumption 3.4.2, there is nothing to prevent f_1 from being very small (or even zero) relative to the other elements of f^1 *and even relative to the elements of f^2*. All that is guaranteed by the theorem is that the sum of squares of the elements of f^2 is small relative to that of *all* the elements of f^1 so that any admissible transformation yields a first equation lying close to that yielded by one with no weight given to equations $\mu + 1, \ldots, \mu + \lambda$. If $\mu = 1$, this means that the transformed equation lies close to the original one and that equation is nearly identified. If $\mu > 1$, this need not be the case.

Next, we add some remarks on the form of the function $G(\epsilon)$ given in Eq. (3.6.1). It is clear that $G(\epsilon)$ is increasing in ϵ and it is easy to show that it is also increasing in μ for small ϵ. This is plausible since the larger either ϵ or μ is, the less tight are the restrictions on the first disturbance variance relative to those on other disturbance variances. The fact that $h'h$ enters as it does at first seems more surprising but can be seen to be plausible from the following argument.

Consider a two-equation example. Take a linear combination of the two equations. Let that combination be P_1 times the first plus P_2 times the second equation. If that combination is to be admissible as a new first equation, it must satisfy the normalization rule on the first equation. This means that it must be divided by $-P'h = P_1 - P_2h_2$ (since the leading element of h is -1 by Assumption 3.4.4). The corresponding disturbance is then also divided by this, and its variance by $(P_1 - P_2h_2)^2$. For h_2 sufficiently large (and positive, say), the bigger h_2, the greater is the maximum relative weight $P_2^2/(P_1^2 + P_2^2)$ consistent with Assumption 3.4.2 which can be put on the second equation in forming the original linear combination, since the greater is the reduction in the transformed disturbance variance consequent on the division required to obey the normalization rule. This is why $h'h$ plays the role it does.

In closing, it may be of some interest to observe that $G(\epsilon)$ is approximately equal to $\mu\epsilon$ for ϵ sufficiently small. Further, $G(\epsilon)$ is capable of being consistently estimated if every element of h either is given by a priori restrictions on equations $2, \ldots, \mu + \lambda$ or is a parameter in an identified equation. If, in addition, $\mu = 1$ and equations $2, \ldots, \mu + \lambda$ are identified, the (narrow) deviation of admissible transformations of the first equation from the true version thereof can be assessed.

3.8. Exact Identification under Such Restrictions; the Necessity of the Assumptions

An interesting question which remains to be discussed is whether the assumptions of Theorem 3.6.1 may not be overly strong. In particular, is Assumption 3.4.3 needed? That assumption requires that *any* appropriately normalized linear combination of certain disturbances have a variance greater than some lower bound, which bound is taken in the theorem to be large relative to the upper bound on the variance of the first disturbance. Would it not suffice to require that only certain linear combinations have that property?

In one way, we have implicitly answered that question. Assumption 3.4.3 restricts only those disturbances which come from equations which are not already such that the first equation is identified with respect to them for other reasons. This suggests immediately the obvious fact that the only linear combinations of disturbances which need be restricted are those which correspond to linear combinations of equations not ruled out by other restrictions as admissible replacements of the first equation. The question of overly strong assumptions thus becomes one of whether this can usefully be expressed in a weaker form than is done in Assumption 3.4.3, which simply restricts all linear combinations of just those disturbances which might otherwise enter into admissible combinations.

The issue will be best highlighted if we leave the question of near-identification for the moment and examine the question of the "full" identification of the first equation under a much stricter restriction on its disturbance variance than we have hitherto imposed. Specifically, we take the limiting case of Assumption 3.4.2 and assume that it is known that

$$\sigma_{11} = 0 \tag{3.8.1}$$

For convenience, we concentrate on the identification of the first equation rather than on its identification with respect to certain equations. The relevance of the discussion to the more general case will be obvious.

Suppose further that there are linear and homogeneous[1] restrictions of the usual type on the elements of A_1:

$$A_1\phi = 0 \tag{3.8.2}$$

Let F_1 be the first row of the matrix of any admissible linear transformation F. (We drop the f notation as no longer required for convenience.) Then F_1 must satisfy

$$F_1(A\phi) = 0 \tag{3.8.3}$$

and

$$F_1\Sigma F_1' = 0 \tag{3.8.4}$$

Since Σ is at least positive semidefinite, however, Eq. (3.8.4) holds if and only if

$$F_1\Sigma = 0 \tag{3.8.5}$$

and we may write Eqs. (3.8.3) and (3.8.5) compactly as

$$F_1[A\phi \ \vdots \ \Sigma] = 0 \tag{3.8.6}$$

If the first equation is to be identifiable, then Eq. (3.8.6) must admit one and only one independent solution. (*How do we know that there is one such solution?*) This is obviously equivalent to:

Theorem 3.8.1 (Generalized Rank Condition): A necessary and sufficient condition for the identifiability of the first equation under the restrictions (3.8.1) and (3.8.2) is that the rank of the matrix $[A\phi \ \vdots \ \Sigma]$ be $M - 1$.

Note that this is guaranteed in the common case in which $\rho(\Sigma) = M - 1$ because the last $M - 1$ disturbances are not linearly dependent.

[1] Note, incidentally, that Eq. (3.8.1) does not necessarily imply a normalization rule on the first equation as would be the case were it in the form of Eq. (3.4.3). It too is a homogeneous restriction.

So much (for the present) for generalizing the rank condition. (*Can you similarly generalize the order condition?*) It is more interesting to derive another identification condition which bears directly on the assumptions of Theorem 3.6.1.

Partition F_1 into $(F_1{}^1 \quad 0)$ (renumbering, if necessary), where the zero elements are those which are required to be zero by Eq. (3.8.3). Let there be $\pi \geq 0$ such zero elements; then the first equation is identified by Eq. (3.8.3) with respect to the last π equations. Correspondingly, partition Σ as

$$\Sigma = \begin{bmatrix} \Sigma^{11} & \Sigma^{12} \\ \Sigma^{21} & \Sigma^{22} \end{bmatrix} \qquad (3.8.7)$$

Then Eq. (3.8.4) is equivalent to

$$F_1 \Sigma F_1' = F_1{}^1 \Sigma^{11} F_1{}^{1\prime} = 0 \qquad (3.8.8)$$

Since Σ^{11} is at least positive semidefinite, this is equivalent to

$$F_1{}^1 \Sigma^{11} = 0 \qquad (3.8.9)$$

Thus:

Theorem 3.8.2: A sufficient condition for the identifiability of the first equation under Eqs. (3.8.1) and (3.8.2) is that after the renumbering and partitioning of equations just described, $\rho(\Sigma^{11}) = M - \pi - 1$. (Why is $\rho(\Sigma^{11}) > M - \pi - 1$ impossible?)

This condition which is the analogue of Assumption 3.4.3 in the present case is sufficient but not necessary. The reason for this is that the condition takes no account of the fact that it may perfectly well be the case that not every $F_1{}^1$ will satisfy Eq. (3.8.3). If that happens, then only by accident (i.e., on a set of measure zero) will a value of $F_1{}^1$ which does satisfy Eq. (3.8.3) also satisfy Eq. (3.8.9) provided that $\Sigma^{11} \neq 0$.

To see this, consider the following three-equation example.

$$u_i = \sum_{j=1}^{3} \beta_{ij} y_j + \gamma_i z \qquad (i = 1, 2, 3) \qquad (3.8.10)$$

Suppose that Eq. (3.8.1) is satisfied and that Eq. (3.8.2) takes the form

$$\gamma_1 = 0 \qquad (3.8.11)$$

Let $F_1 = (F_{11} \quad F_{12} \quad F_{13})$. By Eq. (3.8.11), for an admissible transformation,

$$\sum_{i=1}^{3} F_{1i} \gamma_i = F_{12} \gamma_2 + F_{13} \gamma_3 = 0 \qquad (3.8.12)$$

Assume that $\gamma_2 \neq 0$, then

$$F_{12} = -\frac{\gamma_3}{\gamma_2} F_{13} \qquad (3.8.13)$$

Now, in this case, $\Sigma^{11} = \Sigma$, since Eq. (3.8.11) does not itself identify the first equation with respect to either of the others. Thus also, $\pi = 0$. Suppose that $\rho(\Sigma) < M - \pi - 1 = 3 - 0 - 1 = 2$, because the first disturbance is zero and because, for example, the second and third disturbances are equal. Then, F_1 must satisfy

$$F_1\Sigma = 0 \qquad (3.8.14)$$

or

$$F_{12}\sigma_{22} + F_{13}\sigma_{32} = 0 = F_{12}\sigma_{23} + F_{13}\sigma_{33} \qquad (3.8.15)$$

Since the last two disturbances are equal, this is equivalent to

$$(F_{12} + F_{13})\sigma_{22} = 0 \qquad (3.8.16)$$

or, assuming $\sigma_{22} \neq 0$,

$$F_{12} = -F_{13} \qquad (3.8.17)$$

This is compatible with Eq. (3.8.13) for F_{12} and F_{13} not both zero, however, only if γ_2 just happens to equal γ_3. In the absence of a restriction so specifying, such equality occurs only on a set of measure zero in the parameter space. Moreover, it is possible that the restrictions on the last two equations actually forbid the equality of γ_2 and γ_3. In this case, the first equation is actually identifiable instead of being identifiable almost everywhere despite the fact that the condition of Theorem 3.8.2 fails.

To recapitulate, the condition of Theorem 3.8.2 is sufficient. If $\Sigma^{11} \neq 0$, however, and the restrictions (3.8.2) restrict F_1^1, then the first equation will generally be identified almost everywhere even if that condition fails. This will be true unless there are rather special restrictions on equations 2, . . . , $M - \pi$ (in the example, unless γ_2 is known to equal γ_3). Equally, the first equation will be everywhere identifiable if there are other types of special restrictions in effect implying that the first type is known *not* to hold (in the example, if γ_2 is known *not* to equal γ_3).

We may note that if there are *no* restrictions on A_1, it *is* necessary that $\rho(\Sigma) = M - 1$. This follows both from Theorem 3.8.1 and from observing that this is a case in which $F_1^1 = F_1$ is entirely unrestricted by the (nonexistent) restrictions (3.8.2).

Now we shall return to the case of near-identification and to Assumption 3.4.3. One might think from the preceding discussion that (in the notation of that assumption), provided $\Sigma^{22} \neq 0$, the first equation would be nearly identified except on a set of measure zero in the parameter space. At the least, one might think that, provided Assumption 3.4.3 is not violated for *every* vector d, this would be true. In other words, one might suppose that the first equation would be nearly identified almost everywhere provided that not every appropriately normalized linear combination of the relevant disturbances had a variance less than ρ^2.

Such suppositions are generally false, and this is an important distinction between identification and near-identification. In the case in which the first disturbance was known to be zero, we could assert that if only certain linear combinations of the relevant disturbances are admissible under the restrictions on A_1, then (unless all those disturbances are zero) those admissible combinations would be zero only on a set of measure zero. In the case in which the first disturbance is known only to have a small variance, we cannot make a similar assertion about the probability of encountering a linear combination of the relevant disturbances which is admissible under the restrictions on A_1 and which has a similarly small variance. Smallness of variance, unlike variance equal to zero, can occur on a set of positive measure. Speaking loosely, while it may be true that it is relatively unlikely that a particular admissible linear combination has such small variance, we cannot generally assert that such an event has probability zero in the absence of Assumption 3.4.3.

Of course, it is still possible that the totality of other restrictions on the system implies that such an event does not occur, even if Assumption 3.4.3 fails. This is unlikely to happen in practice and it is difficult to say in general what properties such other restrictions would have to have. Assumption 3.4.3 thus does appear to be the weakest one which will guarantee the desired result, even though it may not be strictly necessary in particular cases. (*Does this statement have to be altered if the first equation is already identified by restrictions on A_1? Why or why not?*)

3.9. The Proximity Theorem and Identification

Just as in the previous chapter we briefly explored the relationship between identification and estimation under the restrictions there considered, so we shall now discuss the similar relationship under the restrictions on disturbance variance discussed in this chapter. Interestingly enough, the appropriate estimator in this case turns out to be ordinary least squares. ("The" is a bit too strong. Other estimators may have as desirable properties as least squares at least when the disturbance variance of the equation in question is only restricted to be small rather than to be zero.)

Consider the case of a single-equation model. In this and the next paragraph only, we shall use the familiar notation of least-squares theory. Let Y be a T-element column vector, each element of which is an observation on the dependent variable in the equation to be estimated; let X be a $T \times n$ matrix, each row of which is an observation on the set of independent variables; let U be a T-element column vector of values of the disturbance; let β be a vector of parameters to be estimated. The model is

$$Y = X\beta + U \qquad (3.9.1)$$

Denoting the least-squares estimator of β by b,

$$b = (X'X)^{-1}X'Y = \beta + (X'X)^{-1}X'U \qquad (3.9.2)$$

Thus, the difference between the least-squares estimator b and the true value of the vector β of parameters to be estimated may be thought of as consisting of the vector of (unobservable) regression coefficients in the regression of the disturbance on the independent variables. The bias of the least-squares estimator is therefore the expected value of that vector of regression coefficients, and the inconsistency of the least-squares estimator is the probability limit of that vector.

The regression coefficients in question, however, may be thought of as follows: Suppose that $X'X$ is bounded away from singularity in the following discussion (a point of crucial importance on which most of the discussion of this section will center). The difference between b and β will then be close to zero if and only if the elements of $X'U$ are close to zero. These elements, however, are the covariances of the disturbance and the regressors. Covariances can be written as correlation coefficients times the product of the standard deviations. In this case, one term in each product is the standard deviation of the disturbance. Further, if $X'X$ is bounded away from singularity, the variance of every regressor is bounded away from zero. Hence, $b - \beta$ will be close to zero if and only if either the standard deviation of the disturbance is close to zero or the disturbance is almost uncorrelated with the regressors, or both. (If both are true, then the two effects help each other, since what matters involves their product.) To make this a statement about the bias of the least-squares estimator, one need only make it a statement after taking expectations; to make it a statement about consistency, one need only make it a statement about probability limits.

For our purposes, it is the consistency statement that is important, since identification is not a property which is affected by sampling. We summarize the result just obtained as a theorem, which, because it speaks of closeness to consistency, is known as the "proximity theorem." It is due to H. Wold.

Wold and Juréen [31, p. 189]; Wold and Faxér [36]. Wold's statements of the theorem are in terms of bias. As stated, we have given it in terms of consistency only because of our particular interest, which follows in this discussion.

The proximity theorem is a basic theorem in the study of specification error. For generalization of the regression coefficient interpretation, see Theil [31, sec. 6B] and [32]. Fisher [8] presents two generalizations of the proximity theorem to simultaneous equation estimators.

Theorem 3.9.1 (Proximity Theorem): If the variance-covariance matrix of the regressors is bounded away from singularity, the least-squares estimator approaches consistency either as the variance of the disturbance approaches zero or as the probability limits of the correlations between the disturbance and the regressors approach zero. The two effects are reinforcing.

The approach envisioned in the theorem is one in which a sequence of models is considered, all with the same true coefficient vector but differing, for example, in the size of the disturbance variance, which approaches zero as the sequence progresses.

Now, what has all this to do with identification? We are here concerned with the part of the proximity theorem which involves the disturbance variance. The apparent implication of the theorem is that least squares applied *even to an equation which is one of a simultaneous set of equations* yields an estimator approaching consistency as the variance of the disturbance term in that equation approaches zero. Indeed, the limit will evidently be reached, so that the theorem apparently implies the existence of a consistent estimator for any equation with no disturbance term. This clearly implies that any such equation is identified.

On the other hand, such a happy result cannot be correct. We saw in the very first chapter that the identification problem arises in nonstochastic equation systems. In general, if the only prior restriction on the equation to be estimated is a zero disturbance term, that equation will not be identified in the presence of one or more other equations in the model which have the same property. In such cases, no consistent estimator of the parameters of the equation in question exists. Yet the proximity theorem apparently implies such existence. Something is wrong somewhere.

The catch lies in the incautious reading of the proximity theorem given two paragraphs above. The proximity theorem carefully includes in its statement the provision that the variance-covariance matrix of the regressors must be bounded away from singularity. It is evident that such a condition is necessary, since, returning to the notation of Eq. (3.9.2) for a moment, $(X'X)^{-1}X'U$ will not approach zero as $X'U$ does unless $(X'X)^{-1}$ is kept from going to infinity at a similar or faster rate.

This immediately suggests that identification of an equation which has a zero disturbance variance is equivalent to the nonsingularity of the appropriate variance-covariance matrix of regressors.

This is indeed the case, and the argument largely parallels that already given for two-stage least squares in Sec. 2.7. Write the equation to be estimated as

$$q = \beta y_1 + \gamma z_1 \qquad (3.9.3)$$

where q is an endogenous variable; y_1 is a column vector of such variables; z_1 is a column vector of exogenous variables; and all exclusion restrictions have already been used—as has a normalization rule. We prove:

Theorem 3.9.2: Least squares is a consistent estimator of the parameters of Eq. (3.9.3) if and only if that equation is identifiable.

Proof: By the foregoing discussion, it suffices to show that identifiability is a necessary and sufficient condition for the nonsingularity of the variance-covariance matrix of the elements of y_1 and z_1. Such nonsingularity is equivalent to the absence of an exact linear relationship connecting these elements.

The proof here is even easier than in the case of two-stage least squares discussed in Sec. 2.7. First suppose that such a relationship exists, so that there exist row vectors c_1 and c_2 such that

$$c_1 y_1 + c_2 z_1 = 0 \qquad (3.9.4)$$

for all y_1 and z_1 satisfying the equations of the model. Addition of any scalar multiple of Eq. (3.9.4) to Eq. (3.9.3) then yields an equation in the same form as Eq. (3.9.3) which thus cannot be identifiable.

Next, suppose that Eq. (3.9.3) is not identifiable. Then there exists a scalar α (which may be zero) and row vectors β^* and γ^* such that

$$\alpha q = \beta^* y_1 + \gamma^* z_1 \qquad (\beta^* \quad \gamma^*) \neq \alpha(\beta \quad \gamma) \qquad (3.9.5)$$

Multiplying Eq. (3.9.3) by α and subtracting from Eq. (3.9.5), we obtain

$$0 = (\beta^* - \alpha\beta)y_1 + (\gamma^* - \alpha\gamma)z_1 \qquad (3.9.6)$$

so that the elements of y_1 and z_1 are connected by an exact linear relationship and their variance-covariance matrix must be singular. This completes the proof of the theorem.

It is further illuminating to show explicitly that the question of whether the variance-covariance matrix of the elements of y_1 and z_1 is bounded away from singularity is intimately connected with the conditions of the principal theorem of this chapter, Theorem 3.6.1, as, of course, it must be.

Note that this will also show the near-consistency of least squares if $\mu = 1$ and the conditions of Theorem 3.6.1 are satisfied. This may be seen as follows:

Suppose those conditions are satisfied but η^2 is large. Multiply all equations by a small positive scalar, say k. Then ϵ is unchanged; the conditions of the theorem still hold; but the upper bound on the first disturbance variance becomes $k^2\eta^2$, which can be made small. The conditions of the proximity theorem are thus satisfied.

To see this connection, it will be helpful to write out that variance-covariance matrix explicitly. Let Y_1 be a $T \times m$ matrix whose rows are observations on the elements of y_1; let Z_1 be a $T \times l$ matrix whose rows are observations on the elements of z_1. As in Sec. 2.7, write that part of the reduced form corresponding to y_1 as

$$y_1 = \Pi^{11}z_1 + \Pi^{12}z_2 + v_1 \tag{3.9.7}$$

where z_2 is a column vector of the $\Lambda - l$ exogenous variables in the model but not in Eq. (3.9.3) and v_1 is a column vector of the appropriate reduced form disturbances. Let V_1 be a $T \times m$ matrix each of whose rows is a set of values for the elements of v_1 at the appropriate observation. The matrix whose distance from singularity is at issue is effectively

$$H = \operatorname*{plim} \left\{ \frac{1}{T} \begin{bmatrix} Y_1'Y_1 & Y_1'Z_1 \\ Z_1'Y_1 & Z_1'Z_1 \end{bmatrix} \right\} \tag{3.9.8}$$

In view of the definition of exogeneity, however,

$$\operatorname*{plim} \left\{ \left(\frac{1}{T}\right) Z_1'V_1 \right\} = 0 \qquad \operatorname*{plim} \left\{ \left(\frac{1}{T}\right) Y_1'V_1 \right\} = \operatorname*{plim} \left\{ \left(\frac{1}{T}\right) V_1'V_1 \right\} \tag{3.9.9}$$

so that we may write

$$H = \operatorname*{plim} \left\{ \frac{1}{T} \begin{bmatrix} (Y_1 - V_1)'(Y_1 - V_1) & Y_1'Z_1 \\ Z_1'Y_1 & Z_1'Z_1 \end{bmatrix} \right\}$$
$$+ \operatorname*{plim} \left\{ \frac{1}{T} \begin{bmatrix} V_1'V_1 & 0 \\ 0 & 0 \end{bmatrix} \right\} \tag{3.9.10}$$

Call the first term on the right H_1 and the second term H_2. H_1, which is the matrix whose nonsingularity is required in two-stage least squares (see Sec. 2.7), can be written as

$$H_1 = \operatorname*{plim} \left\{ \left(\frac{1}{T}\right) [(Y_1 - V_1) \mid Z_1]'[(Y_1 - V_1) \mid Z_1] \right\} \tag{3.9.11}$$

while H_2 can be written as

$$H_2 = \operatorname*{plim} \left\{ \left(\frac{1}{T}\right) [V_1 \mid 0]'[V_1 \mid 0] \right\} \tag{3.9.12}$$

It is thus the case that both H_1 and H_2 are at least positive semidefinite. It follows that H is positive semidefinite and is singular if and only if the same nonzero vector is in the row kernel of both H_1 and H_2.

Now, suppose that the exclusion restrictions are sufficient to identify Eq. (3.9.3). In that case, it follows immediately from Theorem 2.7.2 that H_1 is nonsingular, whence H is also nonsingular. Moreover, since such nonsingularity has nothing whatsoever to do with the properties of the disturbances, it will be maintained if we give Eq. (3.9.3) a nonzero disturbance and consider what happens as the variance of that disturbance approaches zero.

On the other hand, suppose that the exclusion restrictions are not sufficient to identify Eq. (3.9.3). Then (since again this has nothing to do with the disturbances) Theorem 2.7.2 implies the singularity of H_1. Moreover, Theorem 2.7.1 implies the existence of a row vector, say $\mu \neq 0$, such that

$$\mu\Pi^{12} = 0 \tag{3.9.13}$$

Thus
$$\mu y_1 = \mu\Pi^{11}z_1 + \mu v_1 \tag{3.9.14}$$

Now, let y_2 be the column vector of the $M - m$ endogenous variables not included in y_1 (one of these is q) and write the entire reduced form (where the notation not already explained should be obvious)

$$\begin{pmatrix} y_1 \\ y_2 \end{pmatrix} = y = \Pi z + v = \begin{bmatrix} \Pi^{11} & \Pi^{12} \\ \Pi^{21} & \Pi^{22} \end{bmatrix} \begin{pmatrix} z_1 \\ z_2 \end{pmatrix} + \begin{pmatrix} v_1 \\ v_2 \end{pmatrix} \tag{3.9.15}$$

Define
$$\mu^* = (\mu \quad 0) \tag{3.9.16}$$

where the zero vector involved has $M - m$ components. Then

$$\mu^* y = \mu^* \Pi z + \mu^* v = \mu^*(-B^{-1}\Gamma)z + \mu^* B^{-1}u \tag{3.9.17}$$

where the original structure was

$$By + \Gamma z = u \tag{3.9.18}$$

Let
$$\lambda = \mu^* B^{-1} \tag{3.9.19}$$

then
$$\lambda By + \lambda \Gamma z = \lambda u \tag{3.9.20}$$

However, this must be the same as Eq. (3.9.14). Thus Eq. (3.9.20) is a transformation admissible under the exclusion restrictions on Eq. (3.9.3). It follows that $\lambda_i \neq 0$ $(i = 1, \ldots, M)$ only if Eq. (3.9.3) is not identified with respect to the ith structural equation. Note, however, that

$$\mu v_1 = \mu^* v = \lambda u \tag{3.9.21}$$

so that μv_1 is a linear combination of disturbances from equations such that the exclusion restrictions do not identify Eq. (3.9.3) with respect to them.

Now define

$$\eta = (\mu \quad -\mu\Pi^{11}) \tag{3.9.22}$$

By Eq. (3.9.14)

$$\eta \begin{pmatrix} y_1 - v_1 \\ z_1 \end{pmatrix} = 0 \tag{3.9.23}$$

whence, by Eq. (3.9.11),

$$H_1\eta' = 0 \tag{3.9.24}$$

$H_1\eta'$ and not ηH_1 is used here because we defined the observation matrices so as to be able to write the moment matrices in the usual form.

Moreover, it is easy to show (see Sec. 2.7) that if Eq. (3.9.24) holds for any nonzero vector η', then η can be written in the form (3.9.22) with a μ satisfying Eq. (3.9.13). Thus the singularity of H_1 is equivalent to the case we are now discussing.

Now, as stated, H is singular if and only if the same nonzero vector is in the row (or column) kernel of H_1 and H_2. Hence it is only singular if for some η in the form described

$$H_2\eta' = \text{plim}\left\{\left(\frac{1}{T}\right)V_1'V_1\right\}\mu' = 0 \tag{3.9.25}$$

However, by Eq. (3.9.21) and the remarks which preceded it, this means that the variance-covariance matrix of the disturbances from the equations with respect to which Eq. (3.9.3) is not identified by the exclusion restrictions must be singular.

The relationship to Assumption 3.4.3 and to the discussion in Sec. 3.8 should now be clear. That assumption certainly guarantees the nonsingularity (indeed the bounding from singularity) of H. If that assumption fails, H may still be nonsingular, since H_2 can be singular without Eqs. (3.9.25) and (3.9.24) holding simultaneously; but the bounding of H from singularity cannot generally be guaranteed. This was spelled out in Sec. 3.8, in which the problem was discussed at length. It is, of course, natural to reencounter the same range of problems in the present context, because we have been showing that the contexts are in fact the same.

References

The section on identification with respect to a particular equation draws on Fisher [11] and the principal sections of the chapter draw heavily on Fisher [13], although Theorem 3.6.1 has been slightly strengthened. For the proximity theorem see Wold and Faxér [36].

The basic idea that shifts in one equation aid identification of another is in Working [38] and was explored in a rather different way by Metzler [26].

4

Restrictions on the Variance-Covariance Matrix of the Disturbance Terms, II: The Covariances

4.1. Introduction

In this chapter, we shall study the effect on identifiability of restrictions specifying that the disturbances from two different equations are uncorrelated. We have already seen in Sec. 1.3 that such restrictions, at least in the presence of other restrictions, may aid identification.

How can such restrictions arise? They are generally less likely to be immediate consequences of that economic theory which leads to the structure to be estimated than are the restrictions so far discussed (even those in the last chapter). Rather, such restrictions are likely to be present because of notions implicitly held about the real mechanism being subsumed in the disturbance terms. Thus, if the disturbances are thought of as being the net effects of numerous independently acting small influences omitted from the structural part of the equations, the assumption of uncorrelated disturbance terms for two equations is then the assumption that the omitted variables affecting the two equations have no large number of elements in common. Whether this is a reasonable assumption may depend largely on whether the two equations refer to closely related parts of the model—to supply and demand in a single market, for example—or to widely separated parts.

Whether or not such assumptions are plausible, however, their use, as will appear in the discussion of the next two sections, is pervasive, if sometimes only implicit. It is therefore of considerable interest to examine their consequences. Before doing so in general, however, we will first consider the way in which such assumptions of uncorrelated disturbances arise and are used in the context of simultaneous equation models. This will lead us naturally to a reconsideration of what is meant by an "exogenous" or "predetermined" variable.

4.2. The Theory of Recursive Systems

We shall begin by briefly repeating some of the discussion of Sec. 1.5. Let Y, Z, and U be respectively the $T \times M$, $T \times \Lambda$, and $T \times M$ observation matrices whose rows are, respectively, the vectors of observations on the endogenous variables, the predetermined variables, and the disturbances. The model is then compactly written as

$$YB' + Z\Gamma' = U \qquad (4.2.1)$$

Define, as before

$$\Sigma = \text{plim} \left(\frac{U'U}{T} \right) \qquad (4.2.2)$$

as the positive definite (unless otherwise stated) variance-covariance matrix of the disturbances.

We have been assuming (Assumption 1.5.3) and continue to assume that

$$\text{plim} \left(\frac{Z'U}{T} \right) = 0 \qquad (4.2.3)$$

so that the predetermined variables are uncorrelated with the disturbances in the probability limit. It is important to realize at this stage that absolutely nothing we have so far said in this book has depended on any property of the predetermined variables other than this. Indeed, we may go further and observe that—in the terminology of the first chapter—there are as many pieces of observational information available on an equation as there are variables in the system which are uncorrelated in the probability limit with the disturbance *from that equation*. In the general case so far considered, those variables are the same for every equation, namely, the Λ predetermined variables involved in Z. We must now consider the possibility that the prior information on the system is in just such a form as to imply that further variables, endogenous to the whole system, may be predetermined *with respect to a given equation* in the sense of being uncorrelated in the probability limit with the disturbance from that equation. In such a case, such variables can profitably be used to gain information on the equation in question and to aid its identification—a case in which prior information allows the use of posterior information.

Formally:

Definition 4.2.1: A variable will be said to be predetermined with respect to a particular equation if and only if it is uncorrelated in the probability limit with the disturbance from that equation.

Note that predetermined variables are predetermined with respect to every equation in the system.

Now, in general, endogenous variables are not predetermined with respect to any equation in the system, for

$$Y' = (-B^{-1}\Gamma)Z' + B^{-1}U' = \Pi Z' + V' \qquad (4.2.4)$$

so that $\quad \mathrm{plim}\left(\dfrac{Y'U}{T}\right) = \Pi\,\mathrm{plim}\left(\dfrac{Z'U}{T}\right) + \mathrm{plim}\left(\dfrac{V'U}{T}\right)$

$$= B^{-1}\Sigma \qquad (4.2.5)$$

In the general case, $B^{-1}\Sigma$ contains no zero elements. In certain special cases, however, it does. When the ijth element of $B^{-1}\Sigma$ is known to be zero, then the ith endogenous variable is known to be uncorrelated with the jth disturbance. For purposes of identifying the jth equation, therefore, the ith endogenous variable in such a case may be added to the list of Λ predetermined variables. This may be thought of as raising Λ by 1 *and* dropping M by 1, thus reducing for the jth equation the crucial number $(M - 1)$ of pieces of additional prior information required for its identification.

It is clearly time for an example. Suppose that the system consists of only two equations which, after imposing normalization rules, can be written as

$$\begin{aligned} y_1 &= b_{12}y_2 + g_{11}z_1 + u_1 \\ y_2 &= b_{21}y_1 + g_{21}z_1 + u_2 \end{aligned} \qquad (4.2.6)$$

z_1 is predetermined with respect to both equations. Now, consider the second equation; y_1 is not predetermined with respect to it unless further information is available. A pip in u_2 will induce a movement in y_2 which will, in turn, by the first equation, induce a movement in y_1. y_1 and u_2 cannot therefore be assumed to be uncorrelated in the probability limit.

But what if it were known that

$$b_{12} = 0 \qquad (4.2.7)$$

Then a pip in u_2 would still induce a movement in y_2, but that movement would no longer result in a movement in y_1. It is tempting to assert that u_2 and y_1 can then be assumed to be uncorrelated in the probability limit.

Such an assertion would be wrong, however, as we shall see in a minute. Indeed, we know already that it *must* be wrong, for if it were correct, the second equation of Eq. (4.2.6) could be consistently estimated by ordinary least squares and would thus be identifiable. This is obviously impossible, since we have *no* prior information specifically relating to that equation. The restriction (4.2.7) relates to the first equation and does indeed identify it. It cannot alone suffice to identify the second equation unless there is something wrong with great parts of the analysis of Chaps. 1 and 2.

The catch lies in the relations between u_1 and u_2, and this brings us to the subject of this chapter. If u_1 and u_2 are correlated, a movement in u_2 tends to be associated with a movement in u_1 which is obviously associated with a movement in y_1. To put it differently, if some of the variables omitted from the first equation and appearing in u_1 are also represented in u_2, their common effect on u_2 and y_1 prevents us from assuming that the latter two variables are uncorrelated in the probability limit.

This comes out clearly in the algebra. Before setting b_{12} equal to zero, we have

$$y_1 = \frac{1}{1 - b_{12}b_{21}} \{(g_{11} + b_{12}g_{21})z_1 + (u_1 + b_{12}u_2)\} \qquad (4.2.8)$$

so that $\qquad \text{cov}(y_1, u_2) = \dfrac{\sigma_{12}}{1 - b_{12}b_{21}} + \dfrac{b_{12}\sigma_{22}}{1 - b_{12}b_{21}} \qquad (4.2.9)$

where σ_{12} is the covariance of u_1 and u_2 and σ_{22} is the variance of u_2. The second fraction on the right-hand side of Eq. (4.2.9) is the effect of u_2 on y_1 by way of y_2 and the structure of the system; the first fraction is the effect by way of correlation between u_1 and u_2. If Eq. (4.2.7) is imposed, the second fraction becomes zero, but the first does not, becoming simply σ_{12}. If and only if in addition to Eq. (4.2.7) we can assert that the two disturbances are uncorrelated can we take y_1 as predetermined relative to the second equation of Eq. (4.2.6).

We have glossed over the possibility that it just happens that $\sigma_{12} = -b_{12}\sigma_{22} \neq 0$, so that the two effects in Eq. (4.2.9) just cancel each other out. This sort of prior information is never available in practice, as will be clear if the reader considers how such a peculiar fact could ever be known in advance. In terms of the more general discussion, this sort of phenomenon would occur if a particular element of $B^{-1}\Sigma$ were known to be zero without B and Σ having the specialized forms discussed below in which that element is the sum of terms each of which are themselves separately known to be zero.

Suppose, however, that it is indeed known that

$$\sigma_{12} = 0 \qquad (4.2.10)$$

in addition to Eq. (4.2.9). Then y_1 *is* predetermined with respect to the second equation. Accordingly, it is clear that the latter equation can be consistently estimated by least squares and is therefore identifiable. The restriction (4.2.10), in the presence of Eq. (4.2.7), has provided the appropriate prior information on the second equation.

There are two ways of seeing this besides observing the consistency of least squares. Both ways are somewhat illuminating. First, as indicated in our general discussion preceding this example, the two restrictions allow us to take y_1 as predetermined when considering the second equation. This has the effect of reducing M from 2 to 1. Applying the rank condition, since $M - 1$ has become zero, no further restrictions are needed to identify that equation.

Alternatively, proceeding as in Sec. 1.3, note that if a linear combination of the two equations of Eqs. (4.2.6) is to be an admissible substitute for the second equation in the presence of Eq. (4.2.10), then (unless that linear combination involves only scalar multiplication of the true second equation) the admissible structure of which that combination is to be a part must substitute for the *first* equation some other linear combination of the two equations. The latter combination involves the second true equation in a nontrivial way. This is so because if the first equation remains unchanged in the transformed structure, its disturbance will surely be correlated with any linear combination of u_1 and u_2 which gives a nonzero weight to u_1. However, Eq. (4.2.7) clearly implies that the first equation is identified, so that every admissible structure has as its first equation only a scalar multiple of the true first equation. Accordingly, the two restrictions together identify the second equation as well as the first, although neither one separately would suffice.

Return now to the general case. Suppose that:

Assumption 4.2.1: B is a triangular matrix.

Assumption 4.2.2: The disturbances from every distinct pair of equations are uncorrelated in the probability limit, so that Σ is diagonal.

Without loss of generality, we may take B to have zeros above the main diagonal.

If these two assumptions are satisfied, $B^{-1}\Sigma$ is triangular and every endogenous variable is predetermined with respect to every higher-numbered equation, as is the case in the example just discussed when both restrictions are imposed.

Such a system is said to be *recursive*. It clearly has the property that impulses flow only from low-numbered equations to higher-numbered ones. The triangularity of B means that pips in a disturbance act directly through the structure to produce movements only in a single one of the endogenous variables appearing in the equation with that disturbance; the diagonality of Σ guarantees that pips in one disturbance are not associated with pips in another.

It is clear that every equation in such a system is identified. This may be seen in a number of ways. First, the triangularity of B implies that the only endogenous variables appearing in the jth equation are those with numbers less than or equal to j. By the triangularity of $B^{-1}\Sigma$, therefore, the jth endogenous variable is the *only* variable appearing in the jth equation which is correlated in the probability limit with the disturbance from that equation. Accordingly, least squares provides a consistent estimator for the jth equation, which must therefore be identified.

Alternatively, for the jth equation, endogenous variables $1, \ldots,$ $j - 1$ may be thought of as predetermined. This reduces the number of endogenous variables for that equation from M to $M - (j - 1)$. The $M - j$ restrictions that endogenous variables $j + 1, \ldots, M$ do not appear in that equation (which follow by the triangularity of B) then suffice to identify it, by the rank condition. {*How do we know that the rank condition and not just the order condition will be satisfied with $M - (j - 1)$ substituted for M?*}

It is important to notice, however, the crucial role played in such systems by Assumption 4.2.2. The triangularity of B alone does not suffice to identify any equation of the model except the first (as we can already infer from the analysis of previous chapters). This may be driven home most strongly, if we realize that if the model were nonstochastic so that no information on the (zero) disturbances was possible, the model would not be identified without further information.[1] (*The reader should work out how this follows from the analysis of the preceding chapter. What happens to the consistency of least squares in such a case?*) Indeed, our discussion in the example was a little weak, for it suggested that the insufficiency of the triangularity of B was due to the possibility of correlation among the different disturbances, a property missing when those disturbances are identically zero. In fact, the triangularity of B is insufficient to identify any but the first equation of the model even when there are no disturbances. It is not so much the presence of intercorrelated disturbances which prevents identification as it is the knowledge that nonzero disturbances are *not* correlated which permits it. {*Try forming admissible combinations of the equations of Eq.* (4.2.6) *when both u_1 and u_2 are zero, and observe why the argument given above about the effects of Eqs.* (4.2.7) *and* (4.2.10) *fails.*}

We emphasize this point (to which we shall give an alternative rigorous statement below) because it is easy to overlook in empirical work. Too often, investigators who encounter a simultaneous system with a triangular B proceed to use least squares as a consistent estimator, forgetting that such triangularity does not itself suffice even to identify the last

---

[1] We did not trouble to exclude this case in stating Assumption 4.2.2, because we assumed earlier that Σ is positive definite unless otherwise stated.

$M - 1$ equations of the model, let alone imply the consistency of least squares. To apply least squares or, indeed, to identify the last $M - 1$ equations without other information on the coefficients of the model, the assumption of the diagonality of Σ is necessary as well as sufficient. The investigator in such a situation should think carefully about whether he is willing to make such an assumption, particularly if all that is to be gained is the computational convenience and familiarity of ordinary least squares.

4.3. Partitioned Block Triangular and Block Diagonal Matrices

The preceding discussion can readily be generalized in an important way. In order to do so, we must first define a notation for use in treating partitioned matrices and vectors.

Let P be any matrix. Except in special cases when subscripts will be used, we shall partition it as follows:

$$P = \begin{bmatrix} P^{11} & P^{12} & \cdots & P^{1C} \\ P^{21} & P^{22} & \cdots & P^{2C} \\ \cdot & \cdot & \cdots & \cdot \\ \cdot & \cdot & \cdots & \cdot \\ \cdot & \cdot & \cdots & \cdot \\ P^{R1} & P^{R2} & \cdots & P^{RC} \end{bmatrix} \tag{4.3.1}$$

Usually P will be square and we shall take $R = C$. When this is the case, we shall always assume that P^{II} is also square $(I = 1, \ldots, C)$.

Similarly, we shall have occasion to partition vectors. If b is an n-component column vector partitioned into C sets of elements, we write it as

$$b = \begin{bmatrix} b^1 \\ b^2 \\ \cdot \\ \cdot \\ \cdot \\ b^C \end{bmatrix} \tag{4.3.2}$$

Denoting the number of elements in b^I by n_I $(I = 1, \ldots, C)$ and using subscripts to denote individual elements, then

$$b^I = \begin{bmatrix} b_1^I \\ b_2^I \\ \cdot \\ \cdot \\ \cdot \\ b_{n_I}^I \end{bmatrix} \qquad \sum_{I=1}^{C} n_I = n \tag{4.3.3}$$

Now define:

Definition 4.3.1: A partitioned square matrix P is called *block triangular* if $P^{IJ} = 0$ for all $J > I$, $I = 1, \ldots, C$. It is called *block diagonal* if $P^{IJ} = 0$ for all $J \neq I$, $I = 1, \ldots, C$.

In other words, a block triangular matrix, as the name suggests, is one which is triangular (considering whole submatrices as single elements). Indeed, it is the natural generalization of a triangular matrix. Similarly, a block diagonal matrix is the natural generalization of a diagonal matrix. As with triangular and diagonal matrices, the properties of systems with block triangular and block diagonal matrices are possessed by systems with matrices which can be put in those special forms by trivial renumbering of variables and equations. We shall generally assume that such systems are already in their canonical forms without troubling to say so each time.

> Block triangularity and block diagonality are the canonical forms of what are called "decomposability" and "complete decomposability," respectively, in one terminology and "reducibility" and "decomposability," respectively, in another. To avoid confusion, we shall stick to the mnemonically appealing terms "block triangularity" and "block diagonality" which strictly pertain only to the canonical forms themselves.
>
> Incidentally, it should be noticed that the convention that block triangular matrices have their zero submatrices *above* the diagonal blocks is only a convention, since a trivial renumbering of rows and columns would place the zeros below the diagonal.

It is easy to verify that the inverse of a block triangular matrix is block triangular; the inverse of a block diagonal matrix is block diagonal; the product of two block triangular matrices (with the same partitioning) is block triangular; the product of two block diagonal matrices is block diagonal; and the product of a block diagonal and a block triangular matrix (in either order) is block triangular.

4.4. The Theory of Block Recursive Systems

Suppose that in place of Assumptions 4.2.1 and 4.2.2 we make the following (weaker) ones. There is some grouping of equations into blocks of equations and a similar grouping of endogenous variables and disturbances such that, when B and Σ are partitioned according to such blocks,

Assumption 4.4.1: B is block triangular.

Assumption 4.4.2: The disturbance from an equation in any block may be correlated in the probability limit with the disturbances from other equations in the same block, but is known to be uncorrelated in the probability limit with the disturbance from any equation in a *different* block. In other words, Σ is block diagonal.

A system satisfying these two assumptions (which are generalized versions of those for recursive systems) is called *block recursive*. In such systems, blocks of equations and variables play the same role as do single equations and variables in recursive systems.

Thus, write out the partitioned system

$$
\begin{bmatrix}
B^{11} & 0 & \cdots & & 0 \\
B^{21} & B^{22} & 0 & \cdots & 0 \\
\cdot & \cdot & \cdots & & \cdot \\
\cdot & \cdot & \cdots & & \cdot \\
\cdot & \cdot & \cdots & & \cdot \\
B^{C1} & B^{C2} & \cdots & & B^{CC}
\end{bmatrix}
\begin{bmatrix}
y^1 \\
y^2 \\
\cdot \\
\cdot \\
\cdot \\
y^C
\end{bmatrix}
+ \Gamma z =
\begin{bmatrix}
u^1 \\
u^2 \\
\cdot \\
\cdot \\
\cdot \\
u^C
\end{bmatrix}
\tag{4.4.1}
$$

where we have not bothered to partition Γ or z. In this system, the variables in y^1 are jointly determined but causally precede those of y^2, which in turn precede those of y^3, and so forth.[1] More specifically, the block triangularity of B means that movements in any element of u^I lead through effects on the endogenous variables to movements in the elements of y^J if and only if $J \geq I$ $(I = 1, \ldots, C)$. They do not affect the elements of $y^1, \ldots, y^{I-1}$. {Incidentally, note that the (assumed) nonsingularity of B implies (and is implied by) the nonsingularity of every B^{II} (where $I = 1, \ldots, C$).} Similarly, the block diagonality of Σ means that movements in elements of u^I are not systematically associated with movements in the elements of u^J for $J \neq I$. The two together thus allow us to treat endogenous variables from a given block of equations as predetermined with respect to the equations of any *higher-numbered* block.

This somewhat informal reasoning is borne out by examination of the matrix $B^{-1}\Sigma$, which, by Eq. (4.2.5), is the relevant covariance matrix of endogenous variables and disturbances (the rows corresponding to the endogenous variables). Since B is block triangular, so is its inverse, and since Σ is block diagonal, the product $B^{-1}\Sigma$ is block triangular with the same arrangement of zero matrices as B. This is equivalent to the statement that endogenous variables from any block of equations are uncorrelated in the probability limit with the disturbances from any higher-numbered block.

This has the following consequence. Consider the Ith block of equations $(I = 1, \ldots, C)$. By the block triangularity of B, the only endogenous variables appearing in that block are the elements of $y^1, \ldots, y^I$. By the argument just given, however, we may take the elements of

---

[1] The relationship of block triangularity to notions of causality is well explored in H. A. Simon [30].

$y^1, \ldots, y^{I-1}$ as predetermined in dealing with the Ith block. Further, since the elements of $y^{I+1}, \ldots, y^C$ do not appear in the Ith block of equations and since there is no feedback from higher-numbered blocks to the Ith block (the block triangularity of B), we may as well ignore the existence of blocks higher-numbered than I in dealing with the Ith block.[1] But all these facts together suggest immediately that we may forget about the Ith block of equations being embedded in a larger system and treat it in isolation, taking all variables as predetermined, except the elements of y^I. In other words, an equation of the Ith block will be identified by the block triangularity of B and the block diagonality of Σ if it is identified by further restrictions with respect to the other equations of the Ith block. This is a generalization of the remarks made about recursive systems.

Indeed, this is a very natural result. When we write down a system of simultaneous structural equations in econometrics, we do not generally believe that the predetermined variables are nonstochastic. Rather, we are willing to assume that they are determined by equations but are not affected by feedbacks from the endogenous variables of the system in which we are interested. Similarly, we do not generally believe that the endogenous variables of our system influence no variables other than themselves, but merely that variables so influenced do not in turn influence our endogenous variables. In short, we are behaving in estimating less than a universe-embracing equation system as though the larger, universal equation system in which our system is embedded is block recursive, with the predetermined variables coming from lower-numbered blocks than ours and with variables influenced by our endogenous variables but not included in our system coming from higher-numbered blocks. The result for block recursive systems just described enables us to treat our equation system in isolation.

Note, however, the crucial dependence of that result on the block diagonality of Σ. While this is not a necessary or even helpful property as regards ignoring endogenous variables from higher-numbered blocks than the one being estimated, it is indispensable in treating the endogenous variables from lower-numbered blocks as predetermined. This is reasonably clear from the argument as given and will be rigorously proved below. Regardless of what we believe about the systematic causal structure of the larger system which includes ours and which explains the predetermined variables, we are not justified in studying only a part of that structure unless we also believe that the random disturbances which influ-

---

[1] Formally, as we shall show in the formal proof of the theorem now being described, the block triangularity (and nonsingularity) of B implies the identification of every equation of the Ith block with respect to every equation of higher-numbered blocks, by Theorem 3.2.1. The reader may find it a valuable exercise to prove this for himself without waiting for the demonstration given below.

ence the predetermined variables are not correlated with those from the equations under study—the disturbances which influence the endogenous variables.

There is a rather subtle philosophical issue which we are ignoring here. If we *really* had a complete causal system, would disturbances from different equations be correlated? Is it not part of the nature of "true" random disturbances to be uncorrelated with each other? Alternatively, we might ask whether a really complete causal system would have *any* nonzero disturbances. We can evade these questions in the following way. In deciding that certain variables are to be predetermined, the investigator is implicitly deciding that the equations which he, with his incomplete knowledge, would write down to explain those variables would have disturbances uncorrelated with those of the equations he actually intends to estimate. Such unwritten equations would also reveal no structural feedbacks from his endogenous variables to the predetermined ones. What would happen if investigators were omniscient seems not very relevant at the present stage of econometrics.

This implicit willingness to assume that certain pairs of disturbances are uncorrelated is at the foundation of structural estimation. It is therefore clearly worthwhile to make it explicit and explore the consequences for identification of such prior restrictions in general.

Such a general exploration is the task of the next sections of this chapter. After developing the general results, we shall return to the cases of recursive and block recursive systems to show how those results specialize to those already suggested. We shall also investigate the special case in which there is one equation in the model with no restrictions on its coefficients but with a disturbance known to be uncorrelated with any other disturbance therein.

It is interesting to note, before proceeding, that all the cases so far considered—those of recursive and block recursive systems and the two-equation example of Sec. 1.3—have at least one thing in common. In all these cases, the restrictions on the covariances of the disturbances from different equations interact with other restrictions to tie the identification of a particular equation to that of other equations.[1] That such a property should be fairly general seems reasonable, since we are dealing with restrictions which bear on the relationship between two equations. That it is indeed a general property will emerge in our results.

---

[1] This happens directly in the two-equation example. It happens in the recursive or block recursive case in a way involving the triangularity or block triangularity of B. This will be explicit when we come to the proofs, but it should be realized now that the assumed properties of B play the role of identifying a given equation with respect to those of higher-numbered blocks. The identification of the equations of the higher-numbered blocks themselves is accomplished by tying this in through the restrictions on Σ.

4.5. The General Case: Notation and Terminology

We shall turn, then, to the general case of prior restrictions on the covariances of the disturbance terms. Those restrictions are given in the form

$$\sigma_{ij} = 0 \qquad (4.5.1)$$

for certain pairs i and j, $i \neq j$ where σ_{ij} is the ijth element of (the symmetric matrix) Σ. Restrictions in the form (4.5.1) will be referred to as "covariance restrictions."

In addition, we suppose that all other prior restrictions on the model take the form of linear and homogeneous restrictions on particular rows of A. Thus, we suppose that there exist M matrices $\phi^1, \ldots, \phi^M$ such that

$$A_k \phi^k = 0 \qquad (k = 1, \ldots, M) \qquad (4.5.2)$$

expresses the restrictions on the kth row of A (denoted by A_k). Of course, not every row need be restricted, in which case the corresponding ϕ^k can be taken as zero. Restrictions in the form (4.5.2) will be referred to as "coefficient restrictions."

As before, we shall consider the identifiability of the first equation (except where the numbering of the equations matters as in recursive or block recursive systems). Consider the covariance restrictions (4.5.1). Define

$$\begin{aligned} J_2 &= \{j | \sigma_{1j} = 0 \text{ by } (4.5.1); j = 2, \ldots, M\} \\ J_1 &= \{j | 1 \leq j \leq M; j \notin J_2\} \end{aligned} \qquad (4.5.3)$$

Thus J_2 is the set of indices corresponding to disturbances known to be uncorrelated with the first disturbance; J_1 is the set of the remaining indices. Note that $1 \in J_1$. Without loss of generality, we may renumber the equations so that J_1 consists of the indices $1, \ldots, m_1$ and J_2 of the indices $m_1 + 1, \ldots, M$, for some m_1 such that $1 \leq m_1 \leq M$.

Although J_1 and J_2 are defined as sets of indices, we shall avoid unnecessary formalism and speak of particular equations or disturbances as "in" J_1 or J_2 when what is meant is that their subscripts are in these sets. Thus, we shall speak of the first m_1 equations as in J_1 and the last $M - m_1$ equations as in J_2.

Corresponding to J_1 and J_2, we shall partition Σ as

$$\Sigma = \begin{bmatrix} \Sigma_{11} & \Sigma_{12} \\ \Sigma_{21} & \Sigma_{22} \end{bmatrix} \qquad (4.5.4)$$

Finally, let F be an $M \times M$ matrix. We shall partition F in similar fashion as

$$F = \begin{bmatrix} F_{11} & F_{12} \\ F_{21} & F_{22} \end{bmatrix} \qquad (4.5.5)$$

so that F_{12}, for example, has m_1 rows and $(M - m_1)$ columns. The first row of F will be denoted by f.

By the definition of an admissible transformation (Definition 1.7.1), if F is the matrix of an admissible transformation: F must be nonsingular; FA must satisfy all the coefficient restrictions (4.5.2); and $F\Sigma F'$ must satisfy all the covariance restrictions (4.5.1). In particular, since the definition of J_2 implies that the first row of Σ_{12} (or the first column of Σ_{21}) is zero, F must satisfy

$$f\Sigma F_2' = 0 \qquad (4.5.6)$$

where
$$F_2 = [F_{21} \mathbin{\vert} F_{22}] \qquad (4.5.7)$$

Similarly, F must satisfy

$$(fA)\phi^1 = 0 \qquad (4.5.8)$$

We shall shorten the terminology by referring to F itself as admissible when it is the matrix of an admissible transformation.

4.6. The General Case: Necessity Theorems

Conditions which are *both* necessary *and* sufficient for the identifiability of the first equation under Eqs. (4.5.1) and (4.5.2) are not known in the general case, although they are in special cases. We shall begin our discussion with necessary conditions.

Since Eqs. (4.5.6) and (4.5.8) embody all restrictions on f, a necessary condition for the identifiability of the first equation is that, given the other rows of F, they are satisfied for only one independent f. If this did not hold, at least *one* f satisfying the two sets of equations would not be a multiple of e_1 (the vector with a unit leading element and remaining elements zero). We may therefore immediately state:

Lemma 4.6.1: A necessary condition for the identifiability of the first equation under Eqs. (4.5.1) and (4.5.2) is that for every admissible F

$$\rho([\Sigma F_2' \mathbin{\vert} A\phi^1]) = M - 1 \qquad (4.6.1)$$

While the necessity of this condition is evident, it is less obvious that it is not sufficient. That it is not sufficient can be seen as follows. Even if Eqs. (4.5.6) and (4.5.8) admit of only one independent solution in f for every admissible F, there is no guarantee without further conditions that there does not exist an admissible F for which that unique independent solution is not a multiple of e_1. It may easily happen that the restrictions permit us to transform equations other than the first in such a manner that the only equation which can then complete an admissible structure is *not* a scalar multiple of the original first equation.

This has already been seen in the example of Sec. 1.3, the salient features of which we now repeat in the present notation. Suppose that there are only two equations and the only restriction is that the two disturbances are uncorrelated. In this case,

$$\Sigma = \begin{bmatrix} \sigma_{11} & 0 \\ \hline 0 & \sigma_{22} \end{bmatrix} \tag{4.6.2}$$

Suppose that the second row of F is ($\lambda_1 \quad \lambda_2$), so that the second equation is to be replaced by λ_1 times the first equation plus λ_2 times the second. Denote the two elements of f by f_1 and f_2.

If F is admissible, it is nonsingular, so that λ_1 and λ_2 cannot both be zero. However, the matrix of Eq. (4.6.1) is, in this case, just

$$\Sigma F_2' = \begin{bmatrix} \sigma_{11}\lambda_1 \\ \hline \sigma_{22}\lambda_2 \end{bmatrix} \tag{4.6.3}$$

which obviously has rank $1 = M - 1$ for every admissible F. There is no reason, however, why $\lambda_1 = 0$ for every such F without further restrictions. For $\lambda_1 \neq 0$, the Eqs. (4.5.6), which become

$$f_1\sigma_{11}\lambda_1 + f_2\sigma_{22}\lambda_2 = 0 \tag{4.6.4}$$

admit of only one independent solution, but that solution is *not* one with ($f_1 \quad f_2$) proportional to ($1 \quad 0$).

As remarked in Sec. 1.3, if we knew the second equation to be identified, so that any admissible F had $\lambda_1 = 0$, then the condition of Lemma 4.6.1 would be sufficient in addition to this. Without such additional restrictions, that condition is not sufficient.

The fact that the lemma does give a necessary condition implies the necessity part of the following result (which we already know but which we restate in order to make clear its relation to the generalization to ße given in a moment):

Theorem 4.6.1 (Rank Condition): If J_2 is empty, a necessary condition for the identifiability of the first equation under Eqs. (4.5.1) and (4.5.2) is that

$$\rho(A\phi^1) = M - 1 \tag{4.6.5}$$

This is in any case sufficient.

Proofs of sufficiency were, of course, given in Sec. 2.3. If J_2 is empty, the only restrictions on the first equation are coefficient restrictions and we are back in the case of that section. In the general case, however, Lemma 4.6.1 allows us to generalize the rank condition as follows.

Define

$$\Sigma^2 = \begin{bmatrix} \Sigma_{12} \\ \hline \Sigma_{22} \end{bmatrix} \tag{4.6.6}$$

We have

Theorem 4.6.2 *(Generalized Rank Condition):* A necessary condition for the identifiability of the first equation under Eqs. (4.5.1) and (4.5.2) is

$$\rho([\Sigma^2 \;\vdots\; A\phi^1]) = M - 1 \qquad (4.6.7)$$

Proof: Since Lemma 4.6.1 states a necessary condition that must hold for *any* admissible F, that condition is certainly necessary if F is the unit matrix which is always admissible (since we may always replace the original structure by itself). In this case, $F_2 = (0 \quad I)$ and Eq. (4.6.1) becomes Eq. (4.6.7).

The generalized rank condition (GRC) is weaker than the insufficient condition (4.6.1) and is hence not sufficient. However, it will form part of all sufficient conditions given in the next section. As one should expect, it immediately implies:

Corollary 4.6.1 *(Generalized Order Condition):* A necessary condition for the identifiability of the first equation under Eqs. (4.5.1) and (4.5.2) is that

$$\rho(\phi^1) + (M - m_1) \geq M - 1 \qquad (4.6.8)$$

or, equivalently, that

$$\rho(\phi^1) \geq m_1 - 1 \qquad (4.6.9)$$

In the case in which all coefficient restrictions on the first equation are exclusion restrictions and there are $m + 1$ endogenous and l exogenous variables not excluded from that equation, this condition can also be written as

$$\Lambda + (M - m_1) \geq l + m \qquad (4.6.10)$$

Proof: Σ^2 has $M - m_1$ columns (which, incidentally, are independent, since Σ is positive definite). Further, the rank of $A\phi^1$ is no greater than that of ϕ^1. If Eq. (4.6.8) fails, therefore, the GRC cannot hold. The equivalence of Eqs. (4.6.9) and (4.6.10) to Eq. (4.6.8) in the appropriate circumstances is left as a simple exercise to the reader.

We have for convenience given Corollary 4.6.1 the name "generalized" order condition because it does generalize the order condition for the case of linear and homogeneous coefficient restrictions only; however, it is still a special case of the very general order condition given in Condition 1.9.1. It states that the number of independent coefficient restrictions on the first equation plus the number of disturbances known to be uncorrelated with the first disturbance must be at least $M - 1$. In its (4.6.9) version, it becomes the statement that the number of independent coefficient restrictions on the first equation must be as large as the number of members of J_1 other than the first equation, a form whose relation to Corollary 2.3.1 is perhaps the most clear. In the exclusion restriction case, Eq. (4.6.10) states that the number of available independent pieces of posterior information plus the number of covariance restrictions on the first disturbance must be at least as great as the number of parameters left to be estimated after the exclusion restrictions have been used and a normalization rule applied.

As in the case when all restrictions are linear and homogeneous coefficient restrictions, if the prior restrictions are not such as to make the GRC fail identically, the GRC will hold if the generalized order condition holds everywhere except on a set of measure zero in the space of the elements of A and Σ^2. This property was discussed in Sec. 2.5. It is important here for the same reason as previously. The GRC depends on the unknown parameter values; the order condition does not. In checking the GRC in practice, therefore, it is important to know that it almost always suffices to check the generalized order condition *and* to check whether the GRC is known *not* to hold.

So far, the results obtained are highly reminiscent of those secured in Chap. 2, although there have been some interesting differences. The following necessary conditions depart rather more radically from the results of that chapter.

Lemma 4.6.2: A necessary condition for the identifiability of the first equation under Eqs. (4.5.1) and (4.5.2) is that for every admissible F, the first row of the matrix $\Sigma_{11}F'_{21}$ be zero.

Proof: If the first equation is identifiable, then for every admissible F, f is proportional to e_1, that is, $f = (f_1 \quad 0 \cdot \cdot \cdot 0)$, where f_1 is a nonzero scalar. Multiplying out Eq. (4.5.6), we have

$$f\Sigma F'_2 = f \begin{bmatrix} \Sigma_{11} & \vdots & \Sigma_{12} \\ \hline \Sigma_{21} & \vdots & \Sigma_{22} \end{bmatrix} \begin{bmatrix} F'_{21} \\ F'_{22} \end{bmatrix} = f \begin{bmatrix} \Sigma_{11}F'_{21} + \Sigma_{12}F'_{22} \\ \Sigma_{21}F'_{21} + \Sigma_{22}F'_{22} \end{bmatrix} = 0 \quad (4.6.11)$$

In view of the form taken by f, however, this means that the first row of $(\Sigma_{11}F'_{21} + \Sigma_{12}F'_{22})$ must be zero. In view of the definition of J_2 and the way in which Σ was partitioned, the first row of Σ_{12} is known to be zero, whence the first row of $\Sigma_{12}F'_{22}$ is zero and the statement of the lemma is now immediate.

Perhaps one should note that the lemma has nothing to do with the coefficient restrictions (4.5.2); it would be equally true of any set of restrictions which included Eq. (4.5.1) (although, naturally, what constitutes an admissible F depends on the full set of restrictions).

This lemma immediately implies the first of our theorems showing how covariance restrictions tie up the identification of different equations.

Theorem 4.6.3: A necessary condition for the identifiability of the first equation under Eqs. (4.5.1) and (4.5.2) is as follows. Any equation in J_2 which is known to be identified with respect to every equation in J_1 except the first must also be identified with respect to the first equation.

> This is a somewhat stronger result than that stated in Fisher [11, Theorem 2.4, p. 141] in that the condition is here stated separately for *each* equation in J_2 rather than for all such equations taken together.

Proof: Suppose the equation in J_2 in question is the hth ($m_1 + 1 \leq h \leq M$). Since the hth equation is known to be identified with respect to all equations of J_1 except the first, that is, with respect to equations $2, \ldots, m_1$, the hth row of F must have elements $2, \ldots, m_1$ all zero. That row, however, is a row of F_2, since $h \in J_2$; it is the $(h - m_1)$th row, in fact. Thus every element of the $(h - m_1)$th row of F_{21} is zero except the first.

A row of F_{21}, however, is a column of F'_{21}. By Lemma 4.6.2, the first row of $\Sigma_{11} F'_{21}$ must be zero if the first equation is identified. In particular, the $(h - m_1)$th element of that row must be zero. That element, however, is the inner product of the first row of Σ_{11} and the $(h - m_1)$th column of F'_{21}. Since, as shown, all elements of that column are zero except the first, the inner product which must be zero is merely σ_{11} times the leading element of the $(h - m_1)$th column of F'_{21}. Since, by the positive definiteness of Σ, $\sigma_{11} \neq 0$, that leading element must be zero.

Thus the first element of the hth row of F is zero for every admissible F. This is equivalent to the identification of the hth equation with respect to the first—the statement of the theorem.

It should be noted that this theorem can be thought of in two ways. First, it provides a necessary condition for the identification of the first equation. Second, it provides a sufficient condition for the identification of equations of J_2 with respect to the first equation. We shall leave the formal statement of the sufficiency form of the theorem as an exercise to the reader and proceed now to a discussion of other sufficiency theorems.

4.7. The General Case: Sufficiency Theorems

We shall begin this discussion with an important remark. The first equation will clearly be identified under the restrictions (4.5.1) and (4.5.2) if it is identified under only some subset of them. Thus, any sufficiency condition stated in terms of J_1 and J_2 as defined in Eq. (4.5.3) will remain sufficient if it holds after we move some equations from J_2 to J_1. As defined, J_2 contains *all* disturbances known to be uncorrelated with the first disturbance. If the first equation is identified using some of that information, it is certainly identified using all of it. This is important, because many of our results involve the relations between the equations of J_2 and those of J_1 other than the first (as does Theorem 4.6.3, for example). The conditions of the sufficiency theorems involved may not hold for J_1 and J_2 as originally defined, so that the usefulness of the results is greatly enhanced by observing that it always suffices that such conditions hold when J_2 is replaced by some proper subset of itself, say J_2^*, and J_1 is replaced by J_1^*, consisting of J_1 plus all elements of J_2 not in J_2^*.† We shall generally interpret our sufficiency conditions in this way but shall give all formal statements in terms of J_1 and J_2 as originally defined. The possibility of such interpretation should be borne in mind even where not explicitly mentioned.

Our first sufficiency theorem is:

Theorem 4.7.1: A sufficient condition for the identifiability of the first equation under Eqs. (4.5.1) and (4.5.2) is:

(a) The generalized rank condition holds.

(b) Every equation in J_2 is identifiable with respect to every equation in J_1.

Proof: Part (b) of the condition of the theorem is equivalent to $F_{21} = 0$ for any admissible F. Using Eq. (4.5.6)

$$0 = f\Sigma F_2' = f\begin{bmatrix} \Sigma_{11} & \vdots & \Sigma_{12} \\ \hline \Sigma_{21} & \vdots & \Sigma_{22} \end{bmatrix}\begin{bmatrix} 0 \\ F_{22}' \end{bmatrix} = f\begin{bmatrix} \Sigma_{12} \\ \Sigma_{22} \end{bmatrix}F_{22}' = f\Sigma^2 F_{22}' \quad (4.7.1)$$

Since any admissible F must be nonsingular, however, $F_{21} = 0$ implies that F_{22} is nonsingular. Thus

$$f\Sigma^2 = 0 \quad (4.7.2)$$

By Eq. (4.5.8)

$$f(A\phi^1) = 0 \quad (4.7.3)$$

and both Eqs. (4.7.2) and (4.7.3) are satisfied for $f = e_1$. The generalized rank condition is now sufficient to ensure that Eqs. (4.7.2) and (4.7.3) have no solution in f independent of e_1, and the theorem is proved.

This theorem has two immediate corollaries, the first of which follows jointly from it and Theorems 4.6.2 and 4.6.3.

† Note that *every* equation not in J_2^* *must* be in J_1^*. It is *not* sufficient that a condition in terms of J_2 and J_1 hold when restated in terms of J_2^* and J_1. Such conditions must hold in terms of J_2^* and J_1^*. It is this which prevents us from asserting that the discussion in the text always allows us to *strengthen* our sufficiency theorems rather than simply widen their applicability.

Corollary 4.7.1: Suppose that every equation in J_2 is identified with respect to every equation in J_1 except possibly the first. A necessary *and* sufficient condition for the identifiability of the first equation under Eqs. (4.5.1) and (4.5.2) is:

(a) The generalized rank condition holds.

(b) Every equation in J_2 is identified with respect to the first equation.

Corollary 4.7.2: A sufficient condition for the identification of the first equation under Eqs. (4.5.1) and (4.5.2) is:

(a) The generalized rank condition holds.

(b) Every equation in J_2 is identifiable.

We shall interpret the latter corollary in the terms described at the beginning of this section. At first glance, it may appear as if such an interpretation would yield a very strong sufficiency theorem. Provided that the GRC holds, it looks as though it suffices that there be even a single identifiable equation in J_2 so that J_2^* can be taken to contain that equation only. The catch is that the GRC itself is defined in terms of the partitioning of the equations into J_1 and J_2. The correct interpretation is as follows:

Suppose that the GRC holds with J_2 (and hence Σ^2) as originally defined. A sufficient condition for the identifiability of the first equation under Eqs. (4.5.1) and (4.5.2) is that we be able to find a subset of J_2, say J_2^*, such that every equation in that subset is identifiable *and* the GRC continues to hold when the columns of Σ^2 corresponding to equations *not* in that subset are deleted. (*Interpret Theorem 4.7.1 itself in this way.*) We may speak of the latter part of this condition as the GRC holding with respect to J_2^*.

Note that if the generalized order condition (4.6.8) holds when $(M - m_1)$ is replaced by the number of elements of J_2^*, then the GRC will hold with respect to J_2^* with probability 1 (that is, except on a set of measure zero in the appropriate parameter space), unless the GRC fails identically because of Eqs. (4.5.1) and (4.5.2). In the absence of such identical failure, therefore, it suffices with probability 1 to find $\{M - 1 - \rho(\phi^1)\}$ identifiable equations whose disturbances are known to be uncorrelated with the first disturbance. Of course, for this to be possible with a *proper* subset of J_2, the generalized order condition must be overfulfilled when all elements of J_2 are used.

Further, if this can be done, the first equation can be counted as identified with probability 1 in applying the same result to the identification of the remaining equations in J_2 (if any)—the equations not previously identified whose disturbances are uncorrelated with the first one.

An example of this procedure seems in order here. Suppose that the model consists of three equations, which in scalar form are

$$b_{11}y_1 + b_{12}y_2 + b_{13}y_3 + g_{11}z_1 + g_{12}z_2 + g_{13}z_3 = u_1$$
$$b_{21}y_1 + b_{22}y_2 + b_{23}y_3 + g_{21}z_1 + g_{22}z_2 + g_{23}z_3 = u_2 \qquad (4.7.4)$$
$$b_{31}y_1 + b_{32}y_2 + b_{33}y_3 + g_{31}z_1 + g_{32}z_2 + g_{33}z_3 = u_3$$

We suppose the covariance restrictions (4.5.1) to be

$$\sigma_{12} = 0 \qquad \sigma_{13} = 0 \qquad (4.7.5)$$

so that J_1 here consists only of the first equation and J_2 of the second and third.

Suppose further that the coefficient restrictions (4.5.2) are here

$$g_{11} = 0 \qquad g_{22} = 0 \qquad g_{33} = 0 \qquad g_{31} = 0 \qquad (4.7.6)$$

Thus

$$\phi^1 = \begin{bmatrix} 0 \\ 0 \\ 0 \\ 1 \\ 0 \\ 0 \end{bmatrix} \qquad \phi^2 = \begin{bmatrix} 0 \\ 0 \\ 0 \\ 0 \\ 1 \\ 0 \end{bmatrix} \qquad \phi^3 = \begin{bmatrix} 0 & 0 \\ 0 & 0 \\ 0 & 0 \\ 0 & 1 \\ 0 & 0 \\ 1 & 0 \end{bmatrix} \qquad (4.7.7)$$

The generalized order condition is satisfied for the third equation, which is identifiable under Eq. (4.7.6) alone, provided that $g_{13}g_{21} \neq 0$. This occurs with probability 1. The third equation is thus identifiable with probability 1 even without using Eq. (4.7.5).

Now turn to the first equation. Here, $m_1 = 1 = \rho(\phi^1)$, so that the generalized order condition is overfulfilled, since

$$3 = \rho(\phi^1) + (M - m_1) > M - 1 = 2$$

This immediately implies that we may think about selecting a one-equation subset of J_2. Indeed, select J_2^* as the subset of J_2 consisting only of the third equation. Then J_1^* consists of the first two equations. The generalized order condition continues to hold after such replacement, while the generalized rank condition will hold with respect to J_2^* provided that the matrix

$$\begin{bmatrix} 0 & 0 \\ \sigma_{23} & g_{21} \\ \sigma_{33} & 0 \end{bmatrix} \qquad (4.7.8)$$

has rank 2, which occurs with probability 1. Since the only equation in J_2^*, the third, is identifiable with probability 1, Corollary 4.7.2 allows us to conclude that the first equation is also identifiable with probability 1.

Moreover, turn to the second equation. Its disturbance is known to be uncorrelated with the first disturbance. Define J_1 and J_2 *relative to the second equation*, so that J_1 consists of the second and third equations and J_2, the first. The generalized order condition is then certainly satisfied for the second equation. The generalized rank condition is also satisfied provided that the matrix

$$\begin{bmatrix} \sigma_{11} & g_{12} \\ 0 & 0 \\ 0 & g_{32} \end{bmatrix} \tag{4.7.9}$$

has rank 2, which occurs with probability 1.† Since the first equation is identified with probability 1, an additional application of Corollary 4.7.2 allows us to conclude that the second equation is also identified with probability 1.

Note in this example that the identifiability of the third equation, accomplished by coefficient restrictions alone, is carried by the covariance restrictions to aid successively in the identification of the first and then the second equation.

In this example, the presence of coefficient restrictions on an equation in J_2 was thus important. However, the condition of Theorem 4.7.1 can be satisfied even if there are no coefficient restrictions on any such equation, as we shall now see.

Theorem 4.7.2: A sufficient condition for the identifiability of the first equation under Eqs. (4.5.1) and (4.5.2) is:

(a) The generalized rank condition holds.
(b) *Every* disturbance in J_1 is known to be uncorrelated with every disturbance in J_2, that is, Σ_{12} (and not just the first row of Σ_{12}) is zero.
(c) Every equation in J_1 (including the first) is identifiable with respect to every equation in J_2.

Proof: Since $\Sigma_{12} = 0$, every admissible F must be such as to make the upper right-hand block of $F\Sigma F'$ zero. Further, by (c), $F_{12} = 0$. Multiplying out

$$0 = [F_{11} \quad 0] \begin{bmatrix} \Sigma_{11} & 0 \\ 0 & \Sigma_{22} \end{bmatrix} \begin{bmatrix} F'_{21} \\ F'_{22} \end{bmatrix} = F_{11}\Sigma_{11}F'_{21} \tag{4.7.10}$$

Since F must be nonsingular, however, $F_{12} = 0$ implies the nonsingularity of F_{11}. Further, Σ_{11} is nonsingular because Σ is positive definite. It thus follows from Eq. (4.7.10) that $F_{21} = 0$, so that every equation in

† We have used the restrictions in writing the matrix, as was also done in Eq. (4.7.8). Why *must* this be done in this argument?

J_2 is identifiable with respect to every equation in J_1. Together with (a), this makes Theorem 4.7.1 applicable and the desired result is immediate.

It is worth restating separately a remarkable result obtained in the course of the proof just given.

Theorem 4.7.3: Suppose that it is possible to partition the equations (and disturbances) into two mutually exclusive and collectively exhaustive sets, say W_1 and W_2, such that every disturbance in W_1 is known to be uncorrelated with every disturbance in W_2. The equations in W_1 are all identifiable with respect to all the equations in W_2 if and only if all the equations in W_2 are each identifiable with respect to all the equations in W_1.

Returning to the identifiability of the first equation, note that, as before, it suffices to find a subset of J_2, say J_2^*, for which the conditions of Theorem 4.7.2 hold. The catch, of course, is that not only must the generalized rank condition hold with respect to J_2^*, but also every disturbance in J_2^* must be known to be uncorrelated with every disturbance outside it. Further, all equations outside J_2^* must be identifiable with respect to all equations in it.

(Why do we not state the corollary that this last condition can be satisfied if all equations outside J_2^* are identified? What nontrivial corollary can be stated along these lines?)

The last condition of Theorem 4.7.2 is overly strong, however, as the following result shows.

Theorem 4.7.4: A sufficient condition for the identifiability of the first equation under Eqs. (4.5.1) and (4.5.2) is:

    (a) The generalized rank condition holds.
    (b) $\Sigma_{12} = 0$.
and *either*
    (c) Every equation in J_2 is identifiable with respect to every equation in J_1 which is not already known to be identifiable.
or
    (d) Every equation in J_1 is identifiable with respect to every equation in J_2 which is not already known to be identifiable.

Proof: First suppose that (a), (b), and (c) hold. Renumbering if necessary, we may let the last r equations in J_1 be the ones (if any) which are known to be identifiable ($0 \leq r \leq m_1$, but $r = m_1$ is trivial). Then, by (c), the first $m_1 - r$ columns of F_{21} and hence the first $m_1 - r$ rows of F_{21}' are all zero.

Now, consider the matrix $\Sigma_{11}F_{21}'$. By Lemma 4.6.2 (interpreted for *any* identifiable equation of J_1 and not just for the first one), the last r rows of that matrix must be zero.

Denote the matrix consisting of the last r rows of Σ_{11} by $[\hat{\Sigma}_{11} \quad \tilde{\Sigma}_{11}]$ where $\tilde{\Sigma}_{11}$ has r columns. Denote the matrix consisting of the last r rows of F'_{21} by $\tilde{F}'_{21}$. The necessarily zero rows of $\Sigma_{11}F'_{21}$, by the remarks already made, are

$$0 = [\hat{\Sigma}_{11} \quad \tilde{\Sigma}_{11}] \begin{bmatrix} 0 \\ \tilde{F}'_{21} \end{bmatrix} = \tilde{\Sigma}_{11}\tilde{F}'_{21} \tag{4.7.11}$$

Since $\tilde{\Sigma}_{11}$ is a principal submatrix of the positive definite matrix Σ, it is nonsingular. Thus Eq. (4.7.11) implies $\tilde{F}'_{21} = 0$.

We have now shown that the last r rows of F'_{21} are all zero. However, we have already observed that the first $m_1 - r$ rows of that matrix are zero. Thus $F_{21} = 0$ and every equation in J_2 is identifiable with respect to every equation in J_1. This result, combined with (a) and (b), makes Theorem 4.7.2 immediately applicable and demonstrates the identifiability of the first equation.

The proof that (a), (b), and (d) are also sufficient is quite similar and is left as an exercise to the reader. Here one proves that $F_{12} = 0$ and applies Theorem 4.7.1.

Once more, we have obtained an interesting result in the course of the proof which is worth stating separately.

Theorem 4.7.5: Suppose that the partitioning described in Theorem 4.7.3 has been accomplished. Then, if (and only if) every equation in W_1 is identifiable with respect to every equation in W_2 which is not already itself known to be identifiable, every equation in either set is identifiable with respect to every equation in the other set.

Proof: It was shown in the course of the proof of Theorem 4.7.4 (adapting the notation) that the condition of the theorem implies the identifiability of every equation in W_1 with respect to every equation in W_2. The identifiability of every equation in W_2 with respect to every equation in W_1 is then a direct consequence of Theorem 4.7.3.

Of course, the roles of W_1 and W_2 in the statement of the theorem can be interchanged.

4.8. The Case of No Coefficient Restrictions on the First Equation

In this section we shall illustrate our results by applying them to the case in which there are no coefficient restrictions on the first equation. In the remaining sections, we shall give further applications by returning to the question of identifiability in recursive and block recursive systems.

For the remainder of this section, therefore, we shall assume that there are no coefficient restrictions on the first equation. We immediately obtain:

Theorem 4.8.1: If there are no coefficient restrictions on the first equation, then the following is a necessary *and* sufficient condition for the identifiability of that equation under Eqs. (4.5.1) and (4.5.2):

    (a) $\sigma_{1j} = 0$ for all $j = 2, \ldots, M$.
    (b) Every other equation is identifiable with respect to the first.

Proof: That (a) is necessary is an immediate consequence of the generalized order condition (Corollary 4.6.2) and the fact that $\rho(\phi^1) = 0$ here. Further, the generalized rank condition holds if and only if (a) does, since Σ^2 will then consist of the last $M - 1$ rows and columns of the positive definite matrix Σ. Thus (a) is here equivalent to the generalized rank condition and the theorem now follows from the fact that there are no equations in J_1 other than the first and Corollary 4.7.1.

Both conditions in Theorem 4.8.1 are important. The first says that identification of the first equation without coefficient restrictions thereon implies that the first disturbance must be known to be uncorrelated with every other disturbance. The second says that every other equation must be known to be identified with respect to the first one. The two conditions together are sufficient and together they imply that there must not be other equations without coefficient restrictions, as we shall now see.

Corollary 4.8.1: If there are no coefficient restrictions on the first equation, a necessary condition for the identifiability of that equation under Eqs. (4.5.1) and (4.5.2) is that there is no other equation on which there are no coefficient restrictions.

Proof: Suppose that the first equation is identified but there are no coefficient restrictions on the kth equation for some $k \neq 1$. Since (a) of Theorem 4.8.1 is necessary, the first disturbance is uncorrelated with every other disturbance.

Now, the restrictions on the kth equation are all covariance restrictions. However, if the kth equation is identifiable with respect to the first, it surely remains so if we place further restrictions on it.[1] We may therefore consider the case in which the kth disturbance is known to be uncorrelated with every other disturbance. In this case, the kth and first equations may be interchanged, showing that the kth equation is not identified with respect to the first under the (possibly) expanded set of restrictions. Hence it is not so identified under the actual restric-

[1] Note that it is *not* asserted that the identifiability of the *first* equation is necessarily preserved when restrictions on the kth equation are added.

tions. This contradicts the necessity of (b) of Theorem 4.8.1. (An alternate proof can be given along the lines of that of Theorem 4.8.2 below.)

Thus a necessary condition for the identifiability of *any* equation under Eqs. (4.5.1) and (4.5.2) is the existence either of coefficient restrictions on that equation itself or of at least one coefficient restriction on *each* other equation in the system.

It might be thought that one could pursue this line and argue that a necessary condition for the identifiability of the first equation in the present case is that every equation be identifiable with respect to the first equation *by coefficient restrictions alone.* That is, one is tempted to argue that the proof of Corollary 4.8.1 shows that there exists a linear combination of the first and, say, the kth equation which has a disturbance that obeys all covariance restrictions on the kth equation. (Note that there is at least one such restriction.) Thus one might conclude that if coefficient restrictions do not identify the kth equation with respect to the first, covariance restrictions will also not do so. It would then follow that (b) of Theorem 4.8.1 would be violated and the first equation not identifiable.

This is an erroneous argument. The fact that coefficient restrictions do not identify the kth equation with respect to the first does *not* itself imply that there exists a linear combination of *only* those two equations which satisfies all coefficient restrictions on the kth equation (unless, of course, there are only two equations in the system). It may easily happen that all linear combinations involving the first equation and satisfying the coefficient restrictions on the kth equation also involve a third equation. There is then no guarantee that the resulting linear combination of disturbances satisfies the covariance restrictions on the kth equation (if there are more of these than the restriction $\sigma_{1k} = 0$, which is necessary for the identifiability of the first equation). What is true is that the first equation must not *itself* satisfy all coefficient restrictions on the kth equation, since, if the first equation were then identifiable, (a) of Theorem 4.8.1 would lead to a contradiction of (b), as in the proof of Corollary 4.8.1.[1] One could not specify this, however, without coefficient restrictions on the first equation.

A three-equation example may be of aid here. Suppose that the system is

$$b_{11}y_1 + b_{12}y_2 + b_{13}y_3 + g_{11}z_1 + g_{12}z_2 = u_1$$
$$b_{21}y_1 + b_{22}y_2 + b_{23}y_3 + g_{21}z_1 + g_{22}z_2 = u_2 \qquad (4.8.1)$$
$$b_{31}y_1 + b_{32}y_2 + b_{33}y_3 + g_{31}z_1 + g_{32}z_2 = u_3$$

---

[1] Despite the fact that this argument is made in Fisher [11, p. 146], the second statement in Corollary 2 to Theorems 2.1 and 3.1 given there contains the same fallacy. A specific counterexample is about to be given in the text.

with coefficient restrictions

$$b_{23} = 0 \qquad g_{21} = 0 \qquad g_{32} = 0 \qquad (4.8.2)$$

and covariance restrictions

$$\sigma_{12} = 0 \qquad \sigma_{13} = 0 \qquad \sigma_{23} = 0 \qquad (4.8.3)$$

The single coefficient restriction on the third equation does not identify it with respect to the first, since taking the first equation plus $(-g_{12}/g_{22})$ times the second equation yields an equation satisfying that restriction. On the other hand, any admissible replacement of the third equation, other than by scalar multiplication, must involve a linear combination of the first two equations with coefficients proportional to $(1 \quad -g_{12}/g_{22})$. It follows that such replacement of the third equation results in a disturbance which is not uncorrelated with the second disturbance. Since the second equation is identified (except on a set of measure zero), every admissible structure has as its second disturbance a scalar multiple of the true second disturbance. The restriction $\sigma_{23} = 0$ then implies that replacement of the third equation in the way described is in fact not admissible. Thus the third equation is indeed identified with respect to the first one (and, in fact, the first equation is identified) despite the fact that the coefficient restrictions on the third equation do not alone accomplish this.

Note that the first equation is identifiable despite the fact that there is a disturbance other than the first (the third) which is known to be uncorrelated with the remaining disturbances.

On the other hand, note that a covariance restriction on the third disturbance other than $\sigma_{13} = 0$ was required to secure this result. Without that restriction, we could clearly have chosen the *three* coefficients of a linear combination of equations to replace the first equation in such a way as to satisfy the *two* covariance restrictions on the first disturbance even after replacement of the third equation in the way permitted by the coefficient restrictions thereon. Such a construction would always be possible, and we may state as the true result implied by this sort of argument:

Theorem 4.8.2: If there are no coefficient restrictions on the first equation, a necessary condition for the identifiability of that equation under Eqs. (4.5.1) and (4.5.2) is as follows. There exists no $k \neq 1$ such that the coefficient restrictions on the kth equation fail to identify it with respect to the first equation and such that the covariance restrictions on the kth equation at most state $\sigma_{1k} = 0$.

Proof: Suppose that there exists such a k. By (a) of Theorem 4.8.1, it is necessary for the identifiability of the first equation that $\sigma_{1j} = 0$ for all $j = 2, \ldots, M$, so it is certainly necessary that $\sigma_{1k} = 0$. Suppose that there are no other covariance restrictions on the kth disturbance. Since the kth equation is not identified with respect to the first by coefficient restrictions alone, there exists some linear combination of the equations, involving the first, which satisfies all coefficient restrictions on the kth equation. Consider a linear combination of the M equations as a candidate to replace the first one after the kth one has been so replaced. There are M coefficients in such a combination and only $M - 1$ restrictions to satisfy—the restrictions that the constructed first disturbance must be uncorrelated with all other disturbances including the constructed kth disturbance. (Recall that there are no coefficient restrictions on the first equation.) This can clearly be done. Replacing the kth and first equations in the way described then results in a new admissible structure, and since the new kth equation involves the original first equation in a nonzero way, it is easy to see that the new first equation is not simply a scalar multiple of the original one. (*Prove this by writing it out.*) The first equation is therefore not identifiable.

We have already had a necessary and sufficient condition for the identifiability of the kth equation with respect to the first one by coefficient restrictions alone. It was Theorem 3.2.1.

This completes our discussion of the case of no coefficient restrictions on the first equation.

4.9. Identification in Recursive Systems

In this section, we shall apply our results by returning to the case of recursive systems, already discussed in Sec. 4.2. We shall here give formal proof along the lines of the main parts of this chapter of the statements that were made earlier on identification in such systems and proved in part by the existence of a consistent estimator (ordinary least squares).

Since the numbering of the equations is not arbitrary in considering triangular matrices, we can no longer restrict our attention to the first equation. Despite the fact that our results in Secs. 4.6 and 4.7 were stated in terms of that equation, there should be no difficulty in rereading them in terms of an arbitrarily numbered equation, and we shall not bother to redefine explicitly sets such as J_1 and J_2 to refer to equations other than the first because the meaning will be clear from the context.

Theorem 4.9.1: Suppose that the coefficient restrictions (4.5.2) specify that B (the coefficient matrix of the endogenous variables) is triangular. A sufficient condition for the identifiability of the hth equation ($h = 1, \ldots, M$) under Eqs. (4.5.1) and (4.5.2) is that the covariance restrictions (4.5.1) specify

$$\sigma_{hj} = 0 \qquad \text{for all } j \text{ such that } 1 \le j < h\dagger \qquad (4.9.1)$$

Further, if the only restrictions on the hth equation are (4.9.1) and those involved in the triangularity of B, i.e.,

$$B_{hj} = 0 \qquad \text{for all } j \text{ such that } h < j \le M \qquad (4.9.2)$$

then Eqs. (4.9.1) and (4.9.2) are necessary for the identifiability of that equation.

Proof: Here J_2 consists of all equations with numbers lower than h. We begin by observing that Eqs. (4.9.1) and (4.9.2) together just satisfy the generalized order condition, since there are $h - 1$ covariance and $M - h$ independent coefficient restrictions on the hth equation. The necessity of Eqs. (4.9.1) and (4.9.2) in the absence of further restrictions is an immediate consequence of the necessity of the generalized order condition (Corollary 4.6.1).

Moreover, if Eqs. (4.9.1) and (4.9.2) hold, then the generalized rank condition is also satisfied. To see this requires an agreement about numbering, since we are no longer dealing with the first equation. Agreement is most easily achieved by continuing to denote the partitioning of Σ by subscripts which refer to J_1 and J_2, so that Σ_{22} is now the variance-covariance matrix of the disturbances from equations $1, \ldots, h - 1$. As may be seen (if necessary) by renumbering the whole system to correspond to the numbering used in deriving the generalized rank condition, the matrix whose rank is to be tested is

$$[\Sigma^2 \ \vdots \ A\phi^h] = \begin{bmatrix} \Sigma_{22} & 0 \\ & 0 \quad \cdots \quad \quad \quad 0 \\ & B_{h+1h+1} \quad 0 \quad \cdots \ 0 \\ \Sigma_{12} & B_{h+2h+1} \quad B_{h+2h+2} \quad \cdots \ 0 \\ & \vdots \quad \quad \vdots \quad \quad \quad \vdots \\ & B_{Mh+1} \quad B_{Mh+2} \quad \cdots \ B_{MM} \end{bmatrix} \qquad (4.9.3)$$

Denote that matrix by Q. The hth row of Q consists of zeros only. (*Why?*) Consider any vector, say λ, in the row kernel of Q. Partition λ as $(\lambda_1 \quad \lambda_2 \quad \lambda_3)$ where λ_1 has $h - 1$ elements, λ_2 is a scalar, and λ_3 has

---

† This differs trivially from the statement in Fisher [11, p. 147] in that we are here taking triangular matrices to have zeros *above* rather than below the diagonal. Similar differences held throughout this and the following section.

$M - h$ elements.   Then

$$\lambda Q = 0 \qquad (4.9.4)$$

which implies

$$\lambda_3 \tilde{B} = 0 \qquad (4.9.5)$$

where $\tilde{B}$ is the matrix in the lower right-hand corner of Q, that is, the matrix consisting of the last $M - h$ rows and columns of B. Since B is triangular and nonsingular (Assumption 1.5.1), $\tilde{B}$ is nonsingular. (*If you do not see this immediately, write out a proof.*) Thus $\lambda_3 = 0$.

In that case, however, Eq. (4.9.4) implies

$$\lambda_1 \Sigma_{22} = 0 \qquad (4.9.6)$$

and Σ_{22} is nonsingular by the positive definiteness of Σ. Thus $\lambda_1 = 0$ also.

Thus every vector in the row kernel of Q has at most its hth element nonzero. The dimension of that row kernel is thus 1 and since Q has M rows, the fact that the generalized rank condition holds follows from Theorem 1.4.1.

Now consider any equation in J_2, say the kth $(1 \leq k < h)$. We shall show that the kth equation is identified with respect to equations $h, \ldots, M$, whence the identifiability of the hth equation under the triangularity of B and Eq. (4.9.1) will follow immediately from Theorem 4.7.1. Since the kth equation will be identified with respect to such equations if it is so identified neglecting some of the restrictions on it, we may as well assume that the only coefficient restrictions on the kth equation are those implied by the triangularity of B. Thus

$$A \phi^k = \begin{bmatrix} & & & 0 & & & \\ B_{k+1k+1} & 0 & & \cdots & & 0 \\ B_{k+2k+1} & B_{k+2k+2} & 0 & \cdot & \cdot & 0 \\ \cdot & \cdot & & \cdot & \cdot & \cdot \\ \cdot & \cdot & & \cdot & \cdot & \cdot \\ \cdot & \cdot & & \cdot & \cdot & \cdot \\ B_{Mk+1} & B_{Mk+2} & & \cdots & & B_{MM} \end{bmatrix} \qquad (4.9.7)$$

Clearly, the nonsingularity of B implies $\rho(A \phi^k) = M - k$, since the columns of $A \phi^k$ must be independent. On the other hand, it is evident that striking out any of the last $M - k$ rows of $A \phi^k$ reduces the rank. In particular, this is true if any one of the last $M - h + 1$ rows are so stricken. Theorem 3.2.1 thus implies the identifiability of the kth equation with respect to equations $h, \ldots, M$, and the identifiability of the hth equation follows by the remarks already given.

Corollary 4.9.1: If B is triangular and Σ diagonal, every equation is identifiable.

As already remarked in Sec. 4.2, the role of the diagonality of Σ should never be overlooked in practice. The triangularity of B alone is not enough as shown by the necessity part of Theorem 4.9.1.

4.10. Identification in Block Recursive Systems

A similar development holds for block recursive systems; indeed, the proof of the principal result proceeds along the matrix generalization of the lines of that of Theorem 4.9.1, the only complications being introduced by the necessity of dealing with the identifiability of an equation with respect to others in the same block of equations. Whenever we deal with relations among blocks, we are, as one would expect, in a case entirely analogous to that of recursive systems.

As indicated in Sec. 4.4, the principal result here is that the block triangularity of B and the block diagonality of Σ allow us to deal with the separate blocks in isolation. The importance of this result has already been discussed. Formally, we have:

Theorem 4.10.1: Suppose that the coefficient restrictions (4.5.2) specify that B is block triangular. Consider the first equation of the Hth block of equations ($H = 1, \ldots, C$). A sufficient condition for the identifiability of that equation under Eqs. (4.5.1) and (4.5.2) is then

(a) That equation is identifiable with respect to the others of the Hth block.

(b) The covariance restrictions (4.5.1) specify

$$\Sigma^{HJ} = 0 \qquad \text{. for all } J \text{ such that } 1 \le J < H \quad (4.10.1)$$

where Σ^{HJ} denotes the covariance matrix of the Hth and Jth sets of disturbances, with the rows corresponding to H.

Further, if the restrictions on the equation in question are just enough in number to satisfy (a) plus those implied by (b) and the block triangularity of B, then all those restrictions are necessary for the identifiability of that equation.

Proof: Again we begin with the generalized order condition. Since, by (a), the first equation of the Hth block—say equation H_1—is identified with respect to the other equations of that block, there must be at least $m_H - 1$ independent restrictions on that equation, where m_J is the number of equations in the Jth block ($J = 1, \ldots, C$). Since the restrictions on equation H_1 implied by the block triangularity of B and by Eq. (4.10.1) are also satisfied by all other equations in the Hth block, it is evident that there must be at least $m_H - 1$ independent restrictions on that equation in addition to these. The total number of restrictions on the equation in question is thus at least $(m_H - 1)$ from (a), $\sum\limits_{J=1}^{H-1} m_J$ from Eq. (4.10.1), and $\sum\limits_{J=H+1}^{C} m_J$ from the block triangularity of B. Since

$$\sum_{J=1}^{C} m_J = M \tag{4.10.2}$$

there are thus at least $M - 1$ independent restrictions on equation H_1 and the generalized order condition is satisfied. The necessity part of the theorem now follows from the fact that if there are *only* $m_H - 1$ independent restrictions involved in (a), then the generalized order condition is only just satisfied so that the restrictions on equation H_1 implied by block triangularity and the restrictions in (b) are required to satisfy it.

We now show that the conditions of the theorem imply that the generalized rank condition also holds. Unfortunately, while the proof is quite simple in essence, to write it requires a rather burdensome notation. This comes about because of the possibility that the identification of equation H_1 with respect to the other equations of the Hth block is partly accomplished by covariance restrictions other than those involved in Eq. (4.10.1).

Accordingly, suppose that the coefficient restrictions on equation H_1 *other than those implied by the block triangularity of B* are given by

$$A_1{}^H \psi = 0 \tag{4.10.3}$$

where $A_1{}^H$ denotes the first row of the Hth block of rows of A and ψ is a constant matrix of known elements (and is a submatrix of columns of ϕ^{H_1}).

Further, suppose that the H_1th disturbance is known to be uncorrelated with certain other disturbances from the Hth block of equations. Without loss of generality, we may renumber the equations of the Hth block so as to put such equations last in that block. Denote by R_2 the matrix consisting of the columns of Σ^{HH} corresponding to those equations.

Now, since the H_1th equation is identified considering the Hth block of equations in isolation, and since this can have nothing to do with Eq. (4.10.1) or the block triangularity of B,† the generalized rank condition must hold considering *only* the Hth block. That is

$$\rho([R_2 \mid A^H \psi]) = m_H - 1 \tag{4.10.4}$$

where A^J denotes the Jth block of rows of A $(J = 1, \ldots, C)$.

Now, we shall take the rows of Σ in three groups: those corresponding to the first $H - 1$ blocks of equations; those corresponding to the Hth block; and those corresponding to the last $C - H$ blocks. Since J_2 here

† Why?

consists of both the equations in the first $H - 1$ blocks and the special last group of equations in the Hth block (if it exists), we must have columns corresponding to both parts of J_2. We shall denote the submatrix of Σ consisting of the first $H - 1$ blocks of rows and columns by S_1; the submatrix consisting of the Hth block of rows and the first $H - 1$ blocks of columns by S_2; and the submatrix consisting of the last $C - H$ blocks of rows and the first $H - 1$ blocks of columns by S_3. Similarly, the columns corresponding to the special equations of the Hth block will be partitioned into three submatrices: R_1 consisting of the first $H - 1$ blocks of rows; R_2 consisting of the Hth block of rows (as already defined); and R_3 consisting of the last $C - H$ blocks of rows. Note that Eq. (4.10.1) implies

$$R_1 = 0 = S_2 \tag{4.10.5}$$

The reader may find it helpful to write out a three-block example and perform the partitioning, taking $H = 2$.

Denote by P the matrix whose rank is to be tested in the generalized rank condition. With all the above definitions, we have

$$P = \left[\begin{array}{cc|c|ccccc} & & A^1\psi & & & & & \\ & & \cdot & & & & & \\ S_1 & 0 & \cdot & & & 0 & & \\ & & \cdot & & & & & \\ & & A^{H-1}\psi & & & & & \\ \hline 0 & R_2 & A^H\psi & & & 0 & & \\ \hline & & A^{H+1}\psi & B^{H+1\,H+1} & 0 & \cdots & 0 \\ & & \cdot & B^{H+2\,H+1} & B^{H+2\,H+2} & 0 & \cdots & 0 \\ S_3 & R_3 & \cdot & \cdot & \cdot & & \cdots & \cdot \\ & & \cdot & \cdot & \cdot & & \cdots & \cdot \\ & & \cdot & \cdot & \cdot & & \cdots & \cdot \\ & & A^C\psi & B^{CH+1} & B^{CH+2} & \cdots & B^{CC} \end{array} \right] \tag{4.10.6}$$

Note that the first row of the Hth block of rows of P consists of zeros only. (*Why?*)

Consider any vector $\lambda = (\lambda_1 \quad \lambda_2 \quad \lambda_3)$ in the row kernel of P (the partitioning being as that of the rows of P).

$$\lambda P = 0 \tag{4.10.7}$$

Denote the matrix in the lower right-hand corner of P by $\tilde{B}$. Certainly Eq. (4.10.7) implies

$$\lambda_3 \tilde{B} = 0 \tag{4.10.8}$$

However, the nonsingularity and the block triangularity of B imply the nonsingularity of $\tilde{B}$ (*Prove it.*) whence

$$\lambda_3 = 0 \tag{4.10.9}$$

Using the first set of columns of P, Eqs. (4.10.7) and (4.10.9) yield

$$\lambda_1 S_1 = 0 \tag{4.10.10}$$

However, S_1 is the submatrix of Σ consisting of the first $H - 1$ blocks of rows and columns. Since Σ is positive definite, S_1 is therefore nonsingular. Hence

$$\lambda_1 = 0 \tag{4.10.11}$$

Finally, using the middle two sets of columns of P, Eqs. (4.10.7), (4.10.9), and (4.10.11) yield

$$\lambda_2[R_2 \vdots A^H \psi] = 0 \tag{4.10.12}$$

However, $[R_2 \vdots A^H \psi]$ has precisely m_H rows and, by Eq. (4.10.4), has rank $m_H - 1$. By Theorem 1.4.1, therefore, its row kernel has dimension 1, and indeed all λ_2 satisfying Eq. (4.10.12) have only their first element (if any) nonzero.

We have thus shown that λ has at most one nonzero element (the H_1th) and thus that the row kernel of P has dimension 1. (*How do we know that it does not have dimension 0?*) Since P has M rows, the fact that the generalized rank condition holds follows from Theorem 1.4.1.

We now show that the block triangularity of B implies that any equation is identified with respect to all equations from higher-numbered blocks. While we shall show this specifically for equation H_1, the demonstration is obviously quite general, and we shall use the general result.

To see the point in question, observe that it is sufficient to show that such identification can be accomplished using only some of the restrictions on equation H_1. We can therefore take for the moment all coefficient restrictions on that equation as being those implied by the block triangularity of B. The matrix $A\phi^{H_1}$ then becomes

$$A\phi^{H_1} = \begin{bmatrix} 0 \\ 0 \\ \tilde{B} \end{bmatrix} \tag{4.10.13}$$

where $\tilde{B}$ is as before. It is obvious that the rank of this matrix falls if any one of the rows of $\tilde{B}$ is deleted, so that the desired result is an immediate consequence of Theorem 3.2.1.

This immediately implies that each equation of the first $H - 1$ blocks is identified with respect to the equations of blocks $H, \ldots, C$. If the identification of the H_1th equation with respect to the others in its own block is accomplished by coefficient restrictions alone,[1] the theorem is now proved, since the conditions of Theorem 4.7.1 are then satisfied. Unfortunately, in the more general case, the proof is still incomplete,

---

[1] The case covered, for simplicity, in Fisher [11, pp. 150 and 151].

for here there are equations in J_2 which themselves belong to the Hth block and which are *not* known to be identified with respect to all equations in J_1. Since we needed to use the fact that such equations were in J_2 in showing that the generalized rank condition holds, we cannot simply assume that it holds without such use and apply Theorem 4.7.1 with J_1 excluding such equations.

Fortunately, it is easy to adapt the proof of Theorem 4.7.1 to yield the desired result. Let F be an admissible transformation with H_1th row $f = (f_1 \quad f_2 \quad f_3)$ with partitioning corresponding to the first $H - 1$ blocks of equations, the Hth block, and the last $C - H$ blocks. We have just shown that

$$f_3 = 0 \qquad (4.10.14)$$

Let the first $H - 1$ blocks of rows of F be denoted by $G = (G_1 \quad G_2 \quad G_3)$ with the same partitioning. Since all equations, as shown, are identifiable with respect to equations from higher-numbered blocks (by the block triangularity of B),

$$G_2 = 0 = G_3 \qquad (4.10.15)$$

The covariance restrictions (4.10.1), however, clearly imply

$$f\Sigma G' = 0 \qquad (4.10.16)$$

and it is not hard to see (*Write it out.*) that Eqs. (4.10.14) and (4.10.15), plus those restrictions, then imply

$$f_1 S_1 G_1' = 0 \qquad (4.10.17)$$

As already observed, however, S_1 is nonsingular. Further, if F is admissible, it is nonsingular, and Eq. (4.10.15) then implies that G_1 is nonsingular. Thus

$$f_1 = 0 \qquad (4.10.18)$$

We have now shown that the H_1th equation is identifiable with respect to all equations of the last $C - H$ blocks (4.10.14) and with respect to all equations of the first $H - 1$ blocks. Since, by assumption, it is identifiable with respect to all other equations of the Hth block, it is identifiable. Q.E.D.

Strictly speaking, the demonstration that the generalized rank condition holds is irrelevant, since the proof just given does not depend directly thereon. We gave it, nevertheless, both to exemplify that condition and to bring out the parallel with recursive systems. As remarked above, in the simpler case in which the H_1th equation is identified with respect to the other equations in the Hth block by coefficient restrictions alone, the generalized rank condition forms an integral part of a proof by way of Theorem 4.7.1.

Corollary 4.10.1: If B is block triangular and Σ block diagonal, any equation which is identifiable with respect to the other equations in its own block is identifiable.

In such a case—that of a fully block recursive system—each block of equations may be treated separately and all the others ignored.

This completes our discussion of restrictions on the variance-covariance matrix of the disturbance terms.

References

The whole of this chapter is based on Fisher [11]. The theory of recursive systems is due to Wold [35, 36, and other writings]. The generalization to block recursive systems was introduced in Fisher [8], and both systems are discussed in detail in Fisher [15].

5

Nonlinearities in the Variables and the A Priori Restrictions

5.1. Introduction

In this chapter, we shall discuss identifiability criteria when non-linearities are present in one of two special ways in the equation system to be estimated. The two cases considered in detail are: first, and most important, the case in which every equation is linear in its disturbance and the parameters to be estimated but may be nonlinear in the variables; second, the case in which the system is linear in disturbances, parameters, and variables, but the parameters of the equation to be estimated are subject to nonlinear constraints. While, as we shall comment in due course, both these problems, especially the former one, are of independent interest, they also arise if we consider a particular approach to more general nonlinear cases.

Thus, suppose that the first equation of the structure is written in implicit form as

$$G(\alpha_1, \ldots, \alpha_R; x_1, \ldots, x_N; u) = 0 \qquad (5.1.1)$$

where α_i = parameters to be estimated

x_j = observable variables

u = a disturbance

and the time subscript has been omitted for simplicity. It is reasonable to assume that this can be solved explicitly for u:

$$F(\alpha_1, \ldots, \alpha_R; x_1, \ldots, x_N) = u \qquad (5.1.2)$$

If, as will generally (but not always) occur in practice, F can be expanded in convergent Taylor series in the parameters, this can be put in a form in which analysis of our two special cases bears on it. Thus, denoting the vector $(\alpha_1, \ldots, \alpha_R)$ by α and the vector $(x_1, \ldots, x_N)$ by x, and writing F as $F(\alpha,x)$, assume that F can be expanded about $\alpha = 0$ (for simplicity). Denoting partial derivatives with respect to the α_i by subscripts

$$u = F(0,x) + \sum_{i=1}^{R} \alpha_i F_i(0,x) + \frac{1}{2!} \sum_{i=1}^{R} \sum_{j=1}^{R} \alpha_i \alpha_j F_{ij}(0,x)$$
$$+ \frac{1}{3!} \sum_{i=1}^{R} \sum_{j=1}^{R} \sum_{k=1}^{R} \alpha_i \alpha_j \alpha_k F_{ijk}(0,x) + \cdots \quad (5.1.3)$$

By expanding far enough, this may be made as accurate as desired.

Observe, however, that the functions $F(0,x)$, $F_i(0,x)$, $F_{ij}(0,x)$, $F_{ijk}(0,x)$, . . . , are all *known* functions of the variables x_1, . . . , x_N only. They do not depend on the unknown parameters. Define

$$\lambda_i = \alpha_i; \; \lambda_{ij} = \frac{1}{2!} \alpha_i \alpha_j; \; \lambda_{ijk} = \frac{1}{3!} \alpha_i \alpha_j \alpha_k; \; \ldots \qquad (i,j,k = 1, \ldots, R)$$
$$(5.1.4)$$

then Eq. (5.1.3) can be rewritten as

$$u = F(0,x) + \sum_{i} \lambda_i F_i(0,x) + \sum_{i,j} \lambda_{ij} F_{ij}(0,x) + \sum_{i,j,k} \lambda_{ijk} F_{ijk}(0,x) + \cdots$$
$$(5.1.5)$$

where all sums run from 1 to R. Consider the λs as the parameters to be estimated; then Eq. (5.1.5) is a function *linear in the parameters and the disturbance* but not in the variables—the first case to be considered below.

On the other hand, it may be objected that just defining terms like $(1/2!)\alpha_i \alpha_j$ which are *not* linear in the original parameters to be themselves parameters does not make the system linear in the parameters of interest, the α_i. This is very true, and here is where the second of the special cases comes in. The objection just made can be put in another way. Suppose that we estimate Eq. (5.1.5) without regard for its genesis. This will yield estimates of the λs, but those estimates may not lead to unique estimates of the αs. The answer to this is to treat the λs as subject to the following *nonlinear* constraints

$$\lambda_{ij} = \frac{1}{2!} \lambda_i \lambda_j; \; \lambda_{ijk} = \frac{1}{3!} \lambda_i \lambda_j \lambda_k; \; \ldots \qquad (i,j,k = 1, \ldots, R) \quad (5.1.6)$$

When this is done, estimation of the λs is equivalent in every respect to estimation of the αs. We have thus transformed the problem into one in which the equation to be estimated is linear in the parameters and disturbance but not in the variables and in which the parameters are subject to nonlinear restrictions.

A very simple example may be useful. Suppose that Eq. (5.1.2) is of the form

$$u = y - \log (\alpha + x) \qquad (5.1.7)$$

where all symbols are now scalars. Expanding in MacLaurin series in α,

$$u = y - \left\{\log x + \alpha(x^{-1}) + \frac{1}{2!}\alpha^2(-x^{-2}) + \frac{1}{3!}\alpha^3(2x^{-3}) \cdots\right\}^\dagger \qquad (5.1.8)$$

which can be rewritten as

$$u = y - \{\log x + \beta_1(x^{-1}) + \beta_2(-x^{-2}) + \beta_3(2x^{-3}) \cdots\} \qquad (5.1.9)$$

which is an equation linear in u, y, and the β_i, but not in x, and in which the β_i are subject to the nonlinear constraints

$$\beta_2 = \frac{1}{2!}\beta_1{}^2; \, \beta_3 = \frac{1}{3!}\beta_1{}^3; \, \ldots \qquad (5.1.10)$$

It follows that a detailed treatment of identification of the two special cases of systems in which the nonlinearities appear only in the variables or in the constraints will be highly relevant to the general nonlinear case, even if only through the approximative device of Taylor series expansion. In principle, the more general case can be treated by first using such expansion and then applying the results given below. Nevertheless, this procedure lacks at least a certain amount of elegance, and a direct attack on the general case is an interesting prospect for future work in the field.

5.2. Systems with Nonlinearities Only in the Variables

We shall begin our detailed discussion with the case in which non-linearities appear only in the variables. All equations are assumed linear in the parameters and the disturbances, and all constraints are assumed linear, although the latter is necessary only for ease of discussion. Such systems are of considerable interest in themselves aside from their interest as part of a more general analysis, as just discussed. Thus, one might think of systems in which one equation is linear in the variables and another linear in the logarithms thereof; alternatively, there are systems in which price and quantity separately enter some equations, and their product—revenue—enters others.

Of course, there is little point in a discussion of what we might call "trivial" nonlinearities. If every variable in the system appears, for example, only in logarithmic form, then, for our purposes, the system might as well be linear, since we can consider the logs themselves as being the original variables. We are interested rather in systems in

† This converges for $x > \alpha$ Otherwise one would expand about $\alpha = \bar{\alpha}$ for $\bar{\alpha}$ large.

which at least one variable enters in at least two linearly independent functional forms. Thus, in the first of the two examples mentioned above, the nonlinearity of the problem lies in the fact that one equation is linear in the variables and the other linear in the logs of the variables and not simply in the fact that logs appear. Similarly, in the second example, the essential nonlinearity lies in the fact that price and quantity, as well as revenue, appear separately and not merely in the fact that revenue does.

Indeed, even if, in the latter example, revenue and price appeared separately but quantity did not, there would be no essential nonlinearity. We would consider the two appearing variables as separate items and let it go at that for identification purposes. The essential characteristic of the problems we are now treating is that the system is linear in a set of functions of some set of variables and that two or more of the functions appearing in the system are connected by nonlinear identities.

For similar reasons, we have no special interest in systems in which the only variables which enter such identities are predetermined. Since the defining characteristic of a predetermined variable, for our purposes, will be that the current values of the disturbance terms are distributed independently of the current value of such a variable,[1] any function of current predetermined variables is also predetermined. Since, in addition, the only assumption made about the relations between different predetermined variables is that they are not connected by *linear* identities, different functions of the same predetermined variables can merely be renamed as new predetermined variables, for our purposes, and the nonlinearities removed. For this reason, we may as well assume in discussing the problem that among the variables, functions of which enter the nonlinear identities discussed above, there is at least one endogenous variable.

Actually, even if there are no nonlinear identities or even if such identities connect only predetermined variables, our results will be formally correct and relevant. Such results in those cases will only repeat ones already obtained, however,[2] so that we shall assume that we are in a case to which new interest attaches.

We thus consider the following model. (For reasons of convenience we omit the time subscript.) Let x denote a vector of N "basic" or

---

[1] Note that this is stronger than the concept actually employed in earlier chapters (Assumption 1.5.3). There we merely required that current disturbances and current predetermined variables be uncorrelated in the probability limit. In the present chapter, we actually need such noncorrelation to hold not only between current disturbances and current predetermined variables but also between current disturbances and all functions of current predetermined variables. In principle, this is a much stronger assumption than the earlier one. In terms of the reasons which lead one to such considerations in practice, the difference is only negligible.

[2] It is a good exercise for the reader to show this.

"underlying" variables, of which the first M are endogenous and the remaining $\Lambda = N - M$ are predetermined. Let u be a column vector of disturbances (one for each equation). Let $q(x)$ be an N^0-component column vector of exact functions of x. We shall assume the elements of $q(x)$ to have continuous first partials with respect to the nonconstant elements of x everywhere in the range of observations. The form of the model is

$$Aq(x) = u \qquad (5.2.1)$$

where A is an $M \times N^0$ matrix of parameters to be estimated.

Since the model is supposed to be a theoretical statement of the way in which the endogenous variables are determined, given the predetermined variables and the disturbances, we shall assume that it does so. Thus, let y be the subvector of x consisting of the endogenous variables and let z be the subvector consisting of the predetermined variables. We assume:

Assumption 5.2.1: Equations (5.2.1) implicitly determine a vector-valued function $G(z,u)$ continuous in the elements of z such that

$$y = G(z,u) \qquad (5.2.2)$$

is single-valued for all z and u.

A word about this assumption is in order. In the first place, it is a bit too strong when taken literally. Suppose that any y satisfying Eq. (5.2.2) is *locally* unique for given z and u; that is, that G is single-valued in some neighborhood of any point (y,z,u) satisfying Eq. (5.2.1). It is possible that a model which determines the endogenous variables given the predetermined variables and the disturbances does so by yielding several *isolated* solutions for the endogenous variables. Conditions of economic relevance (e.g., that outputs are nonnegative) may then suffice to determine which solutions obtain in the real world. It thus suffices for our purposes to suppose that G is locally single-valued and that unstated side conditions rule out all but one of the solutions.

Further, if the model as written yields several isolated solutions, even if more than one of these cannot be ruled out on outside grounds, we may take Assumption 5.2.1 as asserting that only one is relevant in the real world—even if *which* solution that is is not known. In other words, the assumption implies that only one set of values of the endogenous variables can hold for given values of the exogenous variables and disturbances. Note also that if more than one formal solution of the model can obtain at different times, the model is not complete without a rule for determining which one holds at a given time. With the addition of such a rule, Assumption 5.2.1 is valid, since the rule must run in terms of the value of at least *some* variable or disturbance, which then becomes part of the model if it was not so already.

Next, observe that even local single-valuedness of G implies that A has rank M, since otherwise the Jacobian of $Aq(x)$ with respect to the elements of y would vanish identically.[1] In the case of a linear system, this is all that is required for Assumption 5.2.1, and we have been making that assumption (Assumption 1.5.1) since Chap. 1. For the present nonlinear system, it must be strengthened.

Finally, observe that Eq. (5.2.2) is the generalization of the reduced form equations for linear models. While the reduced form in such models is derived by a linear transformation of the structure, here that transformation is nonlinear as is the reduced form itself. Indeed, $G(z,u)$ will generally be nonlinear in the elements of A, even though the original system (5.2.1) is linear in those elements. G will also generally be nonlinear in u. Continuity of G (the normal case) is needed at one point below.[2]

We now suppose that $q(x)$ can be separated into functions of predetermined variables alone and other functions. Elements of $q(x)$ which are functions of endogenous variables, whether or not they are also functions of predetermined variables, will be termed endogenous functions. We take the number of these to be M^0. The remaining elements of $q(x)$ are termed predetermined functions and their number is represented by $\Lambda^0 = N^0 - M^0$. Note that Assumption 5.2.1 implies (*Why?*)

$$M^0 \geq M \tag{5.2.3}$$

but that a similar inequality need not hold for Λ^0 and Λ. In view of our preceding discussion, it is clear that separate interest only attaches to the case in which the strict inequality holds in Eq. (5.2.3).

In dealing with linear models, we assumed that no linear identities connect the predetermined variables (Assumption 1.5.2). The corresponding assumption on predetermined functions is included in the following:

Assumption 5.2.2: The elements of $q(x)$ are not connected by any linear identity.

The absence of linear identities connecting any set of elements of $q(x)$, not just the predetermined ones, is put in for reasons of convenience. As with the corresponding assumption in the linear case, this is an innocuous assumption, since linear identities can be eliminated by substitution at the outset and the system transformed into an equivalent one which has the required property.

---

[1] And, indeed, the condition of Theorem 5.A.1a below would fail.

[2] It follows from Theorem 5.A.1 and Corollary 5.A.1 below that if all elements of $q(x)$ are analytic, continuity of G is guaranteed almost everywhere (i.e., except for sets of measure zero) by the uniqueness assumption and the differentiability of $q(x)$. Even in such cases, continuity needs to be assumed below to hold at all points.

Note that only *linear identities* are ruled out. The elements of $q(x)$ are certainly allowed to be connected by nonlinear identities; this is the interesting case. Further, nonidentical linear relationships among the elements of $q(x)$ may actually be stated by the model if one or more elements of u are always zero—a case we shall wish to consider.

As our next assumption, we strengthen Assumption 1.5.3 in a way already discussed.

Assumption 5.2.3: The elements of u are distributed independently of the elements of z.

Examples of such systems seem now in order. We present two such examples with which we shall work in later sections. Letting all previously undefined symbols be scalars, the first such example is

$$a_0 + a_1 \log y_1 + a_2 \log y_2 + a_3 z = u_1$$
$$b_0 + b_1 y_1 + b_2 y_2 + b_3 z = u_2 \tag{5.2.4}$$

Here, y_1 and y_2 are endogenous and z is predetermined, as is also a variable identically equal to unity whose coefficients are the constant terms. The vector $q(x)$ is

$$q(x) = \begin{bmatrix} \log y_1 \\ \log y_2 \\ y_1 \\ y_2 \\ z \\ 1 \end{bmatrix} \tag{5.2.5}$$

where the 1 stands for the constant exogenous variable just mentioned. The first four elements of $q(x)$ are endogenous functions and the last two are predetermined functions. $M = 2$, $M^0 = 4$, $N = 4$, $N^0 = 6$, and $\Lambda = \Lambda^0 = 2$. Writing out the matrix A,

$$A = \begin{bmatrix} a_1 & a_2 & 0 & 0 & a_3 & a_0 \\ 0 & 0 & b_1 & b_2 & b_3 & b_0 \end{bmatrix} \tag{5.2.6}$$

Assumption 5.2.1 *can* clearly be satisfied, since the Jacobian of Eq. (5.2.4) with respect to y_1 and y_2 vanishes only along the line

$$a_1 b_2 y_2 = a_2 b_1 y_1 \tag{5.2.7}$$

although this, by itself, only guarantees local uniqueness for points not on that line.

The second example which we shall use is the following:

$$a_0 + a_1 y_1{}^2 + a_2 y_2{}^2 + a_3 y_1 y_2 + a_4 z = u_1$$
$$b_1 y_1 + b_2 y_2 = u_2 \tag{5.2.8}$$

Again, y_1 and y_2 are endogenous and z and the constant variable are predetermined.

$$q(x) = \begin{bmatrix} y_1^2 \\ y_2^2 \\ y_1 y_2 \\ y_1 \\ y_2 \\ z \\ 1 \end{bmatrix} \tag{5.2.9}$$

so that while $M = 2$ and $N = 4$, $M^0 = 5$, $N^0 = 7$, and $\Lambda = \Lambda^0 = 2$. The matrix A is

$$A = \begin{bmatrix} a_1 & a_2 & a_3 & 0 & 0 & a_4 & a_0 \\ 0 & 0 & 0 & b_1 & b_2 & 0 & 0 \end{bmatrix} \tag{5.2.10}$$

As before, Assumption 5.2.1 can be satisfied, the relevant Jacobian vanishing only on a particular line in the space of y_1 and y_2.

5.3. The Limits of Observational Information Reconsidered

In the opening chapter, we proved that in the linear model an equation could be distinguished from the true first equation on the basis of observational information alone if and only if such an equation was not a linear combination of the equations of the model (Theorem 1.6.1). We did this by observing that the information available from observation on the first equation can be summarized by the statement that the true first row of A satisfies the equation

$$A_1 W = 0 \tag{5.3.1}$$

where W is a matrix of (in principle) observable elements derived by setting the covariances of the predetermined variables and the disturbances equal to zero. Since

$$A W = 0 \tag{5.3.2}$$

this does not suffice to distinguish A_1 from the other rows of A, and since the dimension of the row kernel of W was M, the rows of A formed a basis for that row kernel. We observed that Eq. (5.3.1) provided Λ independent pieces of information, so that M more were required from prior restrictions.

What becomes of this analysis in the present case? Clearly, it cannot carry over to the nonlinear model being considered without modification. In the linear model, with N parameters to estimate in the first equation, the Λ independent pieces of observational information left missing precisely the same number of independent pieces of information as of equations. In the present case, however, there are not N but N^0 parameters to be estimated, reflecting the fact that certain endogenous functions appear in Eq. (5.2.1) without *linear* equations to relate them to the predetermined variables and disturbances.

One's first thought, therefore, might be as follows. Treat the Λ^0 predetermined functions of $q(x)$ in the same way as the predetermined variables themselves were treated in the linear model. That is, let W be the $N^0 \times \Lambda^0$ matrix whose ijth element is the expected cross-product of the ith element of $q(x)$ with the jth predetermined function ($i = 1$, $\ldots, N^0$; $j = 1, \ldots, \Lambda^0$).† Then $\rho(W) = \Lambda^0$ and Eqs. (5.3.1) and (5.3.2) still hold. This suggests that prior restrictions must provide not M but $M^0 = N^0 - \Lambda^0$ independent pieces of information, so that, in view of Eq. (5.2.3), the situation is worse than in the linear case.

Such a view is clearly too pessimistic. The procedure just outlined makes use only of the fact that the disturbances and the predetermined elements of $q(x)$ are uncorrelated in the probability limit. This by no means exhausts the possibilities of observational information, however, since, by Assumption 5.2.3, not just those elements but *every* function of current predetermined variables is uncorrelated with the disturbances in the probability limit.

Thus, we might proceed by taking as many linearly independent functions of z as we like[1] and, using Eq. (5.2.1), express the zero correlations just described in the form (5.3.2) where W is expanded so that its jth column now contains the expected cross-products of the elements of $q(x)$ with the jth arbitrary function of z, where $j = 1$, $\ldots, J$ and J can be made as large as desired. One might think that one could proceed in this way until the rank of W was restricted only by Eq. (5.2.3), i.e., until W had rank $N^0 - M$. We could then proceed as in the linear case, since observational information would suffice to distinguish the true first equation from all candidate equations except those which were linear combinations of the structural equations (5.2.1). This would be a happy circumstance were it true, since in the M independent pieces of prior information required to identify the first equation of Eq. (5.2.1) we could clearly use the fact that certain elements of $q(x)$ do not appear in that equation, regardless of the fact that the same variables might appear in other forms in that equation. Thus, for example, both equations of (5.2.4) or (5.2.8) would be overidentified by the familiar rank condition, even though all the basic variables appear in each equation.

Unfortunately this view is too optimistic.[2] This is so for two reasons— one very special and the other more general.

---

† We assume that such cross-products exist and are finite, although this is not strictly necessary. The expected cross-product of any variable and the constant variable is the mean of the former.

[1] Why must such functions be linearly independent?

[2] It was mistakenly adopted in Fisher [9], except for the first of the two cases about to be discussed.

We take the special case first. The happy result just described depends on the existence of many linearly independent functions of the predetermined variables which yield new statements about correlations with the disturbances. If, however, the *only* predetermined variable is the constant one,[1] any function of it is proportional to the variable itself. In this case, W can only have rank $\Lambda^0 = 1$ no matter how many columns we add to it. For this special case, at least, the pessimistic view is the right one, for the *only* independent piece of observational information available is the fact that the disturbances have zero means.

Insight may be gained here if we pause to examine the nonstochastic case in which all disturbances are identically zero. Here, every column of W, analogous to the case in Chap. 1, may be thought of as an observation on the elements of $q(x)$. Since these elements are not connected by linear identities, if there is at least one nonconstant predetermined variable, we can hope to perform useful experiments by setting such variables at different values so that Eq. (5.2.2) grinds out linearly independent observations on $q(x)$ consistent with Eq. (5.2.1). If there are no such variables, then Assumption 5.2.1 assures us that there is only one such independent observation, so that only one restriction can possibly be placed on A_1 by posterior information.

On the other hand, in the more general case, the argument given above amounts to the statement that since Eq. (5.2.1) places only M linear restrictions on such observations, we can choose $N^0 - M$ linearly independent observations and proceed from there. The reason why that argument is not valid in full generality now becomes obvious from consideration of the nonstochastic case.

Consider the quadratic example (5.2.8) with both disturbances zero. It is clear that squaring the second equation and adding it to the first gives a new equation indistinguishable from the first, which therefore cannot be identified. This corresponds to the fact that squaring the second equation produces a new equation linear in the elements of $q(x)$ which is *linearly* independent of the original two equations. The new equation therefore places another implied linear restriction on observations on $q(x)$ which satisfy the original equation. It follows that instead of generating $N^0 - M = 5$ independent observations on $q(x)$, we can only generate at most four such independent observations consistent with the original equations. Whereas in the linear case only *linear* transformations of the original equations generate linear restrictions on the observations, in the present case we must face the possibility that *nonlinear* transformations can generate such restrictions as

---

[1] We shall assume below that the constant variable is always formally present, although its coefficients may all be zero.

well.   Indeed, this is the core of the problem raised for identification by nonlinearities of the present type.

We may now return to the general stochastic case and formalize the difficulty.   The other side of the property that any function of predetermined variables is uncorrelated with the disturbances is that any function of the disturbances is uncorrelated with the predetermined variables (and with any function thereof).   If it so happens that there exists a function of the disturbances which is implied by the equations of the model (5.2.1) to equal a linear function of $q(x)$ and if the vector of parameters of that linear function is linearly independent of the rows of A, then that linear function provides an independent linear restriction on W, however defined.   In other words, such a linear function shares with the original structural equations of the model the property that linear combinations of that function and the structural equations are indistinguishable from the true first equation on the basis of observational information.

Thus, consider any function of the disturbances, say $F(u_1, \ldots, u_M)$, where u_j is the disturbance from the jth equation.   As before, let A_j denote the jth row of A $(j = 1, \ldots, M)$.   Suppose that there exists a constant vector h, such that

$$F(u_1, \ldots, u_M) = F\{A_1 q(x), \ldots, A_M q(x)\} = hq(x) \qquad (5.3.3)$$

for all x satisfying Eq. (5.2.1).   Suppose further that

$$\rho\left(\begin{bmatrix} A \\ \hline h \end{bmatrix}\right) = M + 1 \qquad (5.3.4)$$

Then, letting $\tilde{u} = F(u_1, \ldots, u_M)$, the equation

$$hq(x) = \tilde{u} \qquad (5.3.5)$$

is a linearly independent equation, valid whenever Eq. (5.2.1) is valid. Further, linear combinations of Eq. (5.3.5) and the equations of Eq. (5.2.1) cannot be distinguished from each other on the basis of observational information only, since $\tilde{u}$, like the unobservable u_i, is uncorrelated with any function of the predetermined variables.

The astute reader will perhaps have noticed, however, that there is one formal exception to this statement. Among the predetermined variables is the constant variable. For this variable to have zero cross-product with $\tilde{u}$ requires that the latter have mean zero. Clearly, however, not all nonlinear transformations of the disturbances have zero mean.   This problem (which arises only with respect to the constant variable) is easy to take care of by a convention.   We shall assume that the constant variable is always an element of $q(x)$, although its coefficients (a particular column of A) may be known to be zero.   If the function $F(u_1, \ldots, u_M)$ has a nonzero mean, then we may subtract that mean from both sides of

Eq. (5.3.5) by subtracting it from the element of h corresponding to the constant variable. This will result in an equation in the form of Eq. (5.3.5) in which the disturbance does have zero mean. We shall suppose this already done and shall not trouble explicitly to mention it again. {Note that if the constant term in fact does not appear in the original equations, then the *prior* knowledge that this is the case will serve to identify those equations with respect to any *single* equation (5.3.5) in which this sort of transformation introduces a constant term.}

.   It is possible that such a subtraction just happens to result in a violation of Eq. (5.3.4). This happens only on a set of measure zero and is a subclass of a problem which we shall discuss below.

The fact that knowledge that the original disturbances have zero mean results in this sort of device being required is one example of the fact that if specific things are known about the joint distribution of the original disturbances, then transformations of them as in Eq. (5.3.3) must have corresponding properties. If enough is known about that joint distribution, all such nonlinear transformations may be ruled out. This sort of aid from prior information on the disturbances will be further discussed below.

It is evident, moreover, that if there exists an equation of the form (5.3.5) whose disturbance $\bar{u}$ is distributed independently of the predetermined variables, then it must come from a transformation such as Eq. (5.3.3). Thus, $\bar{u}$ cannot be a function of the variables in x, since it would then not be so distributed. On the other hand, if $\bar{u}$ were a function of some new variable or disturbance, say v, in addition to the elements of u, then there are only two possibilities. Either v influences at least one endogenous variable, contradicting Assumption 5.2.1, or else it is related only to predetermined variables—in which case $\bar{u}$ is not distributed independently of those variables.

Note that in either case the model contains a behavioral equation not written down in Eq. (5.2.1). In the second case, this is possible, but the model is then block recursive (with the definition appropriately generalized to the nonlinear case), and the statement that this is inadmissible in Eq. (5.3.5) may be taken as a statement that any equation of the model is identified with respect to the equations generating the predetermined variables. It may be illuminating to the reader to think this through.

The difficulty in question, therefore, can arise only from the existence of transformations F resulting in equations such as Eq. (5.3.5) which are linearly independent of the original equations. A complete statement is thus as follows:

Suppose that there exist precisely $M^* - M$ functions of the disturbances $F^1, \ldots, F^{M^*-M}$ such that

$$F^i(u_1, \ldots, u_M) = F^i\{A_1 q(x), \ldots, A_M q(x)\} = h^i q(x)$$
$$(i = 1, \ldots, M^* - M) \quad (5.3.6)$$

where the h^i are constant vectors with the property that the matrix

$$A^* = \begin{bmatrix} A \\ \hline h^1 \\ \cdot \\ \cdot \\ \cdot \\ h^{M^*-M} \end{bmatrix} \tag{5.3.7}$$

has rank M^* (that is, A^* has full row rank). Define

$$\bar{u}_i \equiv F^i(u_1, \ldots, u_M) \qquad (i = 1, \ldots, M^* - M) \tag{5.3.8}$$

$$u^* \equiv \begin{bmatrix} u \\ \hline \bar{u}_1 \\ \cdot \\ \cdot \\ \cdot \\ \bar{u}_{M^*-M} \end{bmatrix} \tag{5.3.9}$$

Then the correct generalization of Theorem 1.6.1 is:[1]

Theorem 5.3.1: An N^0-component row vector α can be distinguished from the true A_1 on the basis of a posteriori information if and only if α is not a linear combination of the rows of A^*.

Given this result, identification of A_1 proceeds as in the linear case with the equations

$$A^* q(x) = u^* \tag{5.3.10}$$

replacing the original Eqs. (5.2.1). Thus, for example, if the only prior restrictions on the first equation take the form

$$A_1 \phi = 0 \tag{5.3.11}$$

where ϕ is a known constant matrix, then a necessary and sufficient condition for the identifiability of the first equation of Eq. (5.2.1) {or Eq. (5.3.10)} is that

$$\rho(A^* \phi) = M^* - 1 \tag{5.3.12}$$

and a necessary condition is that

$$\rho(\phi) \geq M^* - 1 \tag{5.3.13}$$

Thus A^* replaces A, and M^* replaces M in the statement of the rank and order conditions.

Note that we are thus entitled to count as valid prior restrictions on the first equation the fact (if true) that certain elements of $q(x)$ do not appear therein. The fact that such elements may be functions also of variables which do appear in the first equation in different form has been

---

[1] Prove that this is indeed a generalization of Theorem 1.6.1.

taken into account in passing from Eq. (5.2.1) to Eq. (5.3.10) and in the restatement of the rank and order conditions.

An important word of warning, however: We saw in Chap. 2 that there were frequent occasions in which the order condition was sufficient in the linear case almost everywhere in the parameter space. These were the occasions in which the rank condition was not known to fail identically. In the present case, such identical failure of the rank condition can readily occur because of the restrictions placed on the other equations *and their effects on* $h^1, \ldots, h^{M^*-M}$. We shall return to this in a later section after discussing the obvious crucial question: How large is $M^* - M$?

5.4. The Size of $M^* - M$

This question is most conveniently studied by consideration of the nonstochastic case in which $u \equiv 0$. That no loss of generality is involved in doing this may be seen in two ways (aside from the fact that the same problems have already been observed to arise in the two cases).

In the first place, the only information about the disturbances which has been employed in the preceding discussion is the fact that they are distributed independently of the predetermined variables. So long as we are careful to do nothing in the nonstochastic case which would violate the implications of this when extended to the stochastic case, we lose nothing by considering the nonstochastic case. To put it differently, it is easy to frame a discussion of the nonstochastic case which corresponds to the use only of such information in the stochastic case—i.e., which corresponds to the discussion at the end of the preceding section. If other information is available concerning the disturbances, it is possible that some of the transformations admissible in the nonstochastic case will, when extended, violate the implications of that information. This should not be treated as a restriction of the present discussion which bears on the question of what observational information can do without further assumptions. Rather it should be taken as a statement that given the present treatment, further *prior* information on the disturbances can certainly aid in identification, in part by ruling out certain transformations which would otherwise be admissible in both the nonstochastic and the stochastic case.

Alternatively, one can look at the matter in this way. The specification that the disturbances are distributed independently of the predetermined variables may be regarded as the specification that the disturbances have zero means at all levels of those variables. Fix the predetermined variables at a particular set of values and take expected values of the elements of $q(x)$ conditional on those values for the predetermined variables.   The resulting vector of values for the elements of $q(x)$ certainly satisfies the nonstochastic equation

$$Aq(x) = 0 \qquad (5.4.1)$$

and we may think of the nonstochastic case as arising from this sort of operation.   The information on the disturbances is thus used by observing that the vector which results from the described operation satisfies Eq. (5.4.1) *whatever* values of the predetermined variables are chosen. The choice of those values then corresponds to the experiment in the nonstochastic case which consists of choosing the same values and letting $q(x)$ be determined by that choice and $G(z,0)$ to satisfy Eq. (5.4.1).

In this section, therefore, we shall deal with Eq. (5.4.1) as the original set of equations.   We restate the problem in this form.

What is the precise number $M^* - M$ such that there exist transformations $F^1, \ldots , F^{M^*-M}$ with the following properties?

$$F^i\{A_1q(x), \ldots ,A_Mq(x)\} = h^iq(x) \qquad (i = 1, \ldots , M^* - M)$$
$$(5.4.2)$$

for *all* x and

$$F^i(0, \ldots ,0) = 0 \qquad (i = 1, \ldots , M^* - M) \qquad (5.4.3)$$

so that $\qquad h^iq(x) = 0 \qquad (i = 1, \ldots , M^* - M) \qquad (5.4.4)$

for all x satisfying Eq. (5.4.1).   Here, $h^1, \ldots , h^{M^*-M}$ are constant vectors and

$$A^* = \begin{bmatrix} A \\ \hline h^1 \\ \cdot \\ \cdot \\ \cdot \\ h^{M^*-M} \end{bmatrix} \qquad (5.4.5)$$

has full row rank.   Moreover, what can be said concerning the vectors $h^1, \ldots , h^{M^*-M}$?

We might consider a direct attack on this problem which essentially utilizes its genesis.   Thus, let $Q(x)$ be an $N^0 \times T$ matrix each of whose columns is an observation on $q(x)$ consistent with Eq. (5.4.1).   Clearly, every h^i satisfies

$$h^iQ(x) = 0 \qquad (i = 1, \ldots , M^* - M) \qquad (5.4.6)$$

We might thus proceed by asking what is the maximal rank permitted to $Q(x)$ by Eq. (5.4.1).   If we require the columns of $Q(x)$ to be linearly independent, how large can T be made by varying the predetermined variables to generate observations?   Since it is obvious that the rows of

A^* form a basis for the row kernel of $Q(x)$, that rank will be precisely equal to $N^0 - M^*$ (by Theorem 1.4.1). In addition, the h^i can be obtained by extending the set of rows of A to form a basis for the row kernel of $Q(x)$.

We have already essentially proceeded in this way to secure some results which may now be recapitulated. First, since there are Λ^0 predetermined elements of $q(x)$ and these are not identically linearly dependent (Assumption 5.2.2), $\rho\{Q(x)\} \geq \Lambda^0$. It follows that:

Theorem 5.4.1: $\qquad\qquad M^0 \geq M^* \geq M$

Proof: By Theorem 1.4.1

$$M^* = N^0 - \rho\{Q(x)\} \leq N^0 - \Lambda^0 = M^0 \qquad (5.4.7)$$

while the fact that M^* is no less than M is trivial.

Thus the worst possible case is that of the pessimistic wrong argument given at the beginning of the preceding section. Here there is a row of A^* for every endogenous function in $q(x)$.

Moreover, we already know that this case certainly holds if there is no nonconstant predetermined variable. We shall now prove this formally.

Theorem 5.4.2: If there is no nonconstant predetermined variable, $M^* = M^0 = N^0 - 1$.

Proof: In this case, Assumption 5.2.1 assures us that there is only one possible observation on $q(x)$, so that $\rho\{Q(x)\} = 1$.

While such results are useful, they seem to exhaust the practical usefulness of considering the row kernel of $Q(x)$. The fact that the unknown rows of A are themselves in that row kernel is itself rather a nuisance in working our particular cases. It is thus preferable to work with a matrix which in general has only the h^i (plus a trivial, known vector) in its row kernel.

In what follows, observe that since the transformations $F^1, \ldots,$ F^{M^*-M} transform differentiable functions of x into differentiable functions, there is no harm in taking them to be differentiable.

Let $Q'(x)$ denote the Jacobian matrix of $q(x)$ with rows corresponding to elements of $q(x)$ and columns corresponding to elements of x. Thus, the ijth element of $Q'(x)$ is the partial derivative of the ith element of $q(x)$ with respect to the jth element of x. Of course, differentiation with respect to the constant variable is impossible, so $Q'(x)$ has only $N - 1$ columns. Further, letting the constant variable be the last element of $q(x)$, the N^0th row of $Q'(x)$ consists of zeros only. In what follows, we shall largely ignore vectors in the row kernel of $Q'(x)$ which have zero everywhere but in the N^0th place and we shall omit the row of $Q'(x)$ in question entirely when doing examples. We shall show that it suffices to consider constant vectors h which satisfy

$$hQ'(x) = 0 \qquad \text{for all } x \text{ satisfying (5.4.1)} \qquad (5.4.8)$$

In other words, we shall show that every h^i can be taken to lie in the row kernel of $Q'(x)$ for every x satisfying the original equations and that any vector which is in that row kernel for all such x is (at least after a trivial transformation) a linear combination of the rows of A^*.

The advantage of doing this is that, except in pathological cases, no linear combination of the rows of A lies in the row kernel of $Q'(x)$ for all x satisfying Eq. (5.4.1) so that the h^i may be taken as a basis for that row kernel (with the addition of the trivial member of that row kernel mentioned earlier). The reason for this is that Assumption 5.2.1 clearly requires that the rows of $AQ'(x)$ not be *identically* linearly dependent, so that no given linear combination of the rows of A will generally lie in the row kernel of $Q'(x)$ for all x satisfying Eq. (5.4.1).[1] Thus that row kernel will generally have dimension $M^* - M + 1$ (the 1 coming from the trivial vector already discussed).

We thus prove:

Theorem 5.4.3: Consider the solutions to Eq. (5.4.8) and form a basis for the set of those solutions, which basis includes the trivial solution (that is, the solution which has only its last element nonzero). Discard from that basis the trivial solution and any vector which is a linear combination of the rows of A (generally, there will not be any of these). The remaining basis vectors are in one-to-one correspondence with the h^i of Eqs. (5.4.2) to (5.4.5) and may be taken to be those h^i after at most a trivial transformation.

Proof: We first show that any nontrivial vector h satisfying Eq. (5.4.8) also satisfies

$$hq(x) = 0 \qquad \text{for all } x \text{ satisfying Eq. (5.4.1)} \qquad (5.4.9)$$

after at most a trivial transformation.

To see this, observe that Eq. (5.4.8) and Assumption 5.2.1 certainly imply that if Eq. (5.4.9) is satisfied for that h and a particular x, say x^0,

---

[1] The equation $y^2 = 0$ is an example of such a pathological case. Here the Jacobian ($= 2y$) is not identically zero and, indeed, there is a unique solution for y, yet the Jacobian just happens to be zero at that solution. (Such problems are discussed in the appendix to this chapter.) Even if such pathological cases do occur in practice, they will be generally easy to recognize. In such cases, the h^i can be taken as the vectors which must be added to certain linear combinations of the rows of A to secure a basis for the row kernel of $Q'(x)$ for all x satisfying Eq. (5.4.1).

satisfying Eq. (5.4.1), then Eq. (5.4.9) is satisfied with that h for all such x.† Thus consider any x^0 satisfying Eq. (5.4.1). Define

$$d^0 = hq(x^0) \tag{5.4.10}$$

Subtract d^0 from the last element of h to secure a new vector, say $\bar{h}$. (This is the trivial transformation referred to in the statement of the theorem. It is an adjustment of a constant term.) Clearly, since the last element of $q(x)$ is always unity,

$$\bar{h}q(x^0) = 0 \tag{5.4.11}$$

and since the last row of $Q'(x)$ is identically zero, $\bar{h}$ satisfies Eq. (5.4.8). Now, form any basis for solutions to Eq. (5.4.8) which includes the trivial solution. The transformation just described when performed on the non-trivial members of that basis cannot make them dependent. (*Prove this.*) Thus, when the trivial solution and linear combinations of the rows of A are discarded, the remaining (transformed) members of the basis can be taken as at least some of the h^i, since they lie in the row kernel of $Q(x)$ for all x satisfying Eq. (5.4.1) and are clearly independent of the rows of A.

This establishes that the set of h^i may be taken to include the independent vectors described in the statement of the theorem. Now we show that every h^i corresponds to precisely one such vector.

To do this, differentiate Eq. (5.4.2) with respect to each element of x (except the last) and write the result in matrix form. After subtraction, this becomes

$$\left\{ h^i - \sum_{j=1}^{M} F_j{}^i(A_1 q(x), \ \dots \ , A_M q(x)) A_j \right\} Q'(x) = 0$$
$$(i = 1, \ \dots \ , M^* - M) \quad (5.4.12)$$

identically in x, where $F_j{}^i$ denotes the partial derivative of F^i with respect to its jth argument $(j = 1, \ \dots \ , M)$. In particular, for any x satisfying Eq. (5.4.1)

$$\left\{ h^i - \sum_{j=1}^{M} F_j{}^i(0, \ \dots \ ,0) A_j \right\} Q'(x) = 0 \qquad (i = 1, \ \dots \ , M^* - M)$$
$$(5.4.13)$$

Define

$$h^{*i} \equiv h^i - \sum_{j=1}^{M} F_j{}^i(0, \ \dots \ ,0) A_j \qquad (i = 1, \ \dots \ , M^* - M) \quad (5.4.14)$$

Then the h^{*i} are clearly solutions to Eq. (5.4.8) as are all linear combinations of them. Indeed, such linear combinations are also solutions to

---

† This is where continuity of $G(z,u)$ is needed. **Under the stated assumptions,** $d\{hq(x)\} = 0$ as x moves to satisfy Eq. (5.4.1).

Eq. (5.4.9). It follows that no such linear combination is a trivial solution to Eq. (5.4.8) (*Why?*), so that the set of the h^{*i} plus the trivial solution is independent if the h^{*i} themselves are.

It remains to show that the h^{*i} are independent and are independent of the rows of A, so that they may be taken to form part of a basis for solutions to Eq. (5.4.8) which includes the trivial solution and may include linear combinations of the rows of A. In other words, we show that the matrix A^* retains full row rank when the h^i are replaced by the h^{*i}, so that, in view of all the foregoing, we may as well take the h^{*i} themselves to be the h^i.

To prove such independence, suppose that it were false. Then there would exist scalars $\lambda_1, \ldots, \lambda_M$ and $\mu_1, \ldots, \mu_{M^*-M}$ not all zero, such that

$$\sum_{j=1}^{M} \lambda_j A_j + \sum_{i=1}^{M^*-M} \mu_i h^{*i} = 0 \qquad (5.4.15)$$

In that case, however,

$$0 = \sum_{j=1}^{M} \lambda_j A_j + \sum_{i=1}^{M^*-M} \mu_i \left\{ h^i - \sum_{j=1}^{M} F_j{}^i(0, \ldots, 0) A_j \right\}$$

$$= \sum_{j=1}^{M} \left\{ \lambda_j - \sum_{i=1}^{M^*-M} \mu_i F_j{}^i(0, \ldots, 0) \right\} A_j + \sum_{i=1}^{M^*-M} \mu_i h^i \qquad (5.4.16)$$

Since A^* has full row rank when the h^i themselves are used for the last $M^* - M$ rows thereof, this implies that

$$\mu_i = 0 \qquad (i = 1, \ldots, M^* - M)$$
$$\lambda_j - \sum_{i=1}^{M^*-M} \mu_i F_j{}^i(0, \ldots, 0) = 0 \qquad (j = 1, \ldots, M) \qquad (5.4.17)$$

which immediately implies that

$$\mu_i = 0 \qquad (i = 1, \ldots, M^* - M)$$
$$\lambda_j = 0 \qquad (j = 1, \ldots, M) \qquad (5.4.18)$$

so that the rows of A and the h^{*i} are independent. This completes the proof of the theorem.

5.5. Two Examples and Some Conclusions

It thus suffices to consider only the vectors h^i satisfying Eq. (5.4.8). To see that this may be relatively easy to work with as opposed to

$$A^*Q(x) = 0 \qquad (5.5.1)$$

we shall work out in detail the two examples given earlier.

The first of these is the quadratic and linear one of Eqs. (5.2.8). Here we have

$$Q'(x) = \begin{bmatrix} 2y_1 & 0 & 0 \\ 0 & 2y_2 & 0 \\ y_2 & y_1 & 0 \\ 1 & 0 & 0 \\ 0 & 1 & 0 \\ 0 & 0 & 1 \end{bmatrix} \tag{5.5.2}$$

where we may obviously forget the N^0th row of zeros. Suppose that there exists a vector $h = (h_1 \cdots h_6)$ such that

$$hQ'(x) = 0 \tag{5.5.3}$$

for all x satisfying Eqs. (5.2.8) with $u_1 = 0 = u_2$. Then, for all such x,

$$\begin{aligned} 2h_1y_1 + h_3y_2 + h_4 &= 0 \\ 2h_2y_2 + h_3y_1 + h_5 &= 0 \\ h_6 &= 0 \end{aligned} \tag{5.5.4}$$

However, for all x satisfying the nonstochastic equivalent of Eqs. (5.2.8),

$$y_1 = \frac{-b_2}{b_1} y_2 \tag{5.5.5}$$

so that
$$\begin{aligned} (b_1h_3 - 2b_2h_1)y_2 + b_1h_4 &= 0 \\ (2b_1h_2 - b_2h_3)y_2 + b_1h_5 &= 0 \end{aligned} \tag{5.5.6}$$

Since y_2 can be made to vary by choosing z in different ways, Eq. (5.5.6) can only be satisfied if the coefficients of y_2 and the constant terms are all zero. Assuming $b_1 \neq 0 \neq b_2$, this implies that h is proportional to the vector $(b_1{}^2 \quad b_2{}^2 \quad 2b_1b_2 \quad 0 \quad 0 \quad 0)$ which gives the coefficients for the extra equation implied by Eq. (5.2.8). (*Why do we expect this result in this example?*) Thus $M^* - M = 1$ here. Note that if the term in y_1y_2 did not appear, the same analysis would show that $h = 0$ and $M^* = M$.

Turning now to the logarithmic and linear example of Eqs. (5.2.4), we have

$$Q'(x) = \begin{bmatrix} \dfrac{1}{y_1} & 0 & 0 \\ 0 & \dfrac{1}{y_2} & 0 \\ 1 & 0 & 0 \\ 0 & 1 & 0 \\ 0 & 0 & 1 \end{bmatrix} \tag{5.5.7}$$

(again ignoring the final row of zeros) so that any $h = (h_1, \ldots, h_5)$ satisfying

$$hQ'(x) = 0 \tag{5.5.8}$$

for all x satisfying Eq. (5.2.4) with $u_1 = 0 = u_2$ must have

$$h_1 \frac{1}{y_1} + h_3 = 0$$

$$h_2 \frac{1}{y_2} + h_4 = 0 \tag{5.5.9}$$

$$h_5 = 0$$

It is evident, however, that choosing z to have several values implies that this is impossible unless $h = 0$. So $M^* = M$ in this case.

The procedure involved in applying Theorem 5.4.3 should now be clear and results in both the value of $M^* - M$ *and* the vectors h^i $(i = 1, \ldots, M^* - M)$.† Although the examples are admittedly very simple ones, they do indicate one or two general conclusions that may be drawn.

In the first place, $M^* - M$ will be zero if the elements of every column of $Q'(x)$ are not implied by Eq. (5.4.1) to be linearly related. This will generally be the case if the functions which are components of $q(x)$ are each functions of only one variable, since the system will not generally imply that such functions are linearly related.[1] This occurs in the logarithmic-linear example just discussed and in the quadratic-linear one if the term in y_1y_2 is absent. It is a fairly general circumstance in practice although by no means a universal one since, for example, prices and quantities multiply to give revenues which may enter into structural equations.

Second, it is tempting to suppose that the only relations that need be considered between rows of $Q'(x)$ are those explicitly stated in Eq. (5.4.1). This is indeed a feature of the first example, but cannot be taken as a general rule. Consider, for example, the case of a linear and a cubic equation. The Jacobian will involve quadratic terms which do not appear in the original system, but the linear equation (when squared) may nevertheless imply dependence of the rows of $Q'(x)$.

Next, it is important to note that the value of $M^* - M$ may not be independent of the specific values of the elements of A. In the quadratic and linear example, $M^* - M = 1$ in general; however, if a_3 just happens

† However, the application of the procedure may be computationally harder in more complicated examples. Note that the procedure does not yield the form of the transformations $F^i(u)$ $(i = 1, \ldots, M^* - M)$ of Eq. (5.3.6). That information is not of much importance, however, once the h^i are known.

[1] Such linear relation can occur on a set of measure zero in the space of the elements of A, however, even if it does not occur in general. We shall return to such problems below.

to be zero, $M^* - M = 0$. Similarly, suppose that, in the same example, a term in $\log y_1$ appears in the second equation with an unknown coefficient. In general, $M^* - M = 0$ in such a case. (*Prove this.*) However, if the term just happens to have a zero coefficient, $M^* - M = 1$. The point is that the value of $M^* - M$ can be different for different values of the parameters. It is evident, however, that the value of $M^* - M$ computed using general parameters and all a priori restrictions will obtain everywhere in the space of the elements of A except on a set of measure zero. Note that the a priori restrictions *must* be used to determine the general value involved.

This brings us to our next point. Corresponding to the necessary and sufficient rank condition (5.3.12) is the necessary order condition (5.3.13) that the number of independent restrictions expressed by Eq. (5.3.11) be at least $M^* - 1$. In general, in the linear case the order condition is used in practice, since it does not depend on the values of the unknown parameters. As in Chap. 2, if the order condition is satisfied in the present case *and if the a priori restrictions do not reduce the rank of $A^*\phi$ identically below $M^* - 1$*, the rank condition (5.3.12) will also be satisfied everywhere in the space of the elements of A except on a set of measure zero. The examples given indicate, however, that it is vital in the present context that the proviso concerning the a priori restrictions not be overlooked. In the quadratic and linear example of Eq. (5.2.8), $M^* = 3$ and there are two independent restrictions on the first equation (that linear terms in y_1 and y_2 do not appear). The order condition (5.3.13) is thus satisfied. The equation constructed to fill out A^*, however, by squaring the linear equation also satisfies those restrictions, and the rank of $A^*\phi$ in this example is identically no greater than 1. It follows that it is not enough to obtain the value of M^*; one must also compute the h^i and determine whether the rank condition is identically violated.

5.6. Do Nonlinearities in the Variables Aid Identification?

We are nearly at the end of our exploration of the case of systems linear in the parameters and disturbances but not in the variables. Before proceeding to other cases, however, it seems interesting to attempt to answer the question of whether identification in such systems is more readily achieved in some sense than in wholly linear systems.

Of course, it is necessary to be precise about the systems which are to be compared. The interesting case seems to be this. Consider the first equation of the system and suppose that it is linear in all respects. Is that equation more likely to be identified if the remainder of the system includes nonlinearities in the variables than if the remainder of the system is also wholly linear? Or is it the other way around?

In part, the foregoing analysis sheds light on this question; it is of some importance to realize, however, that it does not settle it. We assumed in discussing the limits of observational information for the nonlinear model that all that was known about the disturbances was that they were distributed independently of the current predetermined variables. If more precise information on their distribution is available, however, such information can sometimes be used to help identify the first equation in the nonlinear model.

Thus, for example, suppose that all the disturbances from the behavioral equations are assumed normally distributed. In a linear system, the only admissible transformations of the equations are linear transformations, so that the disturbance from any admissible transformation of the disturbances will also be normally distributed. In the present case, however, some nonlinear transformations may be admissible. A nonlinear transformation of normal variables, however, does not produce a normally distributed variable, so such transformations may be ruled out by the assumption of normality.

Note, however, that such information on the distribution of the disturbances cannot rule out *linear* transformations of the original equations in a way different from the case for linear systems.[1]   At best, therefore, it can rule out those transformations, which we have discussed at length, whose admissibility forces us to deal with M^* rather than M. The possible presence of such distributional information, therefore, should be taken as qualifying the following discussion only in those cases in which $M^* > M$.

With this reservation, we may proceed to discuss the point at issue. The simplest case to discuss is that of a system with no nonconstant predetermined variable, and we shall begin with that case.

In such a case, it is clear that nonlinearities do not aid identification in any way. Suppose that we begin with a linear system. Then the order condition specifies that to identify the first equation we must have at least $M - 1$ independent restrictions on it.[2]   Suppose that we have K such restrictions. Now suppose that we have another system identical to the first except that in equations other than the first one there appear $M^0 - M$ nonlinear functions of the variables. Whether or not such functions depend on variables which appear in linear form in the first equation does not matter; we are certainly entitled to count the knowledge that such functions {elements of $q(x)$} do *not* appear as such in the first equation as providing $M^0 - M$ further restrictions on the

---

[1] Of course, if one knew the first disturbance to be normally distributed and the remaining ones to be nonnormal, this would help to identify the first equation. The same statement is equally true of linear and nonlinear systems, however.

[2] For simplicity, we may as well restrict ourselves to the case of homogeneous and linear restrictions on the elements of A_1.

elements of A_1. This knowledge gets us nowhere further, however, for, while we now have $K + M^0 - M$ independent restrictions instead of merely K, Theorem 5.4.2 assures us that in the present case the order condition requires $M^0 - 1$ such restrictions (recalling that $N^0 = M^0$ if there are no nonconstant predetermined variables). Since

$$(M^0 - 1) - (K + M^0 - M) = (M - 1) - K \tag{5.6.1}$$

the order condition is no closer or further from fulfillment after the introduction of the nonlinearities than before. The same thing is true of the rank condition. (*Prove it.*)

Thus, for example, consider the system

$$a_0 + a_1y_1 + a_2y_2 = u_1 \\ b_0 + b_1y_1 + b_2y_2 = u_2 \tag{5.6.2}$$

Here $M = 2$ and there are no restrictions. One more restriction is needed to identify the first equation. Now suppose that the second equation is replaced by

$$b_0 + b_1y_1 + b_2y_2 + b_3 \log y_1 = u_2 \tag{5.6.3}$$

We now have one restriction on the first equation—the fact that $\log y_1$ does not appear therein—but $M^0 = 3$ and a further restriction is *still* needed to identify that equation.

The case is generally different when at least one nonconstant predetermined variable is present. Here the addition of nonlinear functions of the variables to equations other than the first raises the number of restrictions without generally raising the required number of such restrictions by the same amount. Thus, consider the following linear system:

$$a_0 + a_1y_1 + a_2y_2 + a_3z = u_1 \\ b_0 + b_1y_1 + b_2y_2 + b_3z = u_2 \tag{5.6.4}$$

As in the case of Eqs. (5.6.2), $M = 2$ and there are no restrictions, so that one further restriction is required to identify the first equation. Now suppose that the second equation is replaced by

$$b_0 + b_1y_1 + b_2y_2 + b_3z + b_4 \log y_1 = u_1 \tag{5.6.5}$$

We have now added one restriction, the fact that $\log y_1$ does not appear in the first equation.[1] On the other hand, it is easy to show by the methods of this chapter that $M^* = M = 2$ for this system, and the first equation is now identified. (*Show it. Show also that such a demonstration depends on at least one of the coefficients of z being nonzero.*)

Indeed, consideration of the logarithmic and linear example (5.2.4) shows that, in the presence of a nonconstant predetermined variable, altering the second equation of a two-equation system from a linear one

---

[1] This fact was also true of the linear system (5.6.4). Why does it do no good there?

to a log-linear one results in changing a case in which neither equation is identified to a case in which both are *over*identified. In cases such as this, it is clear that nonlinearities do provide powerful aid to identification.

Unfortunately, such cases are not the only ones. As in the quadratic and linear example of Eqs. (5.2.8), the introduction of nonlinearities can, even in the presence of a nonconstant predetermined variable, raise the *required* number as well as the *actual* number of restrictions; i.e., it can raise M^* above M. The limiting case is that in which both numbers are equally raised; this happens when there is no nonconstant predetermined variable—but it is certainly possible even when such a variable is present. While one does expect that limiting case to be the exception rather than the rule, the fact that it obviously can occur means that we are unable to state that nonlinearities *always* aid identification if there is at least one nonconstant predetermined variable. Moreover, the fact that the required number of restrictions may go up when nonlinearities are introduced reduces the amount of such aid even in cases other than the limiting one.

Nevertheless, even in such limiting cases, it is true that the introduction of nonlinearities cannot *hinder* identification, since, by Theorem 5.4.1, the number of restrictions required can at most go up just as much as the number of restrictions added. We may thus summarize by saying that nonlinearities can never hurt and will generally, but not always, help.

This concludes our discussion of systems linear in the parameters and disturbances but not in the variables, although certain of our results will appear in an analogous form when we consider the case of autocorrelated disturbances in Chap. 6.

5.7. Nonlinear Restrictions on A_1: Introduction

We shall now turn to the other special case of nonlinearities to be discussed in this chapter. This is the case in which the model itself is linear in parameters, disturbances, and variables but in which the prior information includes nonlinear restrictions on the parameters of the equation to be identified—nonlinear restrictions on the elements of A_1. We have already seen that such restrictions can arise when a function nonlinear in the parameters is approximated by Taylor series; in addition, there is at least one class of cases in which such restrictions occur in a natural way.

Suppose, for example, that the equation to be estimated consists of the following distributed lag relationship:

$$y_t = \sum_{i=1}^{N} \sum_{\theta=0}^{H} \alpha_{i\theta} x_{it-\theta} + u_t \tag{5.7.1}$$

where we need not be concerned for present purposes about the possible endogeneity of the $x_{i\theta}$. If a particular distributed lag structure is assumed, this may imply the existence of a nonlinear constraint on the parameters $\alpha_{i\theta}$ ($i = 1, \ldots, N; \theta = 0, \ldots, H$).

Thus, to take the best known example, suppose that for each i, the $\alpha_{i\theta}$ are assumed to decline geometrically with θ. This may come about by direct assumption or because Eq. (5.7.1) is the solution (with $H = \infty$ and with an additive disturbance) of the system

$$y_t - y_{t-1} = \lambda(y_t^* - y_{t-1}) \qquad 0 < \lambda < 1$$
$$y_t^* = \sum_{i=1}^{N} \beta_i x_{it} \qquad (5.7.2)$$

where y_t^* represents the desired or equilibrium value of y at time t. In this commonly used model, actual changes in y are fractions of the distance between desired and actual y. In any case, such a lag structure implies the nonlinear restrictions on Eq. (5.7.1):

$$\frac{\alpha_{i\theta+1}}{\alpha_{i\theta}} = \frac{\alpha_{i\theta}}{\alpha_{i\theta-1}} \qquad (i = 1, \ldots, N; \theta = 1, \ldots, H - 1) \quad (5.7.3)$$

and

$$\frac{\alpha_{i\theta+1}}{\alpha_{i\theta}} = \frac{\alpha_{j\theta+1}}{\alpha_{j\theta}} \qquad (i,j = 1, \ldots, N; \theta = 0, \ldots, H - 1) \quad (5.7.4)$$

or, more simply,

$$\alpha_{i\theta+1} = \rho\alpha_{i\theta} \qquad (i = 1, \ldots, N; \theta = 0, \ldots, H - 1) \quad (5.7.5)$$

where ρ is a parameter to be estimated and is independent of both i and θ.

Of course, in such a system, lagging Eq. (5.7.1) by one period, multiplying by ρ, and subtracting from the original version of Eq. (5.7.1) will result in an equivalent equation with the nonlinearities eliminated; nevertheless, such transformations may do undesirable things to the autocorrelation properties of the disturbances, and if the lag structure is more complicated, such transformations may not remove all nonlinearities. (For discussion of such models, see Koyck [24] and Nerlove [27] and [28].)

Thus nonlinear parameter restrictions do arise in cases other than Taylor series approximation. Nevertheless, the relative practical importance of this case is limited and we shall not give it the same extended treatment given to the case of systems nonlinear in the variables. Theorems will be presented and problems will be discussed, but examples will not be worked out, and some proofs and issues will be merely indicated.

We shall consider here restrictions which take the form

$$\phi^i(A_{11}, \ldots, A_{1N}) = 0 \qquad (i = 1, \ldots, K) \qquad (5.7.6)$$

where the function $\phi^i(A_{11}, \ldots, A_{1N})$ will be written as $\phi^i(A_1)$ for brevity. We shall assume that all such functions possess continuous first partial derivatives. We deal principally with the case in which each $\phi^i(A_1)$ is homogeneous of *some* degree in its arguments, although that degree need not be the same for all $\phi^i(A_1)$ and certainly need not be degree 1. The extension of our results to the inhomogeneous case is an easy one and will be indicated later.

5.8. Local versus Unique Identifiability

Up to this point we have considered an equation to be either identified or underidentified, sometimes dividing the identified case into the subcases of just identified and overidentified equations. This was a perfectly reasonable treatment, since the problems considered up to now all had the property that if an equation was not identified, then it could not be distinguished from a whole continuum of equations. More formally, if F is the matrix of a linear transformation, with first row f, identification of the first equation (Definition 1.9.1a) is the property that every admissible f be a scalar multiple of e_1, the M-component vector with a unit element in the first place and zeros everywhere else. In all problems considered up to this point,[1] if the first equation was *not* identified, then not only did the a priori restrictions not suffice to determine any admissible f uniquely up to a scalar multiplication, they allowed an infinite and nondenumerable number of admissible fs differing by other than normalization rules.

To put it another way, identification of the first equation may be thought of as the property that the equations expressing the prior and the observational restrictions on the first equation plus a normalization rule admit of only a unique solution in the elements of A_1. (Cf. the proof of Theorem 2.3.1 by way of Lemma 2.3.1.) In every problem so far considered, those equations had either a unique solution or else an infinite number of solutions forming a continuous variety in the space of the elements of A_1.

In the present case of nonlinear restrictions, however, some of the equations defining the prior and observational restrictions on the first equation are not linear in the elements of A_1. It is therefore possible that those equations while admitting of more than one solution may admit of only a finite number of solutions or while admitting of an infinite number of solutions may only admit of a countable infinity of solutions, each solution being locally isolated. In other words, even if we cannot tell the true A_1 from every other substitute, we may be able to tell it from other vectors which lie close to it.

---

[1] This even includes the problem considered earlier in this chapter if Eq. (5.3.10) is first obtained.

It is worthwhile distinguishing such cases, first, because the knowledge that A_1 is one of a finite set of alternatives is valuable; and second, because inequalities not expressed in Eq. (5.7.6) may in fact rule out all but one of a finite set of alternatives or even all but a few of a countable number of alternatives. That is, if each admissible A_1 (each first row of the matrix of an admissible structure) is locally isolated, notions as to plausibility of results may lead to substantial narrowing of the alternative possibilities—something which is not possible when the alternatives are continuous.

As in previous chapters, and as already indicated, the homogeneous case involves distinguishing the true A_1 only up to a normalization rule. If each $\phi(A_1)$ is homogeneous of some degree, then Eq. (5.7.6) remains satisfied if A_1 is multiplied by a scalar. Thus, in discussing that case, we do not wish to bother distinguishing admissible vectors (either A_1s or fs) which lie on the same ray through the origin. For this reason, we shall restrict our attention until further notice only to vectors of unit length and shall speak of these as "on the unit hypersphere." This is a convenient normalization for present purposes, even if it is less natural than those adopted in earlier chapters. It is to be understood that the fact that the same ray crosses the unit hypersphere twice is to be ignored, so that we shall speak of unique admissible vectors on the unit hypersphere without troubling to qualify this by "unique except for multiplication by -1."

With this understanding, we may now define:

Definition 5.8.1: In the homogeneous case, the first equation of the model is said to be *locally identifiable* under the a priori restrictions if and only if there is some neighborhood of the true A_1 (normalized to have unit length) which contains no other admissible A_1 on the unit hypersphere.

By Theorem 1.7.1, admissible structures and admissible linear transformations are in one-to-one correspondence. It is not hard to show[1] further that the following is an equivalent statement to Definition 5.8.1.

Definition 5.8.1a: In the homogeneous case, the first equation of the model is said to be *locally identifiable* under the a priori restrictions if and only if there is some neighborhood of e_1 which contains no admissible f other than e_1 on the unit hypersphere.

Of course, the unit hyperspheres in question are different in the two definitions. In the following definitions, we shall always assume that the true A_1 is normalized to have unit length and we shall state the definitions in terms of either A_1 or f simultaneously without restating each time.

[1] The correspondence is continuous and invertible.

Definition 5.8.2: In the homogeneous case, the first equation of the model is said to be *uniquely, multiply,* or *countably identifiable* under the a priori restrictions according as there are one, a finite number, or a countable number of admissible A_1s (admissible fs) on the unit hypersphere. (Recall that multiplication by -1 is not considered to introduce a new point.)

Definition 5.8.3: The first equation of the model is said to be *completely identifiable* if and only if it is either uniquely or multiply identifiable.

In the inhomogeneous case, the same definitions will apply, except that the phrase "on the unit hypersphere" should be stricken out.

5.9. Local Identifiability

In this section, we shall consider conditions for local identifiability of the first equation. It should come as no surprise that these conditions turn out essentially to be those of the case of linear restrictions derived using the linear approximation to Eq. (5.7.6) in the neighborhood of the true A_1.

Thus, consider the necessary condition for an M-component row vector f to be admissible. This is

$$\phi^i(fA) = 0 \qquad (i = 1, \ldots, K) \qquad (5.9.1)$$

(*Why is this only a necessary condition for the admissibility of f in the present case? Hint: What becomes of the argument of Sec. 2.3 as to the nonsingularity of F, given f? Does this affect the results below?*)

Let $\phi'(\alpha)$ denote the $N \times K$ Jacobian matrix of the ϕ^i with respect to the elements of A_1 evaluated at $A_1 = \alpha$, with rows corresponding to elements of A_1 and columns to different ones of the ϕ^i. Thus, the element in the rth row and cth column of $\phi'(\alpha)$ is the partial of ϕ^c with respect to A_{1r} evaluated at $A_1 = \alpha$.

Now, suppose that α is admissible so that

$$\alpha = fA \qquad (5.9.2)$$

for some f satisfying Eq. (5.9.1). Consider the $M \times K$ Jacobian matrix of the ϕ^i *with respect to the elements of f*, that is, the matrix whose rcth element is the partial of ϕ^c with respect to f_r. Evaluated at α, it is straightforward to show that this matrix is $A\phi'(\alpha)$.

Now, in the homogeneous case, the rank of $A\phi'(\alpha)$ cannot exceed $M - 1$ at an admissible α. To see this, observe that by Euler's theorem, each element of $fA\phi'(\alpha)$ is some multiple of the corresponding value of $\phi^i(\alpha)$. If α is admissible, these are all zero, whence f is in the row kernel of $A\phi'(\alpha)$.[1] This corresponds to the situation in the linear case

[1] If this is not seen at once, the reader should write out the matrices.

and to the fact that admissible fs (and A_1s) are determined only up to scalar multiplication in the homogeneous case. It is clear by the implicit function theorem, however, that requiring the Jacobian of the ϕ^i with respect to f to have rank $M - 1$ at an admissible f will ensure local uniqueness of that f except for such scalar multiplication (because the imposition of a normalization rule will make the Jacobian have full row rank).[1] We have thus obtained:

Theorem 5.9.1: (*Generalized Rank Condition*): A sufficient condition for the local identifiability of the first equation in the homogeneous case is

$$\rho\{A\phi'(A_1)\} = M - 1 \tag{5.9.3}$$

Unfortunately, the implicit function theorem does not provide a general necessary condition for local uniqueness. Thus, the equation

$$x^2 + y^2 = 0 \tag{5.9.4}$$

has but one solution in the real plane, despite the fact that the Jacobian is identically singular. The suspicion that there is something very special about such cases is justified by the results given in the appendix to this chapter which allow us to proceed to necessary conditions.

Definition 5.9.1: f^0 is called *a regular point of the functions* $\phi^i(fA)$ ($i = 1, \ldots, K$) if and only if for all f in some sufficiently small neighborhood of f^0,

$$\rho\{A\phi'(fA)\} = \rho\{A\phi'(f^0A)\} \tag{5.9.5}$$

In this case, we shall also refer to $\alpha^0 = f^0A$ as a regular point.

Thus, a regular point is one for which there is a small neighborhood in which the rank of $A\phi'(\alpha)$ does not change.[2] It is shown in the appendix that the set of irregular points is of measure zero if every element of $\phi'(A_1)$ is analytic. This will generally be the case in practice.[3]

---

[1] *Proof:* Add to the restrictions on f the requirement that f lie on the unit hypersphere. This adds to the Jacobian a column equal to $2f'$. At an admissible α, suppose $A\phi'(\alpha)$ has rank $M - 1$; then *only* scalar multiples of f lie in the row kernel thereof. But any nonzero scalar multiple of f is not orthogonal to $2f'$, so the addition of the new column means that there are now no independent vectors in the row kernel of the Jacobian which must then have rank M by Theorem 1.4.1.

[2] It might be thought that in the present homogeneous case, the definition should be restricted to neighborhoods on the unit hypersphere. That this is not the case may be seen by observing that if some vector h is in the row kernel of $A\phi'(\alpha)$ for an α on the unit hypersphere, then it is in that row kernel for all scalar multiples of that α. Hence, if there is a neighborhood of a point in which the rank of $A\phi'(\alpha)$ does not change for α on the unit hypersphere, then there is a neighborhood of that point in which the same property holds for all α.

[3] A function is analytic on an open set S if and only if it can be expanded in power series at every point of S.

Note also that if the determinant of a submatrix is nonzero at a point, it is nonzero in some sufficiently small neighborhood of that point. An irregular point is thus essentially one for which there is no neighborhood in which the rank of $A\phi'(\alpha)$ fails to increase. {Replacing $A\phi'(\alpha)$ in the definition by the Jacobian of the left-hand side of Eq. (5.9.4), observe that the origin is the only irregular point.}

The results in the appendix to this chapter enable us to state:

Theorem 5.9.2 (Generalized Rank Condition): If A_1 is a regular point, then a *necessary* (as well as sufficient) condition for the local identifiability of the first equation in the homogeneous case is

$$\rho\{A\phi'(A_1)\} = M - 1 \qquad (5.9.6)$$

An alternative way of putting the theorem is that it is necessary that there exist no neighborhood of A_1 in which the rank of $A\phi'(\alpha)$ is both constant and below $M - 1$ for all α in the row-space of A. (The fact that *constancy* of rank below $M - 1$ in such a neighborhood is involved was overlooked in Fisher [7].)

When the set of irregular points is of measure zero (as will generally be the case in practice), A_1 will almost always be regular unless the restrictions on it and on the other equations imply that it is irregular—a case most unlikely in practice. The generalized rank condition is therefore generally necessary almost everywhere in the parameter space and we may add:

Corollary 5.9.1 (Generalized Order Condition): If the elements of $\phi'(A_1)$ are analytic, then provided that A_1 is not known to be an irregular point, a necessary condition almost everywhere in the parameter space for the local identifiability of the first equation in the homogeneous case is

$$\rho\{\phi'(A_1)\} \geq M - 1 \qquad (5.9.7)$$

A fortiori it is necessary almost everywhere that there be at least $M - 1$ not identically dependent restrictions expressed in Eq. (5.7.6).

This completes our discussion of local identifiability in the homogeneous case. We now turn to the even less well-explored topic of complete identifiability.

5.10. Complete Identifiability

Most of this section involves using the fact that the Jacobian matrix of Eq. (5.9.1) with respect to the elements of f is $A\phi'(A_1)$ to restate certain uniqueness-of-solution theorems in the present context. Before doing so, however, we may proceed to use the local results of the preceding section to obtain an important result on complete—but not necessarily unique—identifiability.

Theorem 5.10.1: A necessary and sufficient condition for the complete identifiability of the first equation in the homogeneous case is that every admissible α on the unit hypersphere be locally isolated with respect to others on the unit hypersphere. In other words, it is necessary and sufficient that if the true A_1 happens to be any particular α, the first equation be locally identifiable.

In particular, a sufficient condition for complete identifiability is

$$\rho\{A\phi'(\alpha)\} \geq M - 1 \tag{5.10.1}$$

for all α, and a necessary condition is that this not fail for any regular admissible α.

Proof: The particular conditions given in the last paragraph of the theorem are immediate consequences of the local results of the preceding section and of the first paragraph of the theorem. It remains to be proved that it is necessary and sufficient for complete identifiability that every admissible α be locally isolated.

Since every admissible α is indistinguishable from the true A_1 on the basis of prior *or* posterior information (this is the definition of admissibility), if some admissible α on the unit hypersphere is not locally isolated, there is obviously an infinite set of admissible αs on the unit hypersphere. Local isolation of admissible αs is therefore necessary for complete identifiability.

On the other hand, suppose that every admissible α on the unit hypersphere is locally isolated. Since the unit hypersphere is compact, if there were an infinite sequence of admissible αs on the unit hypersphere, there would be a convergent subsequence thereof. By the continuity in α of the prior and posterior restrictions, however, the limit of such a subsequence of admissible αs is also admissible. Such an admissible α is thus not locally isolated, which is a contradiction.

> The existence of a limit point is the Bolzano-Weierstrass theorem. Readers unfamiliar with set theory can get the idea of the proof by observing that an infinite sequence of admissible αs can only occur if it goes off to infinity or else piles up on some limit point. The first possibility is ruled out by the fact that the unit hypersphere is bounded—i.e., by normalization rules—while the second would contradict the assumption that all admissible αs are locally isolated with respect to others on the unit hypersphere.

Unfortunately, the condition that Eq. (5.10.1) holds everywhere is not strong enough to guarantee unique identifiability. We now present two overly strong sufficient conditions for unique identifiability in the homogeneous case. As these are merely restatements in the present context of results on uniqueness of solution due to Nikaidô and Gale, the reader is referred to their papers for the principal proofs and for similar results for certain regions smaller than the entire hyperplane discussed here. (See Gale and Nikaidô [17].)

For this purpose it will be convenient to shift normalization rules and give up examination of the unit hypersphere in favor of the hyperplane corresponding to setting a particular element of A_1 equal to unity. Without loss of generality, we may take that element to be the first one. It is evident that provided that element is known to be nonzero, examination of admissible points on that hyperplane is equivalent to examination of the set of admissible rays through the origin. We shall call that hyperplane the "normalizing hyperplane." We shift to it rather than remaining concentrated on the unit hypersphere because it is now quite inconvenient that rays cross that hypersphere twice rather than once.

Definition 5.10.1: A matrix H is called weakly positive quasi-definite if and only if $|H| > 0$ and $\frac{1}{2}(H + H')$ is positive semidefinite.

The first of the Nikaidô-Gale results which we present is:

Theorem 5.10.2: A sufficient condition for the unique identifiability of the first equation in the homogeneous case is that there exist some square submatrix of $A\phi'(\alpha)$ of order $M - 1$ whose determinant is positive and each of whose principal minors is nonnegative for all α on the normalizing hyperplane. An alternative sufficient condition is that there exists such a square submatrix which is weakly positive quasi-definite for all such α.

Further, since if Eq. (5.9.1) has a unique solution in f after some of the equations are multiplied by -1 then the original version likewise has a unique solution, we may add:

Corollary 5.10.1: A sufficient condition for the unique identifiability of the first equation in the homogeneous case is that there exists some square submatrix of $A\phi'(\alpha)$ of order $M - 1$ such that after multiplication of some or all of its columns by -1, its determinant is positive and its principal minors are all nonnegative for all α on the normalizing hyperplane. In particular, it suffices that there exists a square submatrix of order $M - 1$ whose determinant is of sign $(-1)^{M-1}$ and each of whose rth order principal minors is either zero or of sign $(-1)^r$ $(r = 1, \ldots, M - 2)$ for all α on the normalizing hyperplane. Alternatively, it suffices that there exists such a submatrix which, after such multiplications, is weakly positive quasi-definite for all such α.

The last theorem in this section runs in terms of the "nested set" of principal minors of a square matrix rather than in terms of all the principal minors thereof. By the nested set of principal minors we mean the set consisting of principal minors formed by taking elements in the *first r* rows and columns ($r = 1, \ldots, M - 1$), that is, the set of principal minors in the upper left-hand corner of the matrix.

Theorem 5.10.3: A sufficient condition for the unique identifiability of the first equation in the homogeneous case is that there exists some square submatrix of $A\phi'(\alpha)$ such that the absolute value of every member of the nested set of principal minors of that submatrix is bounded away from both zero and infinity as α ranges over all points on the normalizing hyperplane.

This completes our discussion of the homogeneous case.

5.11. The Inhomogeneous Case

As in the case of linear restrictions, the extension of all the above results to the case in which some or all of the ϕ^i are inhomogeneous is readily accomplished. The main issues have been discussed in Chap. 2, and we shall not linger over them here. With one exception, all that there is to be said can be said by observing two things. The first of these is that the definitions of Sec. 5.8 must be altered in this case by removing references to the unit hypersphere, since we now do distinguish points on the same ray through the origin. Second, all previous theorems except Theorem 5.10.1 remain true if all references to normalization rules (the unit hypersphere or the normalizing hyperplane) are deleted and $M - 1$ replaced by M throughout.

Thus, for example, a sufficient condition for local identifiability is now that

$$\rho\{A\phi'(A_1)\} = M \qquad (5.11.1)$$

This is necessary if A_1 is a regular point; and so forth.

The exception to this is Theorem 5.10.1 where the introduction of a normalization rule allowed us to operate in a compact set (the unit hypersphere). That theorem must now be altered as follows:

Theorem 5.11.1: A necessary and sufficient condition for the *countable* identifiability of the first equation in the inhomogeneous case is that every admissible α be locally isolated. If that condition holds and if, in addition, the restrictions (5.7.6) or additional inequalities restrict A_1 to lie in a bounded set, then the first equation is completely identifiable.

Such restriction to a bounded set is of course quite likely in practice, particularly since inhomogeneous restrictions are frequently homogeneous ones with a normalization rule. (Restriction to a bounded rather than to a compact set is all that is necessary, because if A_1 lies in a bounded set it also lies in that set's closure, and local isolation is assumed to apply everywhere.)

While inequalities may be of use in this regard, they may also be treated as in Sec. 2.10. If the inequalities are nonlinear, this is less useful than in the linear case, since the derivatives of the parameters with respect to the distances of inequalities from zero (with respect to the elements of μ in Sec. 2.10) will not be constants and may change sign. We shall thus not pursue this matter further, although the interested reader may work out what is involved by combining the results of this chapter with the analysis of Sec. 2.10.

5.12. Concluding Remarks

Before leaving the subject of nonlinear restrictions, a word might be said concerning the use of the order condition to assure at least local identifiability almost everywhere in the parameter space. In the linear case, we saw that if the rank condition was not known to fail identically, then it held almost everywhere if the order condition did. This was essentially because the relevant determinant was a *linear* function of any unknown parameter.

In the present case, the relevant determinant {of a square submatrix of $A\phi'(A_1)$} is a linear function of each element of the last $M - 1$ rows of A but not of the elements of A_1. The difference that this makes is that it is now not enough to know that the rank condition does not fail identically and that there are at least $M - 1$ not identically dependent restrictions in Eq. (5.7.6) (in the homogeneous case). One must know that the order condition is satisfied *at* A_1 in order to make the analogous argument to that in the linear case and rely on Theorem 5.9.1.

Fortunately, this is overly restrictive. If one knows that the order condition is *itself* satisfied almost everywhere, i.e., that $\rho\{\phi'(\alpha)\} \geq M - 1$ for α everywhere except on a set of measure zero, then one knows that the order condition is satisfied at A_1 with probability 1, so to speak. Note that this can be known without knowing A_1. Indeed, from Theorem 5.A.2 of the appendix, such a property is guaranteed if the elements of $\phi'(\alpha)$ are analytic as will generally be the case in practice. In this case, if the rank condition does not fail identically, one can still assert that the first equation is at least *locally* identifiable everywhere in the parameter space except on a set of measure zero.

A local result is all that seems available through this line of reasoning, however. In particular, the complete identifiability result of Theorem 5.10.1 cannot be claimed to hold almost everywhere on this line of reasoning. (*Why not?*)

This concludes our discussion of the case of nonlinear restrictions on the elements of A_1. It is apparent that this case, and a fortiori the general nonlinear case, is not nearly so well explored as the cases treated in earlier chapters and in the first six sections of the present chapter. In large measure, this reflects the state of the mathematical art as regards uniqueness theorems for the solution of equations. Clearly, much remains to be done.

References

The model of the first part of the chapter is that of Fisher [9] and the discussion is based on Fisher [12]. The second part of the chapter draws on Fisher [7].

A Necessity Theorem for the Local Uniqueness of Solutions to Certain Equations

In this appendix we shall provide the justification for Theorem 5.9.2 by proving a necessity result on the local uniqueness of solutions to equation systems in which the functions involved have continuous first partial derivatives. We shall also show that if these derivatives are analytic, the set of points at which the necessity result does not hold is of measure zero. The notation used is different from that in the rest of the book and is confined to this appendix. (The principal necessity result is a mild generalization of that given in Franklin [16, pp. 344–347]. I am indebted to William T. Martin for this reference.)

Let x be an n-component row vector of variables. Consider the equations

$$F^i(x) = 0 \qquad (i = 1, \ldots, m) \qquad (5.A.1)$$

where each of the F^i has continuous first partial derivatives. Denote the Jacobian matrix of the F^i with respect to the elements of x by $J(x)$, where the rows correspond to the F^i and the columns to the elements of x.

Definition 5.A.1: A point x^0 is said to be *a regular point of the functions* $F^i(x)$ $(i = 1, \ldots, m)$ if and only if for all x in some sufficiently small neighborhood of x^0,

$$\rho\{J(x)\} = \rho\{J(x^0)\} \qquad (5.A.2)$$

We shall show below that the set of irregular points is of measure zero if the elements of $J(x)$ are analytic.

We prove:

Theorem 5.A.1: Let x^0 be a solution to Eq. (5.A.1). If x^0 is a regular point, a necessary (as well as sufficient) condition that x^0 be a locally isolated solution is that

$$\rho\{J(x^0)\} = n \qquad (5.A.3)$$

Proof: That Eq. (5.A.3) is sufficient whether or not x^0 is a regular point is the classic implicit function theorem, so that only its necessity if x^0 is regular here concerns us.

Suppose, therefore, that Eq. (5.A.3) fails, so that $J(x^0)$, which has n columns, has rank below n. If $\rho\{J(x^0)\} = 0$, then, since x^0 is a regular point, every element of $J(x)$ is zero everywhere in some neighborhood of x^0. Thus, the derivative of every F^i with respect to every element of x

163

is zero everywhere in that neighborhood, and it is then trivial that x^0 cannot be a locally isolated solution.

We may therefore consider the case in which $J(x^0)$ has rank r, where $0 < r < n$. $J(x^0)$ certainly has a nonsingular $r \times r$ submatrix. Without loss of generality, we may take that submatrix to lie in the first r rows and columns of $J(x^0)$. Since determinants are continuous functions of their elements, there is some neighborhood of x^0 in which that submatrix is never singular.

Now, denoting the elements of x by $x_1, \ldots, x_n$, the Jacobian of $F^1(x), \ldots, F^r(x)$ with respect to $x_1, \ldots, x_r$, evaluated at x^0, is the submatrix just described. The first r equations of (5.A.1) therefore define $x_1, \ldots, x_r$ as continuously once differentiable functions of $x_{r+1}, \ldots, x_n$ in some neighborhood of x^0. Let S be the hypersurface defined by those functions and note that x^0 is on S.

We now restrict our attention to a neighborhood of x^0 sufficiently small that for all x in that neighborhood: (1) $\rho\{J(x)\} = r$; (2) the leading $r \times r$ principal submatrix of $J(x)$ is nonsingular; and (3) $x_1, \ldots, x_r$ are the unique functions of $x_{r+1}, \ldots, x_n$ defined by the first r equations of Eq. (5.A.1). We shall show that none of the functions $F^i(x)$ change value on the hypersurface S in that neighborhood.

To see this, denote the ith row of $J(x)$ by $J(x)_i$ $(i = 1, \ldots, m)$. For $j = r + 1, \ldots, n$, denote by ξ^j the n-component column vector whose first r components are $\partial x_1/\partial x_j, \ldots, \partial x_r/\partial x_j$ {defined by the solution of the first r equations of Eq. (5.A.1)} and whose remaining components are zero—except for the jth component, which is unity. Differentiate $F^i(x)$ $(i = 1, \ldots, m)$ totally with respect to x_j $(j = r + 1, \ldots, n)$, letting $x_1, \ldots, x_r$ move along S. Then

$$\frac{dF^i(x)}{dx_j} = J(x)_i \xi^j \qquad (i = 1, \ldots, m; j = r + 1, \ldots, n) \quad (5.A.4)$$

By construction, however,

$$J(x)_i \xi^j = 0 \qquad (i = 1, \ldots, r; j = r + 1, \ldots, n) \quad (5.A.5)$$

and it remains to show that this holds for equations $r + 1, \ldots, m$ as well (if there are any such equations).

To see this, let

$$C(x)^i \equiv \begin{bmatrix} J(x)_1 \\ \cdot \\ \cdot \\ \cdot \\ J(x)_r \\ J(x)_i \end{bmatrix} \qquad (i = r + 1, \ldots, m) \quad (5.A.6)$$

and consider the equations

$$C(x)^i \xi^j = \begin{bmatrix} 0 \\ \cdot \\ \cdot \\ \cdot \\ 0 \\ k_{ij} \end{bmatrix} \qquad (i = r + 1, \ldots, m; j = r + 1, \ldots, n) \qquad (5.\text{A}.7)$$

We need only show that $k_{ij} = 0$ for all such i and j.

Since x is in a neighborhood (which exists by the regularity of x^0) in which $\rho\{J(x)\} = r$ and the leading $r \times r$ principal submatrix of $J(x)$ is nonsingular, the first r rows of $C(x)^i$ are independent and the last row is either zero or else can be written as a linear combination of those rows $(i = r + 1, \ldots, m)$. It is then immediate from Eq. (5.A.7) that k_{ij} can only be zero for all relevant i and j, and the theorem is proved.

The necessity part of the theorem may be restated as:

Theorem 5.A.1a: Let x^0 be a solution to Eq. (5.A.1). A necessary condition that x^0 be a locally isolated solution is that there exists no neighborhood of x^0 in which the rank of $J(x)$ is constant and below n.

We turn now to the question of the measure of the set of irregular points.[1] At any such point, some minor of the Jacobian vanishes which fails to vanish identically in any neighborhood of the point. Since such minors are continuous functions of their elements and since those elements are continuous functions of the elements of x, every such minor is a continuous function of the elements of x. This is not enough, however, to ensure that the set of irregular points is of measure zero, since it is possible for a continuous function to have no neighborhood in which it is identically zero and yet to have its zeros a set of positive measure.

Consider the following construction which essentially uses the Cantor perfect set. Take the unit interval and remove from it an interval of width ϵ, with $0 < \epsilon < \frac{1}{2}$, whose midpoint is the midpoint of the unit interval. Define a continuous function which is zero at the endpoints of the subinterval and nonzero in the interior. Now consider the two remaining parts of the unit interval. From each of them similarly remove a centered subinterval of width $\epsilon^2/2$ and make the function zero at the endpoints of the intervals removed and zero in the interiors. There now remain four unused pieces of the unit interval. From each of these remove a centered interval of width $\epsilon^3/4$, and so forth. Passing to the limit, the total length of the intervals in which the function is nonzero is $\epsilon + \epsilon^2 + \epsilon^3 + \ldots = \epsilon/(1 - \epsilon) < 1$, so that the zero points form a set of positive measure.

[1] I am indebted to William Nordhaus for suggesting that the set need not be of measure zero if the functions F^i are only restricted to be continuously once differentiable and to Harold Freeman, John Pratt, Karl Shell, Robert Solow, and Hirofumi Uzawa for helpful discussion of the issues involved.

It does suffice, however, to require the elements of $J(x)$ to be analytic, for then any such minor is an analytic function of x. That the set of irregular points is of measure zero in such a case follows immediately from the next theorem.

Theorem 5.A.2: Let $F(x_1, \ldots, x_n)$ be an analytic function of n real variables which is not identically zero. The zeros of F (the points at which $F = 0$) are then a set of measure zero in the space of $x_1, \ldots, x_n$.

Proof: For $n = 1$, the result is well known, and in this case, the zeros are even known to be denumerable. (See, for example, Apostol [4, pp. 518 and 519]. It is obvious that denumerability does not hold in general for $n > 1$.) We shall thus prove the theorem by induction on n and may assume it true for analytic functions of $n - 1$ variables.

Now, the zeros of F may be partitioned into two sets. The first of these consists of the zeros occurring at values of $x_1, \ldots, x_{n-1}$ for which F is identically zero in x_n, that is, the zeros occurring on lines parallel to the x_n axis along which F is always zero. This set will be denoted by S_1. The second set, denoted by S_2, consists of the remaining zeros. We shall show that each of these sets is of measure zero.

Since F is not identically zero, there exists a point, say $x_1^0, \ldots, x_n^0$, at which

$$F(x_1^0, \ldots, x_n^0) \neq 0 \qquad (5.A.8)$$

Define

$$G(x_1, \ldots, x_{n-1}) \equiv F(x_1, \ldots, x_{n-1}, x_n^0) \qquad (5.A.9)$$

Then G is an analytic function of $n - 1$ variables which is not identically zero. By the induction hypothesis, therefore, the zeros of G are a set of measure zero in the space of $x_1, \ldots, x_{n-1}$. Clearly, however, any value of $x_1, \ldots, x_{n-1}$ at which there are points of S_1 is a zero of G. It is now obvious that S_1 is a set of measure zero in the space of $x_1, \ldots, x_n$.

Now consider zeros of F in S_2. Suppose that $x_1^1, \ldots, x_n^1$ is such a zero. Define

$$\phi(x_n) \equiv F(x_1^1, \ldots, x^1_{n-1}, x_n) \qquad (5.A.10)$$

ϕ is then an analytic function of one variable and is not identically zero. Its zeros are thus denumerable. Number the zeros of ϕ and denote the ith such zero by x_n^i (which of course depends on $x_1^1, \ldots, x^1_{n-1}$). Now define

$$H^i(x_1, \ldots, x_{n-1}) \equiv \begin{cases} x_n^i \text{ where defined} \\ 0 \text{ elsewhere} \end{cases} \qquad (i = 1, \ldots, \text{ad inf.})$$

$$(5.A.11)$$

Consider the set of points defined by

$$x_n = H^i(x_1, \ldots, x_{n-1}) \qquad (5.A.12)$$

for a particular i. This is clearly a set of measure zero, and since the H^i are denumerable, the union of such sets is also of measure zero. Since every zero of F in S_2 is a member of one such set, the theorem is proved.

By the remarks preceding the theorem:

Corollary 5.A.1: If the elements of $J(x)$ are analytic, the set of irregular points is of measure zero.

Since the set of irregular points is of measure zero if the elements of $J(x)$ are analytic, Theorem 5.A.1 shows in what sense examples such as

$$x_1{}^2 + x_2{}^2 = 0 \qquad (5.A.13)$$

are special. Here, the origin is the only real solution, despite the fact that the Jacobian is never of rank greater than 1. However, the origin is also the only irregular point, since the Jacobian is of rank zero there and of rank 1 everywhere else. {The example $x_1 x_2 = 0$ illustrates the fact that local uniqueness *can* fail at an irregular point (the origin). The example $x_1{}^2 x_2{}^2 = 0$ illustrates a case of a nondenumerable number of irregular points which are still a set of measure zero.}

Indeed, Theorem 5.A.1 and Corollary 5.A.1 show in general that a counting rule for equations and variables is almost always necessary for uniqueness if the equations have analytic derivatives. Thus:

Corollary 5.A.2: Except for solutions at irregular points, a necessary condition for the local uniqueness of any solution to Eq. (5.A.1) is that there be at least n independent equations in Eq. (5.A.1).

Note that if the set of irregular points is of measure zero and if there is an irregular point which is a solution, there exists a small perturbation of the functions $F^i(x)$ which will move that solution to a regular point or else remove it completely. Thus, for example, in Eq. (5.A.13), replacing the zero on the right-hand side by any small positive number makes all solutions regular (and not locally unique), while replacing it by any small negative number eliminates all real solutions.

6

Other Topics

6.1. Introduction

In this final chapter, we shall consider a number of topics. For the most part, these concern problems less completely analyzed than those discussed in earlier chapters. We shall try to indicate in what ways present knowledge is incomplete. Because the topics discussed (other than the first and last) are, at least in the present state of knowledge, less important than those covered at length in earlier chapters, our treatment will be correspondingly limited.

6.2. Autocorrelated Disturbances

As far back as Assumption 1.5.3, we introduced the primary characteristic of predetermined variables—that they are uncorrelated with the disturbances in the probability limit. All our later analysis has relied on this. We pointed out when making that assumption, however, that if lagged endogenous variables were treated as predetermined, the assumption of no correlation really hid an assumption that the disturbance terms were not autocorrelated. To see this, observe that current endogenous variables are clearly influenced by current disturbances, so that lagged endogenous variables are influenced by lagged disturbances. If current and lagged disturbances are correlated, then so will be current disturbances and lagged endogenous variables, which cannot then be taken as predetermined for purposes of estimation.

This may be seen formally as follows. Suppose the system to be estimated is

$$By_t + Cy_{t-1} + Dz_t = u_t \qquad (6.2.1)$$

where B is an $M \times M$ nonsingular matrix; C is an $M \times M$ matrix; D is $M \times L$; y_t is an M-component column vector of current endogenous variables; u_t is an M-component column vector of current disturbances; and z_t is an L-component column vector of current truly exogenous variables (i.e., variables uncorrelated with past, present, or future values of the disturbances). We let $\Lambda = L + M$. There is no loss of generality in assuming only one lag in the endogenous variables, since, by redefinition of variables, any higher-order system of difference equations can be put in this form.

For example, if a variable x_{t-2} occurs, one can define x_{t-1} as a new variable $\tilde{x}_t$, add the equation $\tilde{x}_t = x_{t-1}$ to the system, and change x_{t-2} to $\tilde{x}_{t-1}$ wherever it appears. This does involve adding to the system equations with known coefficients and with zero disturbances, but this makes no difference to the discussion.

Solving for y_t in terms of y_{t-1}, z_t, and u_t, we obtain the reduced form equations

$$y_t = \Pi_1 y_{t-1} + \Pi_2 z_t + v_t \tag{6.2.2}$$

where $\qquad \Pi_1 = -B^{-1}C \qquad \Pi_2 = -B^{-1}D \qquad v_t = B^{-1}u_t \tag{6.2.3}$

For simplicity, we shall assume that this is a stable dynamic system,[1] so that, by repeated lagging of Eq. (6.2.2) and substitution, we obtain

$$y_t = \sum_{\theta=0}^{\infty} (\Pi_1)^\theta (\Pi_2 z_{t-\theta} + v_{t-\theta}) \tag{6.2.4}$$

Lagging this once,

$$y_{t-1} = \sum_{\theta=1}^{\infty} (\Pi_1)^{\theta-1} (\Pi_2 z_{t-\theta} + v_{t-\theta}) \tag{6.2.5}$$

As is obvious, y_{t-1} depends in general on all past exogenous variables and disturbances up through time $t - 1$ but does not depend directly on u_t.

Now, if u_t is not correlated with its own past values, this raises no difficulty for the treatment of y_{t-1} as predetermined. In this case, the covariance of the elements of y_{t-1} and u_t is a sum of terms each of which involves the covariance of u_t with either past exogenous variables or with past disturbances. All such terms are zero in the probability limit. On the other hand, if u_t is not known to be uncorrelated with its own past values, then the terms in the covariance of u_t with past v_t will not be zero, in general, and thus y_{t-1} cannot be treated as predetermined.

That this raises problems for the analysis of identification is evident in a general way from the fact that Assumption 1.5.3 has clearly played a

---

[1] The unstable case raises difficulties for proofs of the consistency of estimators even in the case of a single equation. We must also assume that the process-generating u_t is sufficiently stable to guarantee the consistency of the least squares estimation of Eqs. (6.2.5) and (6.2.15) below.

crucial role. If y_{t-1} cannot be taken as predetermined, then use of the information that predetermined variables and disturbances are uncorrelated can only yield L rather than Λ pieces of information. Theorem 1.6.1 thus fails, for posterior information may not now be able to distinguish the true first equation of Eq. (6.2.1) from any equation not a linear combination of the equations of Eq. (6.2.1).

In other words, the reduced form cannot now be consistently estimated by ordinary least squares for essentially the same sorts of reasons that lead to inconsistency if that estimator is applied to a structural equation. Yet the ability of observational information to yield the reduced form parameters was crucial in the proof of Theorem 1.6.1. Without some further condition ensuring that the reduced form can be consistently estimated by some other estimator, equations incapable of generating the true reduced form are observationally admissible. (Such a condition is given below.)

Another way of looking at the matter is to observe that the variables in y_{t-1} must now be considered endogenous. The situation is thus quite analogous to the case considered in the preceding chapter in which there were nonlinear functions of endogenous variables in the system without linear equations to explain them. The analysis of that chapter will not simply carry over to this case, however, for the equations in question are clearly the lagged version of Eq. (6.2.1), and these involve still further endogenous variables, the elements of y_{t-2}.

The sort of problem raised may be clearly seen from the following example[1] in which all symbols are scalars.

$$b_{11}y_{1t} + c_{11}y_{1t-1} + c_{12}y_{2t-1} = u_{1t} \qquad (6.2.6)$$
$$b_{21}y_{1t} + b_{22}y_{2t} = u_{2t}$$

If the y_{it-1} can be taken as predetermined, both equations are obviously identified by the rank condition. On the other hand, lagging the second equation, multiplying it by a scalar λ, and adding it to the first equation yields

$$b_{11}^{*}y_{1t} + c_{11}^{*}y_{1t-1} + c_{12}^{*}y_{2t-1} = u_{1t}^{*} \qquad (6.2.7)$$

where

$$b_{11}^{*} = b_{11} \qquad c_{11}^{*} = c_{11} + \lambda b_{21} \qquad c_{12}^{*} = c_{12} + \lambda b_{22} \qquad u_{1t}^{*} = u_{1t} + \lambda u_{2t-1}$$
$$(6.2.8)$$

If no assumption about the autocorrelation properties of the disturbances are made, then u_{1t}^{*} is indistinguishable from u_{1t} and Eq. (6.2.7) is indistinguishable from the first equation of Eq. (6.2.6), which is therefore not identifiable. On the other hand, if current disturbances are known to be

[1] The example and, indeed, the problem were stated in Koopmans, Rubin, and Leipnik [23, pp. 109 and 110].

uncorrelated with past disturbances, the true disturbances are uncorrelated with lagged endogenous variables, so that u_{1t}^*, being correlated with those variables, *can* be distinguished from u_{1t}, and the first equation is identifiable.

This example reveals the essential feature of the problem that once lack of autocorrelation is dropped, transformations of the equations involving shifts in time may become admissible so far as observational information is concerned.   The study of identifiability criteria when such transformations are admissible remains to be performed.   Clearly, it can usefully employ restrictions on the stochastic process generating the disturbances.   For example, if that process is known to be of the form

$$u_t = Ru_{t-1} + \epsilon_t \tag{6.2.9}$$

where R is an $M \times M$ constant matrix and ϵ_t is an M-component column vector of random disturbances which is known to be nonautocorrelated, this places certain restrictions on the transformations in time which are admissible.   (Cf. Hurwicz [19, pp. 337–339].)   More generally, it should be possible to state identification conditions which are necessary and sufficient to identify the first equation even when transformations in time cannot be ruled out in general.

We shall take a different approach here and establish a necessary and sufficient condition for the general inadmissibility of transformations in time, given that nothing is specified about the process generating the disturbances.   This is a useful result, for it means that if the condition in question is satisfied, Theorem 1.6.1 becomes valid again and all the analysis of the preceding chapters stands without amendment even without the assumption of nonautocorrelated disturbances.

The condition in question makes use of the fact that the example given above has a rather special feature, namely, the equation which is lagged contains no truly exogenous variables.   In more general cases, if one lags one of the equations of Eq. (6.2.1), that transformation will introduce lagged exogenous variables or higher-lagged endogenous variables not in the original system.   Unless such introduction can then be canceled by a further transformation, the result will then be observationally distinguishable from the true first equation.   The condition which we shall give is a necessary and sufficient one for ensuring that such cancelation cannot be performed.

Define

$$\hat{y}_{t-1} \equiv \sum_{\theta=1}^{\infty} (\Pi_1)^{\theta-1}\Pi_2 z_{t-\theta} \tag{6.2.10}$$

so that $\hat{y}_{t-1}$ is the "systematic part" of y_{t-1} from Eq. (6.2.5).   The condition which we shall discuss is:

Condition 6.2.1: The Λ elements of $\hat{y}_{t-1}$ and z_t are not connected by any linear identities.

This condition can be regarded as an extension of Assumption 1.5.2, that no linear identities connect the predetermined variables. It is not an innocuous assumption, however, for it involves not the lagged endogenous variables themselves but certain linear combinations of lagged *exogenous* variables which enter into them. It therefore, for example, rules out the possibility that the exogenous variables are themselves generated by a nonstochastic, linear, first-order difference equation. We shall further discuss Condition 6.2.1 below, after first bringing out its implications in the proof of the main theorem of this section. That theorem is:

Theorem 6.2.1: If nothing is known about the properties of the process generating the disturbances, then observational information can distinguish the true first equation of Eq. (6.2.1) from any equation not a linear combination of the equations of Eq. (6.2.1) if and only if Condition 6.2.1 holds.

In any case, observational information cannot distinguish the true first equation from equations which *are* linear combinations of the equations of Eq. (6.2.1).

Proof: The final sentence of the theorem is merely a reminder that the identification problem is not eliminated by Condition 6.2.1. It is the first statement which requires proof.

(a) Necessity. Suppose that Condition 6.2.1 fails. Then there exists a nonzero Λ-component row vector, say $\lambda = (\lambda_1 \quad \lambda_2)$, such that

$$\lambda_1 \hat{y}_{t-1} + \lambda_2 z_t = 0 \tag{6.2.11}$$

Note that this can*not* be derived by taking a linear combination of the equations of Eq. (6.2.1), since B is nonsingular. Now, define

$$v_t^* = \sum_{\theta=1}^{\infty} (\Pi_1)^{\theta-1} v_{t-\theta} \tag{6.2.12}$$

Then, Eqs. (6.2.5) and (6.2.11) imply

$$\lambda_1 y_{t-1} + \lambda_2 z_t = \lambda_1 \hat{y}_{t-1} + \lambda_2 z_t + \lambda_1 v_t^* = \lambda_1 v_t^* \tag{6.2.13}$$

Define $u_t^* \equiv \lambda_1 v_t^*$; then, since nothing is known about the process generating the true disturbances, u_t^* is indistinguishable from any true disturbance. It follows that the addition of any scalar multiple of

$$\lambda_1 y_{t-1} + \lambda_2 z_t = u_t^* \tag{6.2.14}$$

to the true first equation of Eq. (6.2.1) yields an equation observationally equivalent to that equation. However, as pointed out above, Eq.

(6.2.14) cannot be derived as a linear combination of the equations of Eq. (6.2.1), which establishes the necessity of Condition 6.2.1.

(*Why did we not state Condition 6.2.1 as requiring that $\hat{y}_{t-1}$ and z_t not be connected by a linear equation with a disturbance term uncorrelated with past and present exogenous variables?*)

(*b*) Sufficiency. The proof of the sufficiency of Condition 6.2.1 is rather more interesting and proceeds by establishing that Condition 6.2.1 permits the consistent estimation of the reduced form. The statement of the theorem will then follow immediately, since the ability to secure the reduced form from observational information is the point on which the proof of Theorem 1.6.1 turns. We show that Condition 6.2.1 suffices to ensure consistency of an instrumental variable or quasi-two-stage least-squares estimate of the reduced form.

Suppose, therefore, that Condition 6.2.1 holds. Then certainly the M elements of $\hat{y}_{t-1}$ are linearly independent. It is obvious that this cannot be the case unless among the elements of $z_{t-1}, z_{t-2}, \ldots$, there are at least M which are not identically linearly dependent. Express $\hat{y}_{t-1}$ in terms only of such linearly independent past exogenous variables and observe that this is an exact relationship. Now regress the elements of y_{t-1} on those variables. Since Eq. (6.2.5) certainly is estimated consistently by ordinary least squares, this yields an estimate of $\hat{y}_{t-1}$ which is consistent.

This is where the stability assumptions are needed. Note that if the regression in question is on an infinite number of variables, the stability assumptions guarantee that the coefficients of $z_{t-\theta}$ approach zero as θ goes to infinity, so that $\hat{y}_{t-1}$ can be approximated as closely as desired.

Rewriting Eq. (6.2.2),

$$y_t = \Pi_1\hat{y}_{t-1} + \Pi_2 z_t + (v_t + v_t^*) \qquad (6.2.15)$$

and, in the probability limit, the elements of $\hat{y}_{t-1}$ and of z_t are uncorrelated with those of $(v_t + v_t^*)$, so that the elements of Π_1 and Π_2 can be estimated consistently by ordinary least squares provided that the elements of $\hat{y}_{t-1}$ and of z_t are not connected by any linear identity. The provision that no such identity exists is Condition 6.2.1, and sufficiency is established by the remarks already given.

If the exogenous variables are not connected to their own past values by *any* nonstochastic linear difference equation, then one can proceed a bit differently by showing that in estimating Eq. (6.2.5), one obtains consistent estimates of $(\Pi_1)^{\theta-1}\Pi_2$ for $\theta = 1, \ldots$, ad inf., so that Π_2 is recovered as the first of these matrices. It is then easy to show that Condition 6.2.1

implies that the matrix $P = [\Pi_2 \mid \Pi_1\Pi_2 \mid \Pi_1{}^2\Pi_2 \mid \ldots]$ has a right inverse, so that Π_1 can be recovered from the fact that both P and $\Pi_1 P$ are known. The reader might take the trouble to write out the details.

Note, incidentally, that even the reduced form is not recoverable from observational information if Condition 6.2.1 fails to hold.

We must now discuss the ways in which Condition 6.2.1 can fail. The simplest of these occurs in the example of Eq. (6.2.6). If there are no truly exogenous variables in Eq. (6.2.1), then $\hat{y}_{t-1}$ is identically zero, and the condition fails. Alternatively, even if there are truly exogenous variables in Eq. (6.2.1), the condition fails if those exogenous variables are all perfectly correlated with their own immediately past values. (This is the case, for example, if the only exogenous variable is the constant one always equal to unity.) In this case, $\hat{y}_{t-1}$ is not zero, but every element of $\hat{y}_{t-1}$ can be written as a linear combination of elements of z_t.

More generally, Condition 6.2.1 fails if the exogenous variables are generated by a nonstochastic linear difference equation of so low an order that among the present and past values of the exogenous variables there are not Λ independent elements, that is, M in addition to the L elements of z_t. This is the case, for example, if the only nonconstant exogenous variables are the terms of a polynomial time trend of order r which includes all terms of orders $0, \ldots, r$ or if there is only a monomial time trend of low order.

On the other hand, if the system includes any truly exogenous variable which cannot be written as an exact linear function of its own past values, Condition 6.2.1 *can* hold, since there will be more than Λ independent elements of $z_t, z_{t-1}, \ldots$. (Note the analogy with the case of systems nonlinear in the variables discussed in the preceding chapter. In both cases, the presence of a truly exogenous variable is a considerable help.)

Unfortunately, Condition 6.2.1 requires more than this. It requires that the current exogenous variables and certain linear functions of past exogenous variables be linearly independent. This is a natural requirement which plays a role quite analogous to that of the difference between the rank and order conditions of previous chapters. Without such a requirement, the difficulties introduced by autocorrelated disturbances could always be trivially overcome by the introduction of exogenous variables with zero coefficients. That such a device accomplishes nothing is plain, since it adds to L and therefore to Λ by adding elements to z_t without adding any independent movements to the elements of $\hat{y}_{t-1}$. Thus, if Condition 6.2.1 failed before such introduction, it fails after it. Formally, this occurs because the columns added to Π_2 will all be zero. It is for this reason that Condition 6.2.1 must involve the parameters of the model. {Perhaps the strongest analogy is with Theorem 2.7.1. In both cases, the reduced form is required to be such that certain transformations cannot eliminate certain exogenous variables (present or past).}

Nevertheless, as in the case of the order condition, the necessary condition on independently moving present and past exogenous variables is worth stating separately. Not only can it be checked without knowledge of the unknown parameters, but also, as we shall see in a moment, it is almost always enough to check it and to be sure that Condition 6.2.1 does not fail identically. We thus state separately:

Corollary 6.2.1: A necessary but not a sufficient condition for the conclusions of Theorem 6.2.1 is that among the present and past truly exogenous variables there be at least Λ which are not connected by any linear identity.

If this is satisfied and if the prior restrictions on the matrices B, C, and D are not such as to make Condition 6.2.1 fail identically, that condition will hold everywhere in the space of the elements of those matrices except on a set of measure zero. This may be seen by observing that, writing Z_t as an $L \times T$ matrix each of whose T columns is an observation on the elements of z_t, Condition 6.2.1 states that the rank of the matrix

$$
Q \equiv \begin{bmatrix} \sum_{\theta=1}^{\infty} (\Pi_1)^{\theta-1}\Pi_2 Z_{t-\theta} \\ \hline Z_t \end{bmatrix} = \begin{bmatrix} 0 & \vdots & \Pi_2 & \vdots & \Pi_1\Pi_2 & \vdots & \Pi_1{}^2\Pi_2 & \vdots & \cdots \\ \hline I & \vdots & 0 & \vdots & 0 & \vdots & 0 & \vdots & \cdots \end{bmatrix} \begin{bmatrix} Z_t \\ Z_{t-1} \\ \cdot \\ \cdot \\ \cdot \end{bmatrix}
$$

(6.2.16)

shall be Λ. Since the determinant of a submatrix is a linear function of the elements in any row, this will be satisfied almost everywhere if it does not fail identically.

We have thus successfully dealt with the case in which the condition of Corollary 6.2.1 is satisfied and Condition 6.2.1 does not fail identically. This is probably the most common case in practice. Nevertheless, the analysis of identification in the case in which Condition 6.2.1 is known to fail is of considerable interest. It is as yet unperformed.

6.3. Restrictions Involving the Parameters of More than One Equation

Nearly all our discussion has centered on cases in which the a priori information relating to a particular equation was in the form of restrictions on its parameters only. This was not the case in Chap. 4, where the restrictions examined took the form of statements that the covariances of particular *pairs* of disturbances were zero; but it was the case wherever the prior information related to the elements of A_1. In practice, except for such covariance restrictions, restrictions which relate the parameters of one equation to those of one or more others are extremely rare. There is no reason in principle why such cases cannot occur, however, and it may be worthwhile devoting a very short discussion to them. (This discussion is based on that in Koopmans, Rubin, and Leipnik [23, pp. 93–106].)

For ease of discussion, we shall assume that every restriction either bears on the parameters of a single equation or relates the parameters of two equations. The case in which more than two equations are involved presents no great difficulty and no essential difference, since the known results are in any case extremely meager.

Indeed, except for the case of covariance restrictions, which we treated at length in Chap. 4, very little is known of identification in the cases under discussion. What is known consists of the application of rules for counting equations and variables; and such counting rules turn out to be of very little help.

Thus, without being overly formal, one proceeds by looking for subsets of equations with the following properties. First, assign to every equation in the subset all restrictions (including normalization rules) bearing on its parameters alone. Second, considering only restrictions which relate the parameters of two equations *both* in the subset, assign each such restriction to one of the equations on which it bears. If this can be done in such a way that every equation in the subset has at least M restrictions[1] assigned to it, then the restrictions are said to be adequate in number and variety with respect to the subset in question.

In other words, if the restrictions are adequate in number and variety with respect to some subset of equations, then considering only the restrictions which bear on equations in that subset and relate them to each other and ignoring all restrictions which involve an equation outside that subset, the following is true. First, there are at least as many restrictions as there are elements of linear combinations of all the structural equations to be fixed, that is, M times the number of equations in the subset. Second, every one of the linear combinations to be fixed has at least M restrictions bearing on it; i.e., the large number of restrictions bearing on the equations in the subset is not achieved because most of them bear on a few equations while too few of them bear on others.

Now, clearly, a subset of equations with this property is not necessarily unique. Indeed, the union of two such subsets is another such subset. One therefore wants to distinguish maximal such subsets. This is done by calling a subset of equations *completed* if and only if (1) it has the above

[1] Recall that normalization rules are being counted as restrictions.

property, and (2) it is not included in any larger subset which has that property.

Completed subsets may then be constructed as follows: Take any equation with M or more restrictions relating only to it. Add any other equation which has a total of at least M restrictions either relating only to it or to the given equation; and so forth. After this, go back and look at pairs of equations, triplets, and so forth.

The question naturally arises as to how many completed subsets there are. In fact, it is easy to prove:

Theorem 6.3.1: There is at most one completed subset of equations.

Proof: Suppose that there are two, say S_1 and S_2. Obviously one cannot be a proper subset of the other. Further, they cannot be disjoint, for then they would be proper subsets of their union, which would also have the property discussed and thus they would not be completed. There remains only the case in which they have a nonempty intersection, i.e., they each contain a particular third subset of equations, say S_3.

In this case, take the restrictions bearing on the equations in S_1 and assign them to give S_1 the appropriate property. Consider the set of equations in S_2 but not in S_3; call this S_4. Assign to each equation in S_4 the same restrictions which were assigned to it in deciding that S_2 had the appropriate property. Note that none of these restrictions have already been assigned, since they either relate to equations in S_4 alone or relate equations in S_4 to equations in S_3. Then the union of S_1 and S_2 has the appropriate property, so that neither of these two sets was completed.

This is a convenient result. It states that the equations can always be divided into two subsets (one of which may be empty). For one of these subsets, counting criteria are satisfied; for the other, they are not.

Unfortunately, counting criteria are not very useful. Thus, as numerous examples in preceding chapters make clear, an equation can easily be in a completed subset yet fail to be identifiable. For example, an equation on the parameters of which there are M independent linear restrictions (counting any normalization rule) is clearly a member of any completed subset. Yet all we know in such a case is that the order condition is satisfied. The rank condition may yet fail identically because of other restrictions on other equations (either in or out of the completed subset), in which case the equation in question is not identifiable.

Moreover, equations which are *not* in completed subsets can be identifiable. In the first place, an inequality of equations and unknowns does not guarantee even local nonuniqueness of solution. On the other hand,

Corollaries 5.A.1 and 5.A.2 make it clear in what sense local uniqueness in such cases is special. More important, there can be M restrictions involving the parameters of an equation so that the number of equations and the number of unknowns is the same and that equation can be identifiable even though it does not belong to a completed subset.

This can come about in the following way. Consider a block recursive system with two blocks. Thus, B, the matrix of coefficients of current endogenous variables, is block triangular, with the zeros above the diagonal, and Σ, the variance-covariance matrix of the disturbances, is block diagonal. Corollary 4.10.1 then assures us that any equation in either block is identifiable if and only if it is identifiable with respect to the other equations in its own block. Now suppose that there are K equations in the first block and $M - K$ in the second. There is no reason why an equation in the second block cannot be identified with respect to the other equations in its block by $M - K$ linear restrictions on its parameters alone. Suppose that these are the only restrictions on that equation, other than the restrictions implied by block recursiveness, namely, that the relevant row of Σ has K zero elements. There are then M restrictions involving the equation in question, and that equation is in fact identifiable. Yet K of those restrictions relate the parameters of that equation to those of equations of the first block. If there are no further restrictions on the equations of the first block, those equations and the one in question cannot belong to a completed subset. (*Why not?*)

Indeed, block recursive systems are only one example of this sort of thing. Others may readily be constructed from Theorems 4.7.1 to 4.7.5. All of these examples use the nonsingularity of B and Σ in crucial ways. Whether such nonsingularity can enter into still other examples to produce identifiability of equations not in a completed subset is an open question, but even the present examples make it clear that the usefulness of Theorem 6.3.1 is practically nil.

Thus, except for the case of covariance restrictions, worked out in some detail and presented in Chap. 4, the theory of the identifiability of a structural equation when restrictions relate the parameters of more than one equation to each other largely remains to be developed (although the discussion in the next section bears on this problem).

6.4. Identifiability of Individual Parameters

Up to now, we have been concerned with the identifiability of an equation as a whole. This is the most important concern in practice. Nevertheless, it must not be overlooked that one or more parameters of a given equation may be identifiable, even if the entire equation is not. In other words, every admissible substitute for the given equation may have the same value for a particular parameter. In this case, we shall speak of that parameter as identifiable.

A trivial example of this is easy to produce. Suppose that the restrictions on the first equation do not suffice to identify it, but suppose that one of these restrictions specifies a particular parameter to be zero. That parameter is then identifiable.

This example is trivial because no recourse to observation is necessary to decide the value of the identifiable parameter. It is trivial in the same sense as the statement that a sufficient condition for the identifiability of the first equation is that one knows all its parameters in advance.

There do exist less trivial examples, however. One such was given at the end of Sec. 2.6, where the restrictions on the reduced form implied by the restrictions on the first two equations of a three-equation model sufficed to yield the ratio of two parameters of the unidentifiable third equation in terms of the observable reduced form parameters.

The problem of nontrivial criteria for the identifiability of a single parameter is therefore of some interest. Unfortunately, it is not well explored and the only known result is essentially a general result on local uniqueness of the value of a particular variable in the solution of certain equations, which restatement in the present context does not seem immediately to add much to our understanding of the problem. So much as is known is the contribution of A. Wald in [34], which we shall restate here.

As stated, the nontrivial result involved is a local one, so that we must state what is meant by local identifiability of a given parameter. We shall speak of a parameter as locally identifiable if and only if every admissible structure in some neighborhood in parameter space of the true structure replaces the true value of that parameter by itself.

We may now proceed. It is evident from the discussion in Chap. 1 that the only things which can be obtained from observational information are the matrix of reduced form coefficients Π and the variance-covariance matrix of residuals from the reduced form equations, which we shall call Ω.† These matrices are related to the true structure by (in the usual notation)

$$\Pi + B^{-1}\Gamma = 0 \qquad \Omega - B^{-1}\Sigma B^{-1\prime} = 0 \qquad (6.4.1)$$

These equations are the only restrictions placed by observational information on any parameter of the structure. (*Show that this is implied by Theorem 1.6.1.*)

---

† Actually, the full joint distribution of those disturbances is observable, in principle. However, if the disturbances from the structural equations are jointly normally distributed with mean zero (the case usually assumed), Ω is a sufficient statistic. In the nonnormal case, the analysis below would proceed in a similar fashion using all relevant parameters of the two distributions.

Now, write the prior restrictions, including all normalization rules, as

$$\phi^i(A,\Sigma) = 0 \qquad (i = 1, \ldots ,K) \qquad (6.4.2)$$

Then an admissible structure is one which satisfies Eqs. (6.4.1) and (6.4.2). It is then trivial to observe that identifiability of a particular parameter is equivalent to the property that every solution of these equations has the same value of that parameter. A similar statement holds for local identifiability.

Assume that the functions in Eq. (6.4.2) are all continuously once differentiable. Write the elements of A and Σ out as a vector, and call that vector θ. Denote by $J(\theta)$ the Jacobian matrix of Eqs. (6.4.1) and (6.4.2) with respect to the elements of θ, so that the ijth element of $J(\theta)$ is the partial derivative of the ith function in Eqs. (6.4.1) and (6.4.2) with respect to the jth element of θ.

Denote the value of θ at the true A and Σ by $\bar{\theta}$. For convenience, we concentrate on the local identifiability of the first element of $\bar{\theta}$; this involves no loss of generality.

Consider the equation

$$\theta_1 - \bar{\theta}_1 = 0 \qquad (6.4.3)$$

Denote by $Q(\theta)$ the Jacobian matrix of Eqs. (6.4.1), (6.4.2), *and* (6.4.3) with respect to θ. Thus, $Q(\theta)$ is formed by adding to $J(\theta)$ a row consisting of a unit element in the first column and zero elements everywhere else.

The theorem which we shall prove gives a rigorous statement of the intuitive idea that $\bar{\theta}_1$ is locally identifiable if and only if adding Eq. (6.4.3) to Eqs. (6.4.1) and (6.4.2) adds no new information in some neighborhood of $\bar{\theta}$ and thus fails to raise the rank of $J(\theta)$ in that neighborhood.

Let $H(\theta)$ denote the submatrix of $J(\theta)$ formed by striking out the first column thereof.

Definition 6.4.1: A point θ^0 is called a *normal point* of Eqs. (6.4.1) and (6.4.2) if and only if for all θ in some sufficiently small neighborhood of θ^0, the rank of $J(\theta)$ is the same as that of $J(\theta^0)$ and also the rank of $H(\theta)$ is the same as that of $H(\theta^0)$.

A normal point is one which satisfies stronger conditions than do the regular points discussed in Chap. 5. θ^0 would be a regular point but not a normal point if it satisfied the condition on the rank of $J(\theta)$ but not that on the rank of $H(\theta)$. If the elements of $H(\theta)$ are analytic functions, the set of abnormal points is of measure 0. {*See Theorem 5.A.2. Prove that θ^0 is a normal point of Eqs. (6.4.1) and (6.4.2) if and only if it is a regular point of Eqs. (6.4.1) and (6.4.2) and also a regular point of Eqs. (6.4.1) to (6.4.3).*}

Of course, the fact that $H(\theta)$ rather than some other submatrix of $J(\theta)$ is involved in the definition simply reflects the fact that we are concentrating on the local identifiability of $\bar{\theta}_1$ rather than on that of some other parameter.

Theorem 6.4.1: If $\bar{\theta}$ is a normal point of Eqs. (6.4.1) and (6.4.2), then a necessary and sufficient condition for the local identifiability of $\bar{\theta}_1$ is

$$\rho\{Q(\bar{\theta})\} = \rho\{J(\bar{\theta})\} \qquad (6.4.4)$$

(Observe that $\rho\{Q(\theta)\} \geq \rho\{J(\theta)\}$ for all θ.)

Proof: (a) Sufficiency. Suppose that Eq. (6.4.4) holds and let the common rank of the two matrices at $\bar{\theta}$ be r. In view of the nature of the row added to $J(\theta)$ to form $Q(\theta)$, it is evident that the first column of $J(\theta)$ is not zero and cannot be written as a linear combination of the remaining columns. It follows that $H(\bar{\theta})$ has rank $r - 1$. Further, since $\bar{\theta}$ is a normal point, this is true for all θ sufficiently close to $\bar{\theta}$.

Now, $J(\bar{\theta})$ has an $r \times r$ nonsingular submatrix, in which some part of the first column must be included. Without loss of generality, we can renumber equations and elements of θ other than the first, so that it is the leading $r \times r$ principal submatrix of $J(\bar{\theta})$ which is nonsingular. This submatrix, however, is the Jacobian matrix of the first r equations of Eqs. (6.4.1) and (6.4.2) with respect to the first r elements of θ, evaluated at $\bar{\theta}$. By the implicit function theorem, therefore, those elements, including θ_1, are determined by the first r equations as unique and continuously once differentiable functions of the remaining elements of θ (if any) in some neighborhood of $\bar{\theta}$. If there are no remaining elements, $\bar{\theta}$ and a fortiori, $\bar{\theta}_1$ are locally identifiable, so we may as well assume that θ has $n > r$ elements.

Consider the hypersurface defined by the r functions just described and call that hypersurface S. $\bar{\theta}$ is on S, and in some sufficiently small neighborhood of $\bar{\theta}$, the first r equations of Eqs. (6.4.1) and (6.4.2) are satisfied at all points of S and at no other points. Further, by a proof precisely that given in the course of the proof of Theorem 5.A.1, the normality of $\bar{\theta}$ assures that the remaining equations will also be satisfied at all points of S sufficiently close to $\bar{\theta}$. Thus all admissible θ in some neighborhood of $\bar{\theta}$ lie on S.

It remains to be proved that all points of S sufficiently close to $\bar{\theta}$ have the same value of θ_1. To do this, differentiate the first r equations of Eqs. (6.4.1) and (6.4.2) (the equations defining S) totally with respect to θ_j for any $j = r + 1, \ldots, n$ and solve for $\partial\theta_1/\partial\theta_j$ evaluated at any θ in the relevant neighborhood. By Cramer's rule, the result is minus the ratio of two determinants. The denominator is the leading $r \times r$ principal minor of $J(\theta)$, which we know to be nonzero. The numerator is the same determinant with the first column replaced by the first r elements of the jth column of $J(\theta)$, that is, the determinant of some $r \times r$ submatrix of $H(\theta)$. We have already seen, however, that Eq. (6.4.4) and the normality of $\bar{\theta}$ imply that $H(\theta)$ has rank $r - 1$ in some sufficiently small neighborhood of $\bar{\theta}$. Thus all such numerators and all such derivatives must be identically zero in that neighborhood, which is equivalent to the desired result.

(b) Necessity. Suppose that Eq. (6.4.4) fails and again denote the rank of $J(\bar{\theta})$ by r. In this case, the first column of $J(\bar{\theta})$ is either zero or else can be written as a linear combination of the remaining columns, so that the rank of $H(\bar{\theta})$ is r.† It is therefore the case that r of the elements of θ *other than the first* are uniquely defined as continuously once differentiable functions of θ_1 and the remaining elements in some neighborhood of $\bar{\theta}$, by r of the equations in Eqs. (6.4.1) and (6.4.2).

We denote by S the hypersurface defined by those functions. By the argument of the proof of Theorem 5.A.1, the normality of $\bar{\theta}$ implies that all the Eqs. (6.4.1) and (6.4.2) remain satisfied for all points on S in some sufficiently small neighborhood of $\bar{\theta}$. In view of the way in which S was constructed, however, it is clear that starting at $\bar{\theta}$ as θ_1 moves from $\bar{\theta}_1$, a continuous movement on S is generated. Thus $\bar{\theta}_1$ cannot be locally identifiable and the theorem is proved.

The requirement that $\bar{\theta}$ be a normal point or even a regular point of Eqs. (6.4.1) and (6.4.2) is needed for the proof of sufficiency but not for the proof of necessity. For the latter purpose, all that is required is that the submatrix of $J(\theta)$ consisting of the first column and some set of $\rho\{H(\bar{\theta})\}$ independent columns not change rank in some sufficiently small neighborhood of $\bar{\theta}$, even if $J(\theta)$ can itself change rank in some other way.

Unfortunately, it is hard to see how Theorem 6.4.1 can be used to obtain further understanding of the problem. Further, the order of the matrices which must be examined is very large, since there is a column for each different element of A and Σ. This and the analysis of nonlocal results on the identifiability of individual parameters are important subjects for further work.

† Indeed, an equivalent statement of Eq. (6.4.4) is

$$\rho\{J(\bar{\theta})\} = \rho\{H(\bar{\theta})\} + 1 \qquad (6.4.4a)$$

which bypasses Eq. (6.4.3) entirely. Note the analogy with the condition of Theorem 3.2.1. There we were concerned with identifiability with respect to a particular equation, and the condition was that the rank of the relevant Jacobian decrease when the corresponding row is removed. Here we are concerned with the identifiability of a particular parameter, and the condition is that the rank of the relevant Jacobian decrease when the corresponding column is removed.

6.5. Stochastic Prior Restrictions and Bayesian Analysis

All the cases studied in this book have had one thing in common. They have all involved exact, known prior restrictions on the true structure. Even our discussion of inequalities in Sec. 2.10 and in Chap. 5 ran in terms of exact, known bounds on certain functions of the parameters. Yet such knowledge is likely to be only apparently exact. Do we *really* know that certain variables do not appear in a given equation, for example? Or do we not know merely that they appear with very small coefficients? Even more to the point: do we *really* know that the disturbances from two different equations are uncorrelated? Or do we not merely know that their correlation is not large? Yet we have generally ignored this and have treated approximate knowledge as though it were exact.

One approach to this problem is implicitly taken when exact restrictions are used in practice and has been implicitly taken in this book. This is to observe that the use of restrictions which are approximately valid leads to results which are approximately correct. Thus, for example, we saw explicitly in Chap. 3 that a restriction which stated that a particular disturbance variance was relatively small led to *near*-identification instead of the full identification that would have occurred if that disturbance had been known to be zero. Similarly, it is clear from the discussion in Chap. 2 that replacement of identifying exclusion restrictions by inequalities which specify the relevant coefficients to be absolutely small leads to near-identification if the bounds on the absolute values of the coefficients approach zero. Similar results are obviously true of all the restrictions which we have considered. This situation is reflected in the fact that estimators which are consistent under exact and correct restrictions are nearly so when those restrictions are known to be at most slightly in error.[1] Thus approximately correct restrictions lead to results with only negligible error.

On the other hand, while this argument is a perfectly valid defense of the practice of treating approximate restrictions as if they were exact, it is possible that insight is to be gained by an explicit treatment of approximate knowledge as approximate. If nothing else, such treatment leads to a correct statement of the reliability of the results of estimation—a statement which takes account of variability in the prior restrictions as well as sampling fluctuations.

Such a treatment is in principle afforded by a Bayesian analysis of

---

[1] The estimators are nearly consistent in the sense that the distances between the relevant probability limits and the true parameters are close to zero. See Fisher [8].

simultaneous equation estimation. That analysis is as yet in its infancy.[1] Ideally, it would proceed in the following manner.

Instead of expressing prior restrictions as exact statements, express them in the form of a prior *distribution* on the elements of A and Σ. Bayesian estimation of the structure then combines this prior distribution with sample data from which Π and Ω (the latter being the variance-covariance matrix of the reduced-form disturbances) can be estimated to derive a posterior, unconditional distribution on A and Σ.

What of identification in this context? The problem in this context reappears in a natural way, for Drèze [6] has shown that the sample information, however large the sample, can only affect the posterior distribution of A and Σ by affecting that of Π and Ω (which, as we have seen, are the only things which can be obtained from observational information). The *conditional* distribution of A and Σ, given Π and Ω, is unaffected by observational information and depends only on the prior distribution of A and Σ. Thus, as with exact restrictions, observational information can at most affect estimates of the structure by affecting estimates of the reduced form.

This much is not different from the exact restriction case. The way in which a stochastic restriction approach is different is that concentration on exact identifiability loses its significance. If only stochastic restrictions are employed, only stochastic results will be obtained; and instead of either one or many structures which satisfy the restrictions, there will be many structures which are more or less likely, given the prior distribution of the parameters.

On the other hand, the identifiability or lack thereof of a set of parameters (for convenience, we may think of identification of a particular equation) does have a parallel in the Bayesian case. In that case, one is clearly interested in whether the posterior distribution of the relevant parameters has a unique mode—whether there is one set of parameter values that is most likely after all prior and observational information have been combined. It seems evident that this will be the case if and only if with the variance of the prior distribution reduced to zero (the restrictions made exact), the set of parameters in question would be uniquely identifiable. A similar statement can be made about multiple or local identifiability.

Thus, discussion of identifiability using exact restrictions is relevant even if restrictions are not, in fact, exact. The Bayesian approach to simultaneous equation estimation, however, does promise to lead to new estimation methods and does integrate identification and estimation in a way somewhat different from that of older approaches.

[1] Papers in this area include Drèze [6], Rothenberg [29], and Ando and Kaufman [3]. The paper by Drèze is the only one that discusses identification in the Bayesian context. The following discussion follows it in outline.

6.6. Tests of Prior Restrictions

The preceding section discussed some consequences of the fact that prior restrictions used to identify may not be exact. We saw that the consequences were not great if the restrictions were approximately right. If, however, the restrictions are not even approximately correct, the consequences are more serious. It is therefore desirable to have tests of them. In addition, it is desirable to be able to test the identification of a single equation, since, for example, the rank condition may fail for reasons overlooked by the investigator, even if the order condition holds. This and the next section discuss such tests for the case of exclusion restrictions. This is the only case for which results are available; we saw in Chap. 2, however, that all linear restrictions on the elements of A_1 could be put in this form by a simple transformation.

It is to be hoped, however, that the announcement of the subject of tests of identifying restrictions has already left the reader with an uneasy feeling. If such restrictions can be *tested*, the data can tell us something about their validity. Yet, we already know that the data can at most yield information on the reduced form and that the transformation from the reduced form to the structure *cannot* be tested by the data. To put it another way, if the data can be used to test identifying restrictions, the data can be used to *find* such restrictions. Where then is the identification problem? Where is Theorem 1.6.1?

Of course, such objections are well taken. The data yield no information about the validity of a restriction if identification depends on that restriction. On the other hand, the data clearly can yield information about the validity of a restriction which *over*identifies or which adds nothing to identification, since the equation to be estimated can be consistently estimated without it. To put it another way, such cases imply the existence of restrictions on the reduced form.[1] By seeing if the reduced form obeys such restrictions (i.e., by testing whether violation of such restrictions can be due to sampling error), the restrictions on the structure can be tested. The test of identifying restrictions discussed here might therefore better be called a test of overidentifying or extra restrictions, for we shall see explicitly that it yields no information in the just identified or underidentified case. In the overidentified case, it has the merit (or the defect) of being a test which treats all restrictions symmetrically, as opposed to being a test which might proceed by estimating the equation in question without using a particular restriction and testing whether violation of the unused restriction was due to chance.

[1] See Sec. 2.6. In the case in which such restrictions are implied without overidentification, Theorem 2.6.1 assures us that as many prior restrictions on the structure as there are restrictions on the reduced form may be dropped without affecting the distance from identification. It is natural that this should lead to just so many testable propositions.

Because of such symmetric treatment, the test is a convenient one to use, and this convenience is enhanced by the fact that the statistic involved is the same one which is computed in the test of identification which we shall also discuss.

Such symmetric treatment may be a defect if some restrictions are believed to be more firmly based than others. If the firmly based restrictions are sufficient to identify the equation in question, a better test may be to estimate that equation using only those restrictions and test the result to see if the unused restrictions are satisfied. At present, such a test can only be performed asymptotically since the relevant small sample distributions are not known in general. (A similar statement is true of the test under discussion.)

Before proceeding to the tests, it will be convenient to digress and prove a theorem about quadratic forms which generalizes the theorem that the smallest characteristic root of the matrix of a quadratic form is the smallest value taken on by the form over all vectors of unit length.

Suppose that P and Q are each real symmetric $n \times n$ matrices and that Q is positive definite. Consider the determinantal equation

$$|P - \lambda Q| = 0 \qquad (6.6.1)$$

where λ is a scalar. This is a generalization of the characteristic equation of P. It is known as the characteristic equation of the regular pencil of quadratic forms (P,Q).† Let λ_{min} denote the algebraically smallest root of Eq. (6.6.1). The theorem of interest for our purposes is:

Theorem 6.6.1: Let x be any n-component column vector. Then

$$\lambda_{min} = \min_{x \neq 0} \left(\frac{x'Px}{x'Qx} \right) \qquad (6.6.2)$$

This is a generalization of the property already used in Sec. 3.4 that the smallest latent root of the matrix of a quadratic form is also the smallest value taken on by that form over all vectors of unit length.

Proof: Since the right-hand side of Eq. (6.6.2) is homogeneous of degree zero in the elements of x, we may as well proceed by imposing

$$x'Qx = 1 \qquad (6.6.3)$$

and minimizing $x'Px$ subject to this constraint.

To do this, form the Lagrangian function

$$V = x'Px - \lambda(x'Qx - 1) \qquad (6.6.4)$$

† See Gantmacher [18, vol. I, pp. 310–326] for a discussion of pencils and their properties and for the generalization of the theorem about to be given.

The first-order conditions for a minimum then yield {in addition to Eq. (6.6.3)}

$$(P - \lambda Q)x = 0 \qquad (6.6.5)$$

which have a solution in x if and only if $(P - \lambda Q)$ is singular, i.e., if and only if the Lagrange multiplier λ is a root of Eq. (6.6.2).

Now, suppose that x satisfies Eqs. (6.6.3) and (6.6.5). Premultiply Eq. (6.6.5) by x' and rearrange the result to obtain

$$x'Px = \lambda(x'Qx) = \lambda \qquad (6.6.6)$$

so that, at any x satisfying the first-order conditions, λ is the value of the minimand. Since, as shown, λ is also a root of Eq. (6.6.1), the smallest value of the minimand must be the smallest root of Eq. (6.6.1), or $\lambda_{\min}$, and the theorem is proved. (An alternative proof proceeds by simultaneous diagonalization of P and Q. See below, p. 193.)

An immediate consequence of this is:

Corollary 6.6.1: $\lambda_{\min} > 1$ if and only if $(P - Q)$ is positive definite. $\lambda_{\min} = 1$ if and only if $(P - Q)$ is positive semidefinite.

Proof: If $(P - Q)$ is positive definite, then $x'Px > x'Qx$ for all nonzero x. If $(P - Q)$ is positive semidefinite, then $x'Px \geq x'Qx$, with $x'Px = x'Qx$ for at least one nonzero x. Since Q is positive definite, $x'Qx > 0$, and division of the inequalities just established by $x'Qx$ yields the desired result as an easy consequence of Theorem 6.6.1.

In the context in which we shall use Corollary 6.6.1, $x'Px$ and $x'Qx$ can be interpreted as the variances of the same linear combination of two different sets of residuals from regression equations, where the same and possibly more right-hand variables have been used in obtaining the second set of residuals as in obtaining the first. It is therefore natural in that context that the first variance should not be less than the second, no matter what linear combination is taken; and, by Corollary 6.6.1, this corresponds to the positive semidefiniteness of the difference of the variance-covariance matrices of the two sets of residuals. The context will be clear in a moment.

We shall now return to the identification problem. Suppose that the restrictions on the first equation of the model are all exclusion restrictions and that, after such restrictions have been used and a normalization rule employed, the equation in question is

$$q - \beta y_1 - \gamma z_1 = u_1 \qquad (6.6.7)$$

where q is an endogenous variable whose coefficient has been normalized;[1]

---

[1] Normalization is employed here for the convenience of using a notation already employed in Sec. 2.7. The discussion could just as well proceed without it.

y_1 is an m-component column vector of other endogenous variables appearing in the equation; z is an l-component column vector of exogenous variables appearing in the equation; β and γ are row vectors of unknown parameters to be estimated; and u_1 is the disturbance in the given equation. As we have generally, we will denote the total number of endogenous variables in the model by M and the total number of exogenous variables in the model by Λ.

Now, regress q and each of the elements of y_1 on the elements of z_1, using ordinary least squares. Let W_1' denote the $(m + 1) \times T$ matrix, whose first row consists of T values of the residual from the regression of q on the elements of z_1 and whose remaining rows are similarly T values of the residuals from the regressions of the elements of y_1 on the elements of z_1. Letting P be the sample variance-covariance matrix of such residuals, then

$$P = \frac{1}{T} W_1'W_1 \qquad (6.6.8)$$

Similarly, regress q and each of the elements of y_1 on *all* the Λ exogenous variables in the model, both those included in z_1 and those (if any) not so included. Let W' denote the $(m + 1) \times T$ matrix whose first row consists of T values of the residual from the regression of q on all the exogenous variables and whose remaining rows consist of T values of the residuals from the regressions of the elements of y_1 on those variables. Letting Q be the sample variance-covariance matrix of such residuals, then

$$Q = \frac{1}{T} W'W \qquad (6.6.9)$$

Now, let H' denote the $(m + 1) \times T$ matrix whose first row consists of the T sample values of q and whose remaining rows consist of the T sample values of the elements of y_1. Note that by the definitions, $H - W_1$ has for columns sample values of the $(m + 1)$ linear combinations of the elements of z_1 obtained in the first set of regressions. Similarly, $H - W$ has for columns sample values of the $(m + 1)$ linear combinations of the elements of z—the vector of all the exogenous variables in the model. Since least squares has the property that the sample residuals are uncorrelated *in the sample* with the variables used as regressors,

$$W_1'(H - W_1) = 0 \qquad W'(H - W) = 0 \qquad (6.6.10)$$

Further, since the elements of z_1 are included in the elements of z, the sample residuals from the *second* set of regressions are uncorrelated with the elements of z_1 in the sample, whence

$$W'(H - W_1) = 0 \qquad (6.6.11)$$

as well. It follows that

$$W'W = W'H = W'W_1 \qquad (6.6.12)$$

and, since $W'W$ is symmetric,

$$W'W = W_1'W \qquad (6.6.13)$$

Thus

$$\frac{1}{T}(W_1 - W)'(W_1 - W) = \frac{1}{T}(W_1'W_1 - W'W_1 - W_1'W + W'W)$$

$$= \frac{1}{T}(W_1'W_1 - W'W) = P - Q \qquad (6.6.14)$$

Thus, $(P - Q)$ is at least positive semidefinite and is positive definite unless $(W_1' - W')$ has dependent rows. By Corollary 6.6.1, an equivalent statement is that λ_{min}, the smallest root of

$$|P - \lambda Q| = 0 \qquad (6.6.15)$$

is at least 1 and is greater than 1 unless $(W_1' - W')$ has dependent rows.

Will such rows be dependent? If Eq. (6.6.7) is a valid equation, that is, if the exclusion restrictions used in obtaining it are valid, the answer is *asymptotically* in the affirmative. This may be seen as follows:

If Eq. (6.6.7) is valid, the residual for any observation from the regression of q on any set of variables will be the sum of the residuals from the regressions of the elements of y_1 on the same set of variables, premultiplied by β, plus the residuals from the regressions of the elements of z_1 on the same set of variables, premultiplied by γ, plus the residual from the regression of u_1 on that same set of variables. Since the regression of any variable on itself (and any additional variables) gives a perfect fit, the residuals from the regressions of the elements of z_1 on those same elements or on the elements of z are all zero, so the corresponding term in the sum just described is zero for the regressions performed in obtaining W_1 and W. Further, since the elements of z (and of z_1) are exogenous, u_1 is uncorrelated with those elements in the probability limit. Thus, as the sample size grows, the residual from the regression of u_1 on z_1 or on z approaches u_1 itself.

It follows that the first row of W_1' equals the remaining rows, premultiplied by β, plus a vector the elements of which approach the true values of u_1 as the sample size goes to infinity. Similarly, the first row of W' equals the remaining rows, premultiplied by β, plus a vector the elements of which also approach the true values of u_1 as the sample size goes to infinity. Thus the first row of $(W_1' - W')$ approaches the remaining rows premultiplied by β, since the terms in u_1 cancel in the subtraction. If Eq. (6.6.7) is valid, therefore, $(P - Q)$ approaches singularity as the sample size goes to infinity, whence

$$\text{plim } \lambda_{\min} = 1 \qquad (6.6.16)$$

Now, what if Eq. (6.6.7) is *not* valid; i.e., what if one or more of the exclusion restrictions used in obtaining it is in error? The answer here depends on the degree of identification, as it must. Writing the restrictions in the familiar form

$$A_1\phi = 0 \qquad (6.6.17)$$

the answer depends on $\rho(A\phi)$ in the case in which Eq. (6.6.17) is false. If that rank is less than or equal to $M - 1$, there is at least one nonzero vector in the row kernel of $A\phi$. The corresponding linear combination of the equations of the model then yields an equation which (except for normalization) is indistinguishable from Eq. (6.6.7) *whether or not* the restrictions are correct. Using the new equation in place of Eq. (6.6.7) in the argument just given shows that Eq. (6.6.16) holds in this case, independently of the validity of the restrictions.

Now, what determines the rank of $A\phi$ when the restrictions are false? The most obvious thing is the rank of ϕ. If this rank is not above $M - 1$ (that is, if the order condition for identifiability is at most just satisfied), the rank of $A\phi$ cannot exceed $M - 1$ either. On the other hand, even if the rank of ϕ exceeds $M - 1$, the rank of $A\phi$ may be reduced to at most $M - 1$ by the presence of *valid* restrictions on the *other* equations of the model. In this case, were Eq. (6.6.17) valid, the rank of $A\phi$ would be below $M - 1$ and the first equation underidentified. Thus $\lambda_{\min}$ provides no information on the validity of Eq. (6.6.17) if the first equation would be underidentified with Eq. (6.6.17) valid or if it would be just identified with the order condition just met.

Indeed, if the rank of ϕ does not exceed $M - 1$, $\lambda_{\min}$ will be unity even in the sample. This is because in such a case *any* set of reduced form parameters, including the sample estimates thereof, is consistent with an equation in the form of Eq. (6.6.7). In this case, the reduced form is unrestricted without the explicit application of restrictions on equations other than the first and at least one linear combination of the reduced form equations will yield an equation in the form of Eq. (6.6.7). Furthermore, that derived equation will have as a disturbance a corresponding linear combination of the sample reduced form residuals. Instead of u_1, a disturbance known only to be uncorrelated with the exogenous variables in the probability limit, therefore, the derived equation in the form of Eq. (6.6.7) will have a disturbance which, by its derivation, is uncorrelated *in the sample* with the exogenous variables. Using the derived equation in place of Eq. (6.6.7), the analysis which showed that $(W_1' - W')$ had asymptotically dependent rows now shows that it has dependent rows in the sample. Hence λ_{min} is unity even in the sample in this case. (*Write out such an equation and repeat the former argument explicitly.*)

On the other hand, if the order condition is overfulfilled and if the restrictions on the other equations would not identically reduce the rank $A\phi$ below $M - 1$ if Eq. (6.6.17) were valid, then the invalidity of Eq. (6.6.17) implies that the rank of $A\phi$ is M everywhere in the parameter space except on a set of measure zero. Thus, in this case, no equation in the form of Eq. (6.6.7) can be derived from the structural equations and hence plim λ_{min} exceeds unity. In this case (but only in this case), the validity of the restrictions (6.6.17) can be tested by testing whether λ_{min} deviates significantly from unity. It is known that if Eq. (6.6.17) is valid, $T \log \lambda_{min}$ is distributed *asymptotically* as χ^2 with $\Lambda - (l + m)$ degrees of freedom where T is the sample size.[1] Note that since there is no point in the test unless the order condition is more than satisfied, the number of degrees of freedom involved is always positive where relevant, by Corollary 2.4.1b.

The test just described is appropriate, as shown, if the order condition is overfulfilled and the rank condition would not be violated identically if the restrictions to be tested were valid. If these conditions do not hold, the test fails since there then exist equations in the form of Eq. (6.6.7) whether or not the restrictions are valid. In most cases, the absence of such a test is entirely reasonable. As already remarked, it is clear that no restriction which contributes to the identifiability of an equation can be tested. On the other hand, the test just discussed fails in one class of cases in which there are restrictions which do not so contribute, the cases in which $\rho(\phi)$ exceeds $\rho(A\phi)$ but the latter rank would fall short of $M - 1$ if the restrictions were valid. In such cases, Theorem 2.6.1 assures us that there are as many restrictions on the reduced form as there are structural restrictions not contributing to identification, that is, precisely $\rho(\phi) - \rho(A\phi)$ such restrictions. Since the reduced form can be consistently estimated, those implied restrictions can be tested in principle, although no study of this problem is presently available. It is of some interest to have such a test, since if the rank of $A\phi$ falls short of that of ϕ for reasons other than the overfulfillment of the order condition, the validity of the structural restrictions on the given equation may well bear on the identifiability of other equations of the model.

[1] See Koopmans and Hood [22, Sec. 8 and Appendix G] and Anderson and Rubin [2].

6.7. Testing the Identifiability of a Structural Equation

Much of the preceding discussion also aids in establishing a test of the identifiability of the first equation of the model under the exclusion restrictions (6.6.17). This test is based on the fact that the identifiability of the first equation is equivalent to the existence of one and only one independent equation in the form of Eq. (6.6.7) and that this in turn is equivalent to the existence of one and only one vector asymptotically in the row kernel of $(W_1' - W')$.

The first equivalence is obvious. To see the second, observe that Eq. (6.6.7) yields $(1 \quad -\beta)$ as the vector asymptotically in the row kernel of $(W_1' - W')$. Similarly, any equation in the same form with β and γ replaced by β^* and γ^*, respectively, yields $(1 \quad -\beta^*)$ as a vector asymptotically in that row kernel. There are thus two independent vectors asymptotically in that row kernel, provided we can show that $\beta \neq \beta^*$. This is easy to show, however. Since the reduced form matrix Π is defined as

$$\Pi = -B^{-1}\Gamma \qquad (6.7.1)$$

premultiplication of Π by minus the first row of B yields the first row of Γ. Because two admissible versions of the first equation must both be consistent with the same reduced form, this immediately implies that if $\beta = \beta^*$, then $\gamma = \gamma^*$, so that the two equations would be the same if this were true. This establishes that underidentification leads to two independent row vectors asymptotically in the row kernel of $(W_1' - W')$.

On the other hand, suppose that there is a vector independent of $(1 \quad -\beta)$ asymptotically in that row kernel. Call that vector η. Then

$$d \equiv \eta \begin{bmatrix} q \\ y_1 \end{bmatrix} \qquad (6.7.2)$$

is a linear combination of the endogenous variables appearing in Eq. (6.6.7) which has asymptotically the same residual when regressed on all the elements of z as when regressed on the elements of z_1 only. This can only happen if the structural equations imply

$$d - \gamma^* z_1 = u_1^* \qquad (6.7.3)$$

for some vector γ^* and u_1^* uncorrelated in the probability limit with any of the elements of z. Since η is independent of $(1 \quad -\beta)$, addition of some nonzero scalar multiple of Eq. (6.7.3) to Eq. (6.6.7) and division (if necessary) by the resulting coefficient of q† yields an equation independent of Eq. (6.6.7) but indistinguishable from it. Thus the existence

† How do we know that coefficient is nonzero?

of more than one independent vector asymptotically in the row kernel of $(W_1' - W')$ implies underidentification.

Furthermore, any vector in the row kernel of $(W_1' - W')$ is in the row kernel of $(P - Q)$ which has $m + 1$ rows. Hence, if the first equation is identifiable, the rank of $(P - Q)$ is asymptotically m; while if that equation is not identifiable, that rank is less than m. It can be shown, however, that the multiplicity of any root λ of

$$|P - \lambda Q| = 0 \qquad (6.7.4)$$

is equal to $\{m + 1 - \rho(P - \lambda Q)\}$, that is, to the dimension of the null space of $(P - \lambda Q)$.† It follows immediately that the identifiability of the first equation corresponds to unity being asymptotically a simple root of Eq. (6.7.4) and that underidentification of that equation corresponds to unity being asymptotically a multiple root.

Accordingly, let λ_2 be the second smallest root of Eq. (6.7.4). On the hypothesis that the equation in question is *not* identifiable (so that the test is strictly one of lack of identification rather than of identification), it is known that both $T \log (\lambda_2 \lambda_{min})$ and $T(\lambda_{min} + \lambda_2 - 2)$ are distributed asymptotically as χ^2 with $\Lambda - (l + m) + 1$ degrees of freedom, provided that unity is a double and not a triple (or greater multiple) asymptotic root of Eq. (6.7.4), i.e., provided that the first equation is not *so* underidentified that there is more than one other independent admissible substitute.[1] Note that if the number of degrees of freedom involved is zero or negative, there is no point in making the test, since the order condition then fails.

Indeed, the question may well be raised: why bother to make the test anyway? If the order condition is not satisfied, then the test cannot be made and is unnecessary. If the order condition is satisfied but the rank condition fails identically, the test will (asymptotically) fail to

---

† Since Q is nonsingular, there exists a matrix C such that $C'QC$ is the unit matrix. Consider $C'PC$. This is a real symmetric matrix and is hence orthogonally similar to a diagonal matrix D. Thus there is an orthogonal matrix E such that

$$E'C'PCE = D \text{ and } E'E = I$$

Let $R = CE$. Then

$$R'(P - \lambda Q)R = D - \lambda I \qquad (6.7.4a)$$

Since the rank of $(P - \lambda Q)$ and $(D - \lambda I)$ are the same, a value of λ is a root of Eq. (6.7.4) if and only if it is a diagonal element of D. Further, it is a root of multiplicity r if and only if it appears r times on the diagonal of D. In this case,

$$\rho(P - \lambda Q) = \rho(D - \lambda I) = m + 1 - r$$

as stated.

[1] See Koopmans and Hood, *loc. cit.*, and Anderson [1].

reject the hypothesis of underidentifiability;[1] but this can be told in advance by examination of the form of the matrix $A\phi$. While such examination is cumbersome if the system is large, it is unlikely to be any more cumbersome than the computation of the roots of Eq. (6.7.4). Finally, if the rank and order conditions do not fail identically, they fail only on a set of measure zero in the parameter space. The test is thus guaranteed to reject the hypothesis of underidentifiability with probability 1. Since the outcome of the test can thus be predicted with certainty or probability 1 in every case, why bother to make it?

There are two at least partially satisfactory answers to this cogent argument. First, if one has not been careful about specifying all the prior restrictions on the model, one may have ignored restrictions which make the rank condition fail identically. In this case, the test may reveal that the prior investigation which revealed that the rank condition was satisfied was in error.

Second, if the test fails strongly to reject the hypothesis of under-identification, the matrix $(P - Q)$ will be near singularity. Such closeness to singularity will also hold for the matrices which have to be inverted to obtain the estimates. (See, for example, Theorem 2.7.2.) Such near-singularity can occur even if the equation in question is identifiable, since it can be produced by multicollinearity in the exogenous variables in the sample data. The failure of the test to reject underidentifiability may then be taken as a signal that *in the sample at hand* there are not enough independent movements in the predetermined variables to permit identification, even if identification is present in principle.

To put it another way, the ability of the observational information to yield Λ independent pieces of information on the parameters of the first equation (Theorem 1.6.1) is predicted on the validity of the assumption that no linear identities connect the predetermined variables (Assumption 1.5.2). If those variables are sufficiently collinear, the situation is very close to one of underidentification. This cannot be told a priori but will be revealed by the test which thus provides a convenient summary of the harmfulness of the relevant collinearities.

On the other hand, such a situation of collinearity or of underidentification will in any case reveal itself when the asymptotic standard errors of the coefficients are computed. If a nearly singular matrix is to be inverted, those standard errors will turn out very large. Provided that care has been taken to check the order and rank conditions in advrnce, so that the misleading appearance of estimates (even with large standard errors) of an unidentifiable equation is avoided, nothing seems to be lost

---

[1] We ignore the slight problem raised by the fact that the given distribution of the test statistic is valid only if unity is not asymptotically more than a double root of Eq. (6.7.4).

in bypassing the test and simply computing all estimates and standard errors except a rather convenient summary of how bad things are.

Historically, the test described was constructed when the limited-information, maximum likelihood estimator was the only known one in standard use. (See Koopmans and Hood [22].) Since this estimator requires the extraction of the roots of Eq. (6.7.4), the computations for this test (and for that discussed in the preceding section) are not particularly expensive, compared with proceeding to calculate the relevant estimates and asymptotic standard errors. When other estimators, such as two-stage least squares, are used, however, it is rather more expensive to perform the test than to simply go ahead and get the estimates and asymptotic standard errors. On the other hand, while the usefulness of the test of identifiability seems limited, the test of restrictions described in the preceding section is clearly a useful one, and because the same roots must be extracted for both tests, one may as well perform the identifiability test at the same time as one tests the restrictions. Indeed, with modern computing equipment, computational expense is not a very strong argument against performing the test, so perhaps it should be performed if any of the arguments in its favor are thought to have substantial merit.

References

References for the topics discussed in this chapter are given in the course of the discussion.

Bibliography

[1] Anderson, T. W.: "The Asymptotic Distribution of Certain Characteristic Roots and Vectors," in Jerzy Neyman, ed., *Proceedings of the Second Berkeley Symposium on Mathematical Statistics and Probability*, University of California Press, Berkeley, Calif., 1951, pp. 103–130.

[2] Anderson, T. W., and H. Rubin: "The Asymptotic Properties of Estimates of the Parameters of a Single Equation in a Complete System of Stochastic Equations," *Annals of Mathematical Statistics*, vol. 21, no. 4, December, 1950.

[3] Ando, Albert, and Gordon M. Kaufman: "Extended Natural Conjugate Analysis of the Multivariate Normal Process," paper presented at Econometric Society Winter Meetings, 1964.

[4] Apostol, Tom M.: *Mathematical Analysis*, Addison-Wesley Publishing Company, Inc., Reading, Mass., 1960.

[5] Bronfenbrenner, Jean: "Sources and Size of Least-squares Bias in a Two-equation Model," chap. IX in W. C. Hood and T. C. Koopmans, eds., *Studies in Econometric Method*, John Wiley & Sons, Inc., New York, 1953 (Cowles Commission Monograph 14).

[6] Drèze, Jacques: "The Bayesian Approach to Simultaneous Equations Estimation," Office of Naval Research, Research Memorandum 67, Northwestern University, Evanston, Ill., September, 1962.

[7] Fisher, Franklin M.: "Generalization of the Rank and Order Conditions for Identifiability," *Econometrica*, vol. 27, no. 3, July, 1959.

[8] Fisher, Franklin M.: "On the Cost of Approximate Specification in Simultaneous Equation Estimation," *Econometrica*, vol. 29, no. 2, April, 1961; reprinted as Chap. 3 in A. Ando, F. M. Fisher, and H. A. Simon: *Essays on the Structure of Social Science Models*, The M.I.T. Press, Cambridge, Mass., 1963.

[9] Fisher, Franklin M.: "Identifiability Criteria in Nonlinear Systems," *Econometrica*, vol. 29, no. 4, October, 1961.

[10] Fisher, Franklin M.: *A Priori Information and Time Series Analysis: Essays in Economic Theory and Measurement*, North Holland Publishing Company, Amsterdam, 1962.

[11] Fisher, Franklin M.: "Uncorrelated Disturbances and Identifiability Criteria," *International Economic Review*, vol. 4, no. 2, May, 1963.

[12] Fisher, Franklin M.: "Identifiability Criteria in Nonlinear Systems: A Further Note," *Econometrica*, vol. 33, no. 1, January, 1965.

[13] Fisher, Franklin M.: "Near-identifiability and the Variances of the Disturbance Terms," *Econometrica*, vol. 33, no. 2, April, 1965.

[14] Fisher, Franklin M.: "Restrictions on the Reduced Form and the Rank and Order Conditions," *International Economic Review*, vol. 7, no. 1, January, 1966.

[15] Fisher, Franklin M.: "Dynamic Structure and Estimation in Economy-wide Econometric Models," (1) chap. XV in J. Duesenberry, G. Fromm, E. Kuh, and L. Klein, eds., *The Brookings Quarterly Econometric Model of the United States*, Rand McNally & Company, Chicago, and North Holland Publishing Company, Amsterdam, 1965; (2) *Study Week on the Econometric Approach to Development Planning*, Pontifical Academy of Sciences, Vatican City, 1965, pp. 385–447; (3) a shortened version, "The Choice of Instrumental Variables in the Estimation of Economy-wide Econometric Models," *International Economic Review*, vol. 6, no. 3, September, 1965.

[16] Franklin, Philip: *A Treatise on Advanced Calculus*, John Wiley & Sons, Inc., New York, 1940.

[17] Gale, D., and H. Nikaidô: "The Jacobian Matrix and Global Univalence of Mappings," Osaka University, Institute of Social and Economic Research, March, 1965; to be published in *Mathematische Annalen*.

[18] Gantmacher, F. R.: *The Theory of Matrices*, Chelsea Publishing Company, New York, 1959.

[19] Hurwicz, L.: "Prediction and Least Squares," chap. 7 in T. C. Koopmans, ed., *Statistical Inference in Dynamic Economic Models*, John Wiley & Sons, Inc., New York, 1950 (Cowles Commission Monograph 10).

[20] Johnston, J.: *Econometric Methods*, McGraw-Hill Book Company, New York, 1963.

[21] Koopmans, T. C.: "Identification Problems in Economic Model Construction," chap. II in W. C. Hood and T. C. Koopmans, eds., *Studies in Econometric Method*, John Wiley & Sons, Inc., New York, 1953 (Cowles Commission Monograph 14).

[22] Koopmans, T. C., and W. C. Hood: "The Estimation of Simultaneous Linear Economic Relationships," chap. VI in W. C. Hood and T. C. Koopmans, eds., *Studies in Econometric Method*, John Wiley & Sons, Inc., New York, 1953 (Cowles Commission Monograph 14).

[23] Koopmans, T. C., H. Rubin, and R. B. Leipnik: "Measuring the Equation Systems of Dynamic Economics," chap. 2 in T. C. Koopmans, ed., *Statistical Inference in Dynamic Economic Models*, John Wiley & Sons, Inc., New York, 1950 (Cowles Commission Monograph 10).

[24] Koyck, L. M.: *Distributed Lags and Investment Analysis*, North Holland Publishing Company, Amsterdam, 1954.

[25] Malinvaud, E.: *Méthodes Statistiques de l'Econométrie*, Dunod, Paris, 1964.

[26] Metzler, Lloyd A.: "The Assumptions Implied in Least Squares Demand Techniques," *Review of Economic Statistics*, vol. 22, no. 3, August, 1940.

[27] Nerlove, Marc: *The Dynamics of Supply: Estimation of Farmer's Response to Price*, The Johns Hopkins Press, Baltimore, 1958.

[28] Nerlove, Marc: *Distributed Lags and Demand Analysis for Agricultural and Other Commodities*, U.S. Department of Agriculture Handbook 141, 1958.

[29] Rothenberg, Thomas J.: "A Bayesian Analysis of Simultaneous Equation Systems," Econometric Institute, Netherlands School of Economics, Rotterdam, Report 6315, May, 1963.

[30] Simon, H. A.: "Causal Ordering and Identifiability," chap. III in W. C. Hood and T. C. Koopmans, eds., *Studies in Econometric Method*, John Wiley & Sons, Inc., New York, 1953 (Cowles Commission Monograph 14); reprinted as chap. 1 in H. A. Simon, *Models of Man*, John Wiley & Sons, Inc., New York, 1957; and as chap. 2 in A. Ando, F. M. Fisher, and H. A. Simon, *Essays on the Structure of Social Science Models*, The M.I.T. Press, Cambridge, Mass., 1963.

[31] Theil, H.: *Economic Forecasts and Policy*, 2d rev. ed., North Holland Publishing Company, Amsterdam, 1961.

[32] Theil, H.: "Specification Errors and the Estimation of Economic Relationships," *Review of the International Statistical Institute*, vol. 25, 1957.

[33] Theil, H., and A. S. Goldberger: "On Pure and Mixed Statistical Estimation in Economics," *International Economic Review*, vol. 2, no. 1, January, 1961.

[34] Wald, A.: "Note on the Identification of Economic Relations," chap. 3 in T. C. Koopmans, ed., *Statistical Inference in Dynamic Economic Models*, John Wiley & Sons, Inc., New York, 1950 (Cowles Commission Monograph 10).

[35] Wold, H.: "Ends and Means in Econometric Model Building," in U. Grenander, ed., *Probability and Statistics; The Harald Cramer Volume*, John Wiley & Sons, Inc., New York, 1959, pp. 354–434.

[36] Wold, H., and P. Faxér: "On the Specification Error in Regression Analysis," *Annals of Mathematical Statistics*, vol. 28, no. 1, March, 1957.

[37] Wold, H., in association with L. Juréen: *Demand Analysis: A Study in Econometrics*, John Wiley & Sons, Inc., New York, 1953.

[38] Working, E. J.: "What Do Statistical 'Demand Curves' Show?" *Quarterly Journal of Economics*, vol. 41, no. 1, February, 1927.

Index